Scandalous™

Written by
J. Torres

Illustrated by
Scott Chantler

book design & cover by
Keith Wood

edited by
Jamie S. Rich

afterword by
Ande Parks

published by
Joe Nozemack

Acknowledgements

J.: I'd first like to thank Scott, my co-director, chief cinematographer, set designer, and wardrobe mistress for making it all look so good; I'd also like to thank Jamie, my manager, for all the years of support and encouragement; Joe, our producer, for believing in me and always coming through with the financing for the pictures; Keith, my stylist, for this dress; James, my assistant, for pressing the dress; also, my family, friends, and fans, especially my fiancée... I love you, baby! I hope I haven't forgotten anyone... I love you all! Thank you!

Scott: First and foremost, I'd like to thank my wife, Shari. It takes a special kind of person to be married to an artist, weathering a wildly fluctuating income and a spouse who's constantly restless and distracted by their own work. She has done so for nine years with understanding, patience, and grace. All creative professionals should be so lucky. I've had a lot of encouragement and support from many great people over the years. Those people know who they are, and to them, I offer a very heartfelt, "thank you."

There were also a lot of people who said I couldn't do it. They, too, know who they are. To them, equally heartfelt, I say, "Shove it, jerks."

lettering font - Blambot.com

senior editing - James Lucas Jones

managing editing - Randal C. Jarrell

editorial assistance - Ian Shaughnessy

Visit the author at www.jtorresonline.com.

Visit the illustrator at www.scottchantler.com.

ONI PRESS, INC.
6336 SE Milwaukie Avenue, PMB30
Portland, OR 97202
USA

www.onipress.com

First edition: August 2004
ISBN 1-929998-98-8

1 3 5 7 9 10 8 6 4 2

PRINTED IN CANADA.

Act I

"The way to become famous
fast is to throw a brick at
someone who is famous."
- Walter Winchell

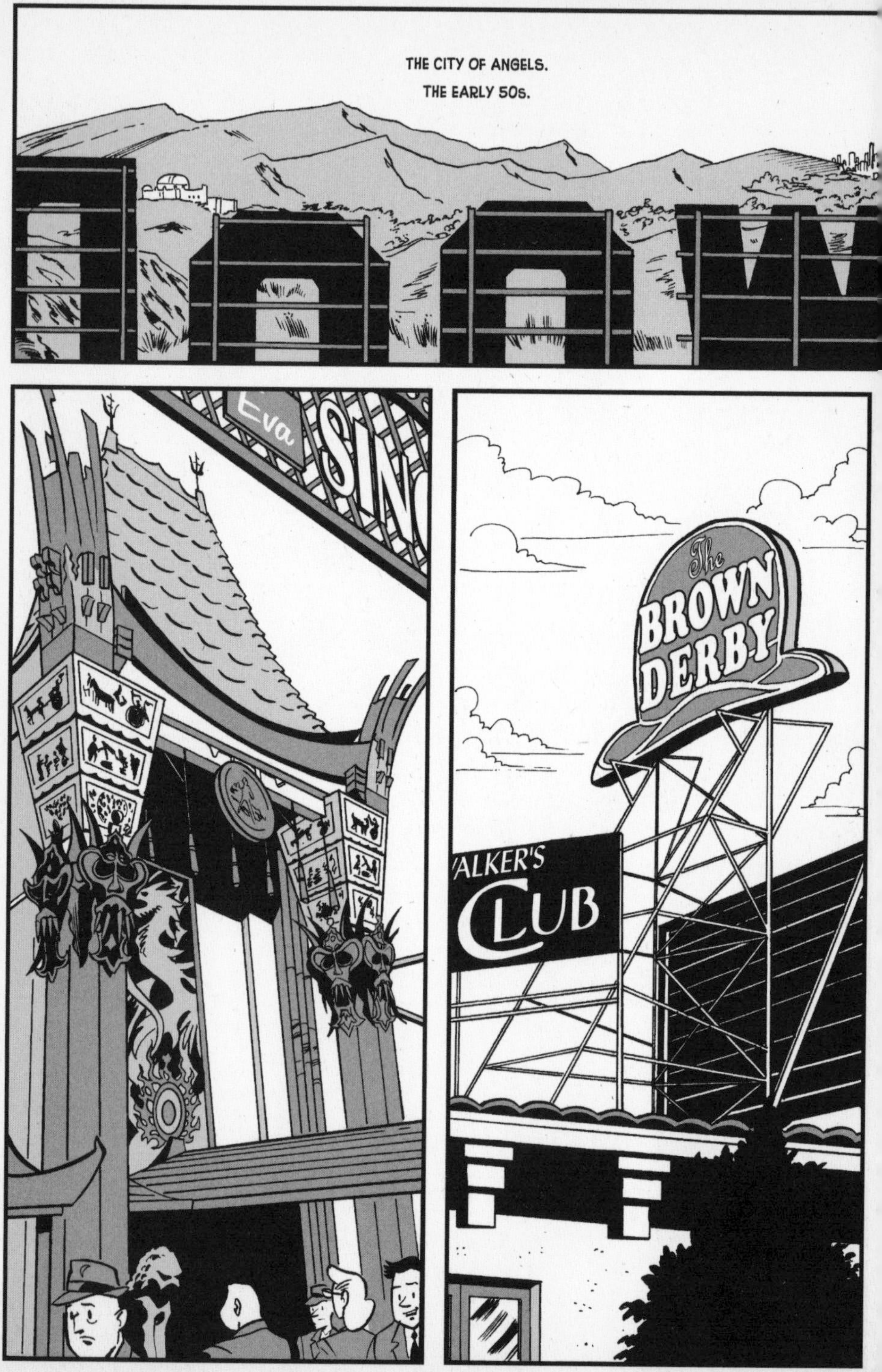
THE CITY OF ANGELS.
THE EARLY 50s.
Eva
SIN
The BROWN DERBY
ALKER'S
CLUB

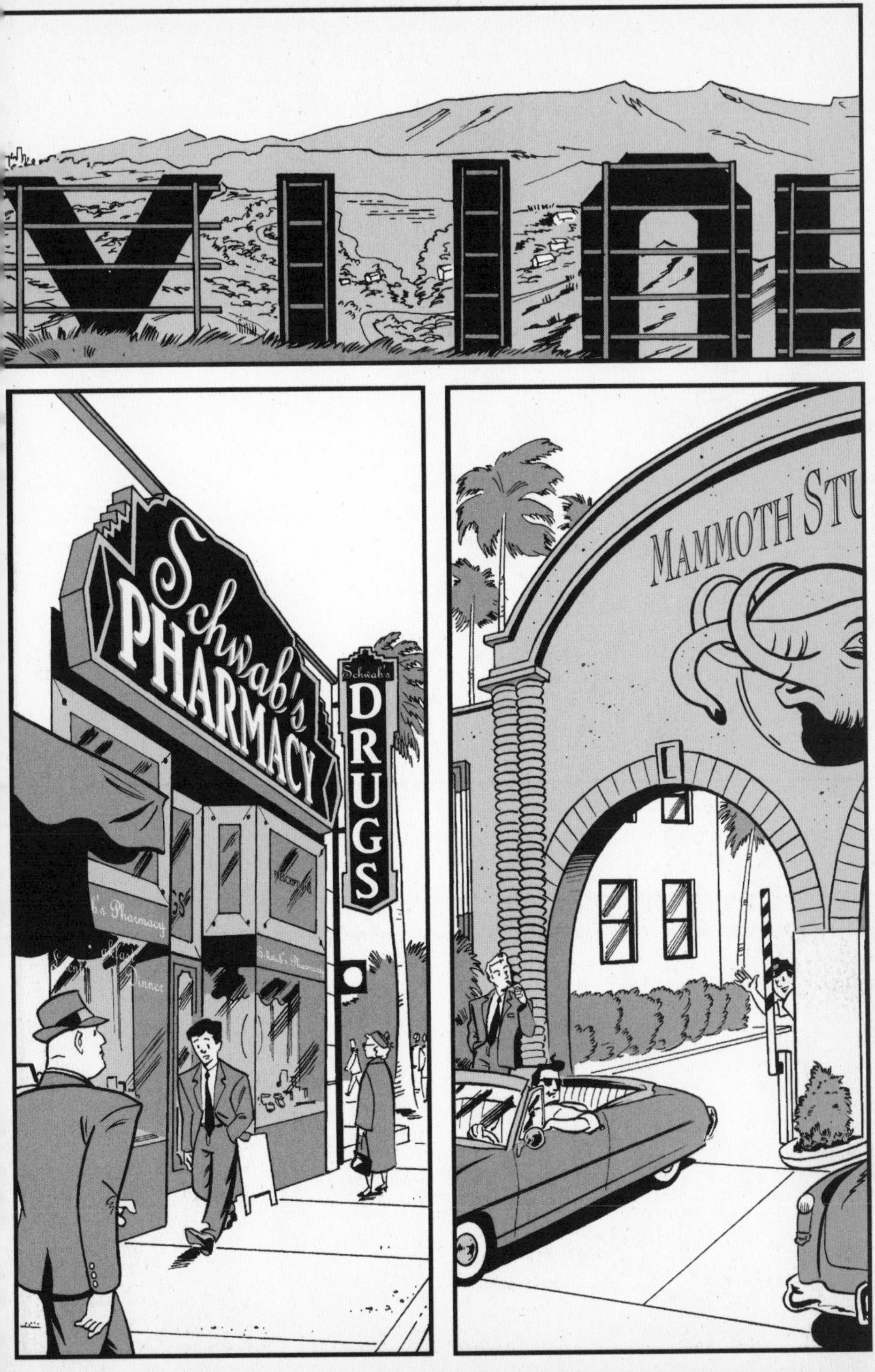

Schwab's
PHARMACY
Schwab's
DRUGS
PRESCRIPTIONS
MAMMOTH STU

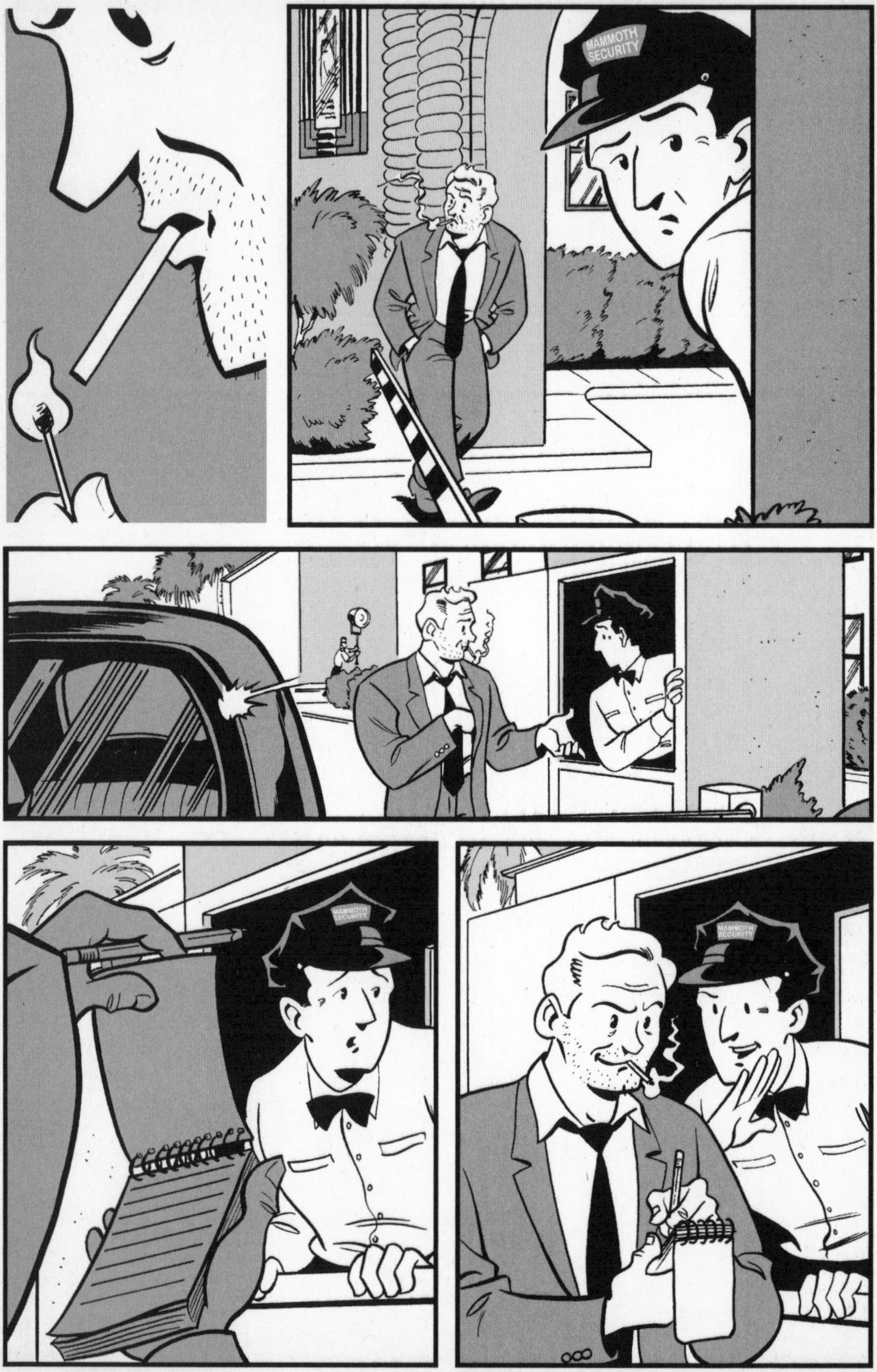
MAMMOTH SECURITY
MAMMOTH SECURITY
MAMMOTH SECURITY

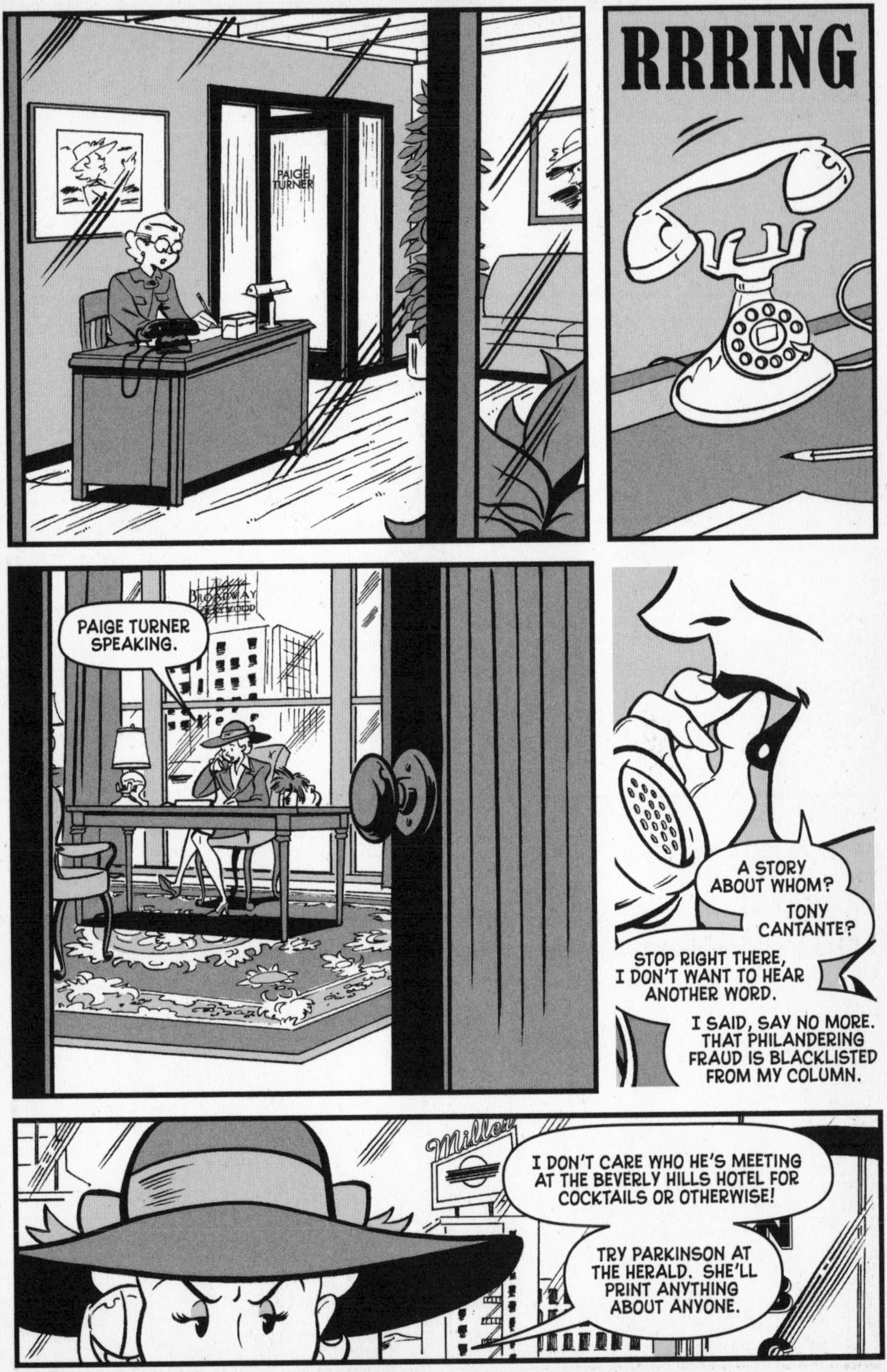
PAIGE TURNER
RRRING
BROADWAY
PAIGE TURNER SPEAKING.
A STORY ABOUT WHOM?
TONY CANTANTE?
STOP RIGHT THERE, I DON'T WANT TO HEAR ANOTHER WORD.
I SAID, SAY NO MORE. THAT PHILANDERING FRAUD IS BLACKLISTED FROM MY COLUMN.
I DON'T CARE WHO HE'S MEETING AT THE BEVERLY HILLS HOTEL FOR COCKTAILS OR OTHERWISE!
TRY PARKINSON AT THE HERALD. SHE'LL PRINT ANYTHING ABOUT ANYONE.

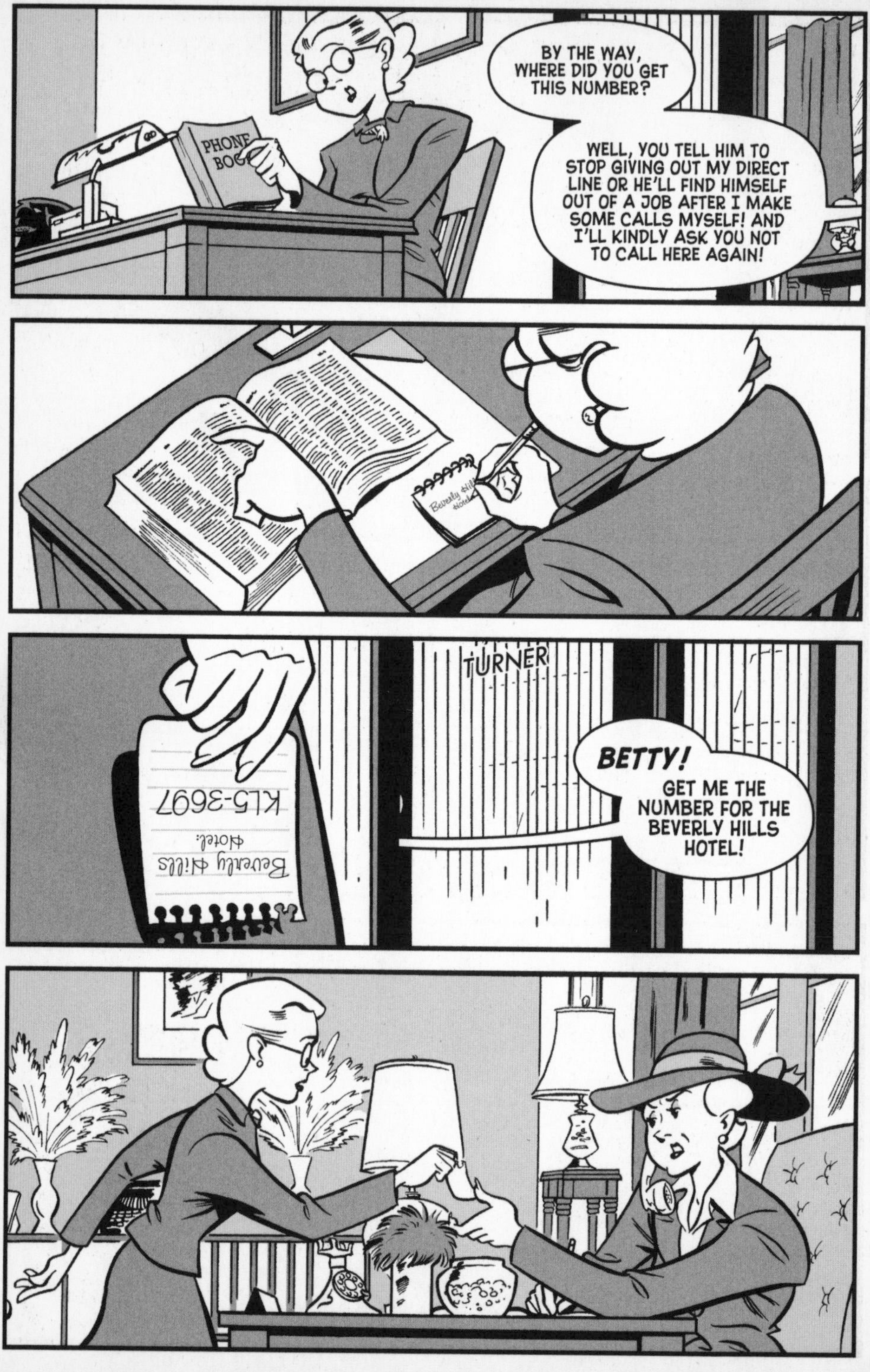
BY THE WAY, WHERE DID YOU GET THIS NUMBER?
WELL, YOU TELL HIM TO STOP GIVING OUT MY DIRECT LINE OR HE'LL FIND HIMSELF OUT OF A JOB AFTER I MAKE SOME CALLS MYSELF! AND I'LL KINDLY ASK YOU NOT TO CALL HERE AGAIN!
TURNER
Beverly Hills Hotel
KL5-3697
BETTY! GET ME THE NUMBER FOR THE BEVERLY HILLS HOTEL!

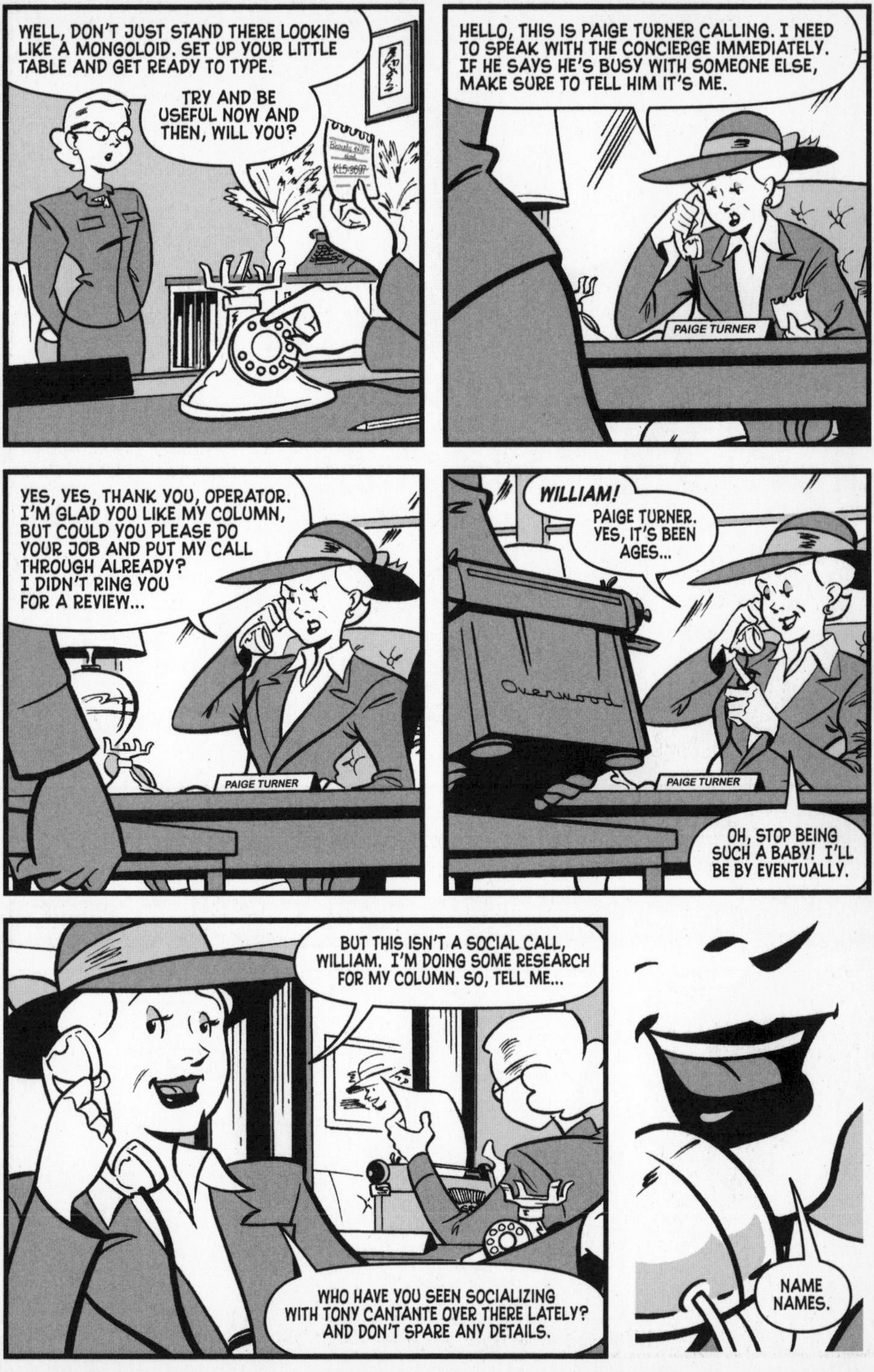
WELL, DON'T JUST STAND THERE LOOKING LIKE A MONGOLOID. SET UP YOUR LITTLE TABLE AND GET READY TO TYPE.
TRY AND BE USEFUL NOW AND THEN, WILL YOU?
HELLO, THIS IS PAIGE TURNER CALLING. I NEED TO SPEAK WITH THE CONCIERGE IMMEDIATELY. IF HE SAYS HE'S BUSY WITH SOMEONE ELSE, MAKE SURE TO TELL HIM IT'S ME.
PAIGE TURNER
YES, YES, THANK YOU, OPERATOR. I'M GLAD YOU LIKE MY COLUMN, BUT COULD YOU PLEASE DO YOUR JOB AND PUT MY CALL THROUGH ALREADY? I DIDN'T RING YOU FOR A REVIEW...
PAIGE TURNER
WILLIAM!
PAIGE TURNER. YES, IT'S BEEN AGES...
Overwood
PAIGE TURNER
OH, STOP BEING SUCH A BABY! I'LL BE BY EVENTUALLY.
BUT THIS ISN'T A SOCIAL CALL, WILLIAM. I'M DOING SOME RESEARCH FOR MY COLUMN. SO, TELL ME...
WHO HAVE YOU SEEN SOCIALIZING WITH TONY CANTANTE OVER THERE LATELY? AND DON'T SPARE ANY DETAILS.
NAME NAMES.

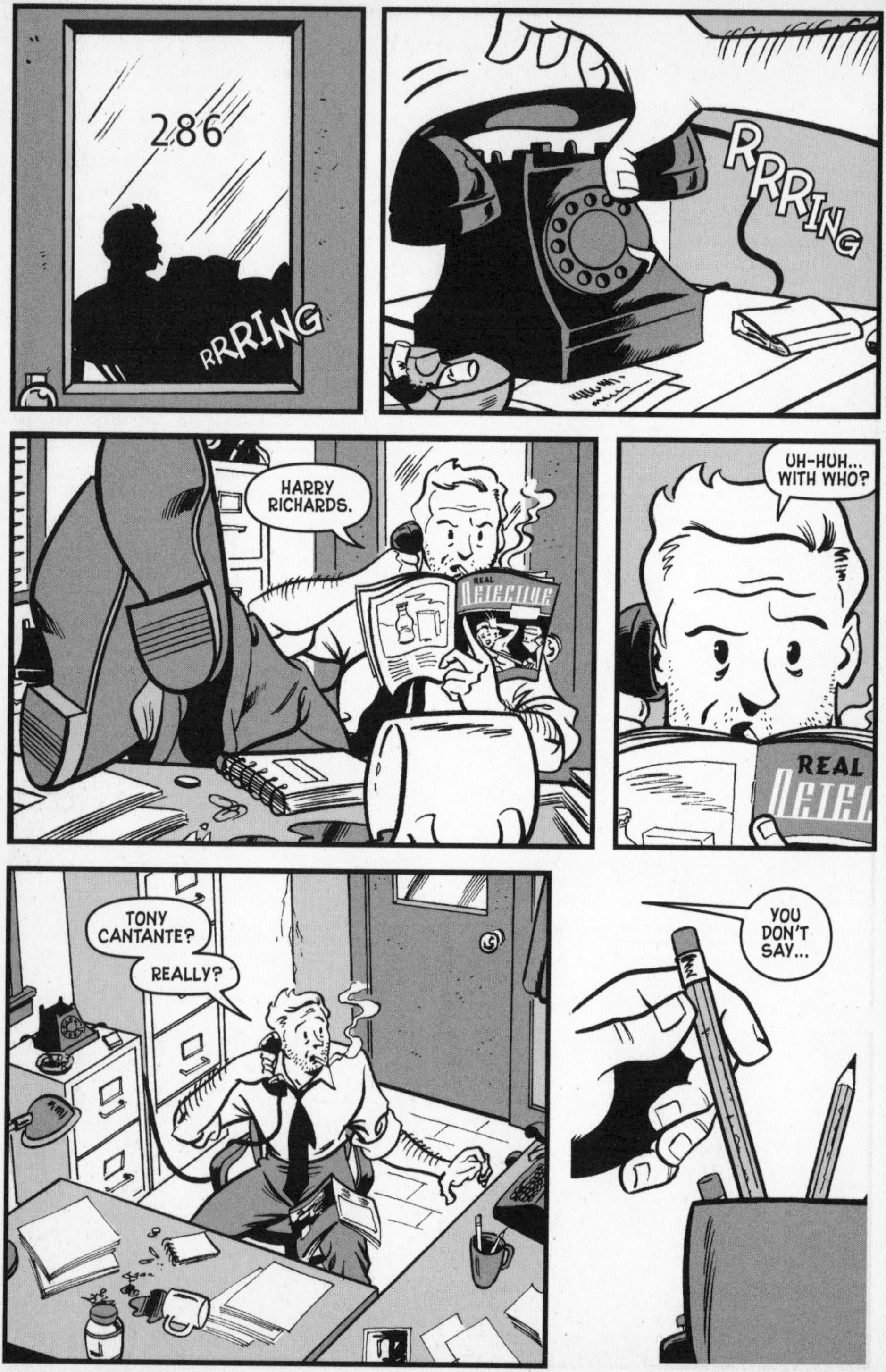
286
RRRING
RRRING
HARRY RICHARDS.
REAL DETECTIVE
UH-HUH... WITH WHO?
REAL DETECTIVE
TONY CANTANTE?
REALLY?
YOU DON'T SAY...

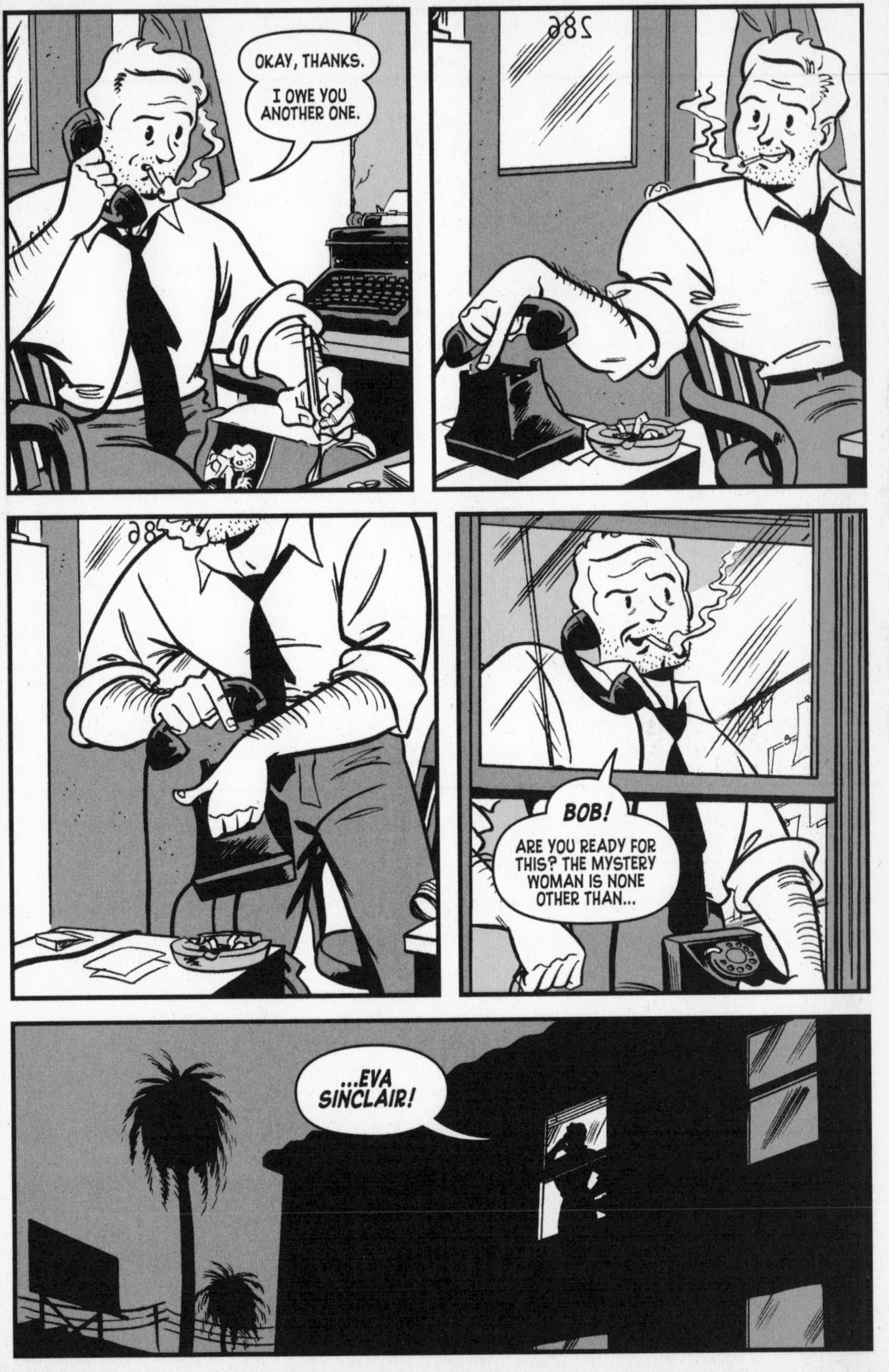
OKAY, THANKS.
I OWE YOU ANOTHER ONE.
BOB!
ARE YOU READY FOR THIS? THE MYSTERY WOMAN IS NONE OTHER THAN...
...EVA SINCLAIR!

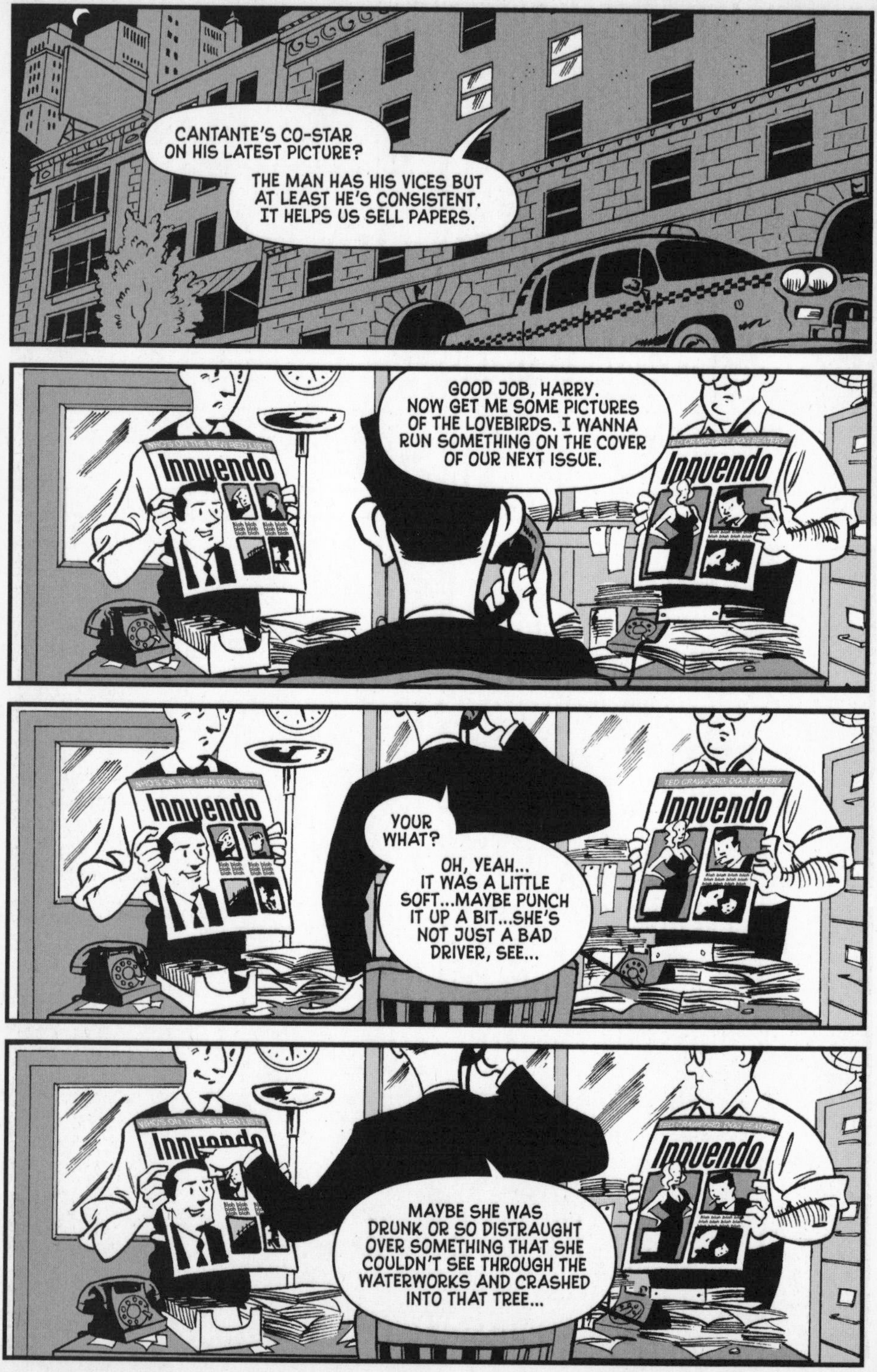
CANTANTE'S CO-STAR ON HIS LATEST PICTURE?
THE MAN HAS HIS VICES BUT AT LEAST HE'S CONSISTENT. IT HELPS US SELL PAPERS.
WHO'S ON THE NEW RED LIST?
Innuendo
GOOD JOB, HARRY. NOW GET ME SOME PICTURES OF THE LOVEBIRDS. I WANNA RUN SOMETHING ON THE COVER OF OUR NEXT ISSUE.
TED CRAWFORD: DOG BEATER?
Innuendo
YOUR WHAT?
OH, YEAH... IT WAS A LITTLE SOFT...MAYBE PUNCH IT UP A BIT...SHE'S NOT JUST A BAD DRIVER, SEE...
MAYBE SHE WAS DRUNK OR SO DISTRAUGHT OVER SOMETHING THAT SHE COULDN'T SEE THROUGH THE WATERWORKS AND CRASHED INTO THAT TREE...

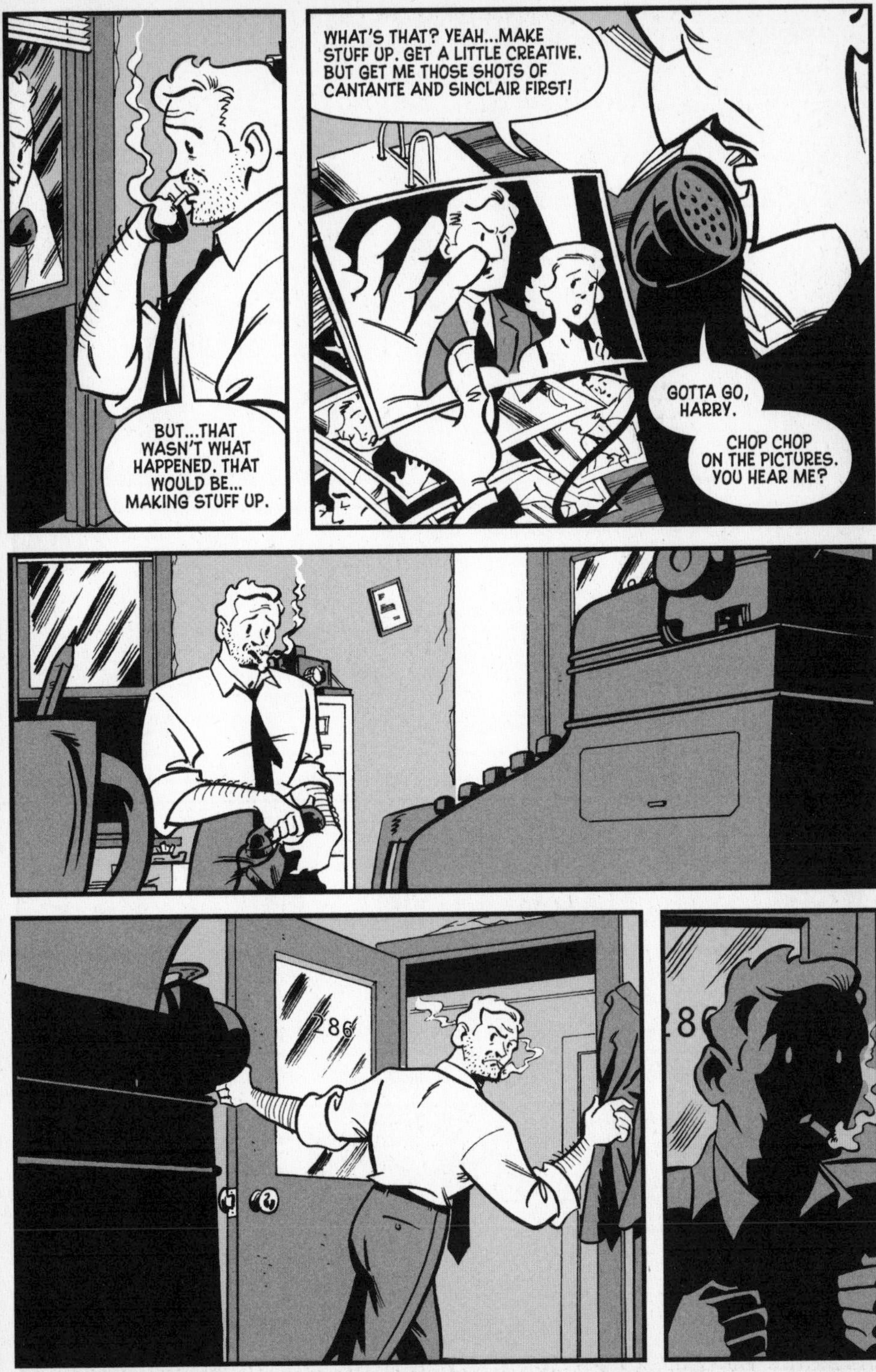
BUT...THAT WASN'T WHAT HAPPENED. THAT WOULD BE... MAKING STUFF UP.
WHAT'S THAT? YEAH...MAKE STUFF UP. GET A LITTLE CREATIVE. BUT GET ME THOSE SHOTS OF CANTANTE AND SINCLAIR FIRST!
GOTTA GO, HARRY.
CHOP CHOP ON THE PICTURES. YOU HEAR ME?
286
28

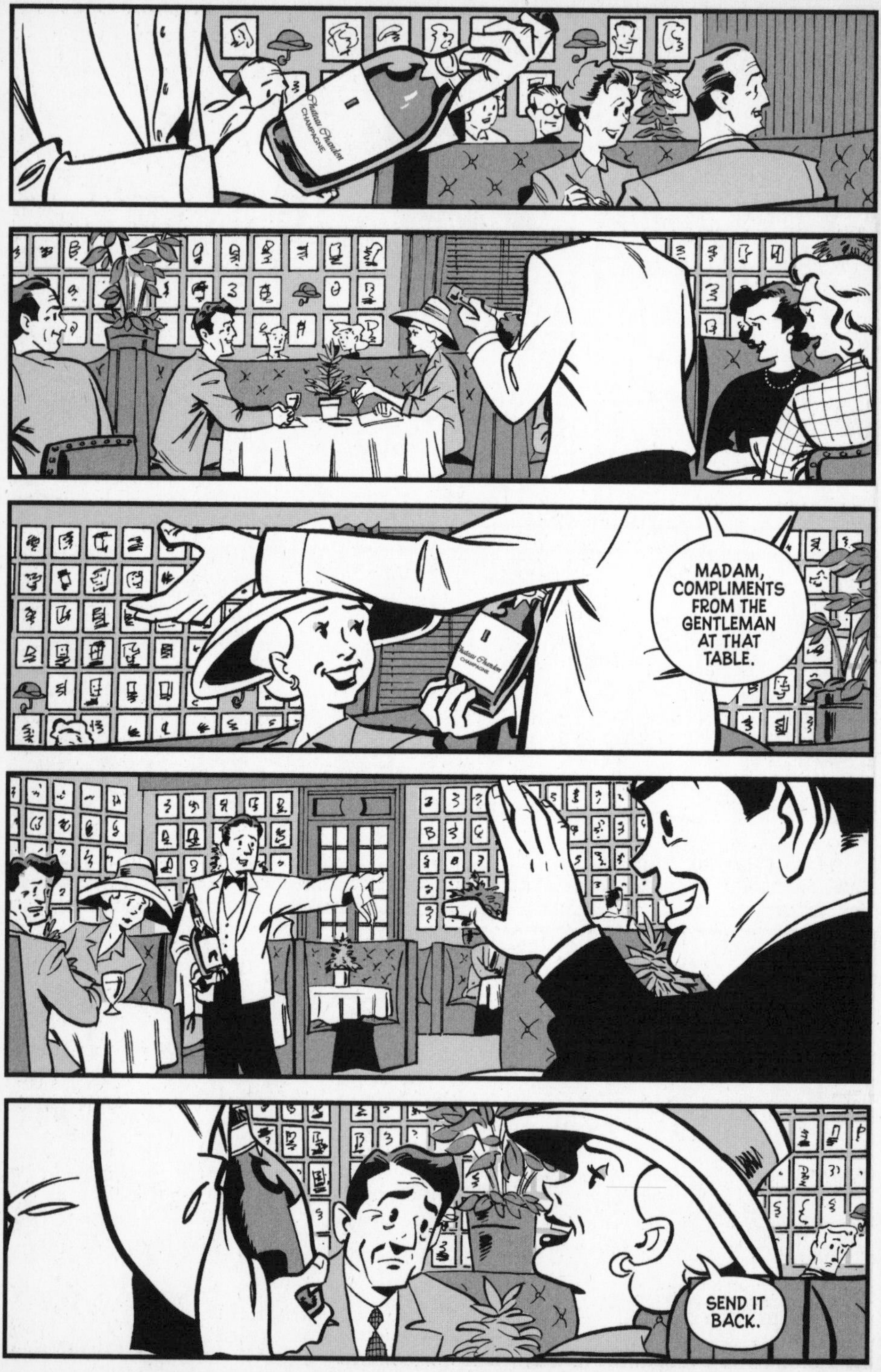
Chateau Chandon
CHAMPAGNE
MADAM, COMPLIMENTS FROM THE GENTLEMAN AT THAT TABLE.
SEND IT BACK.

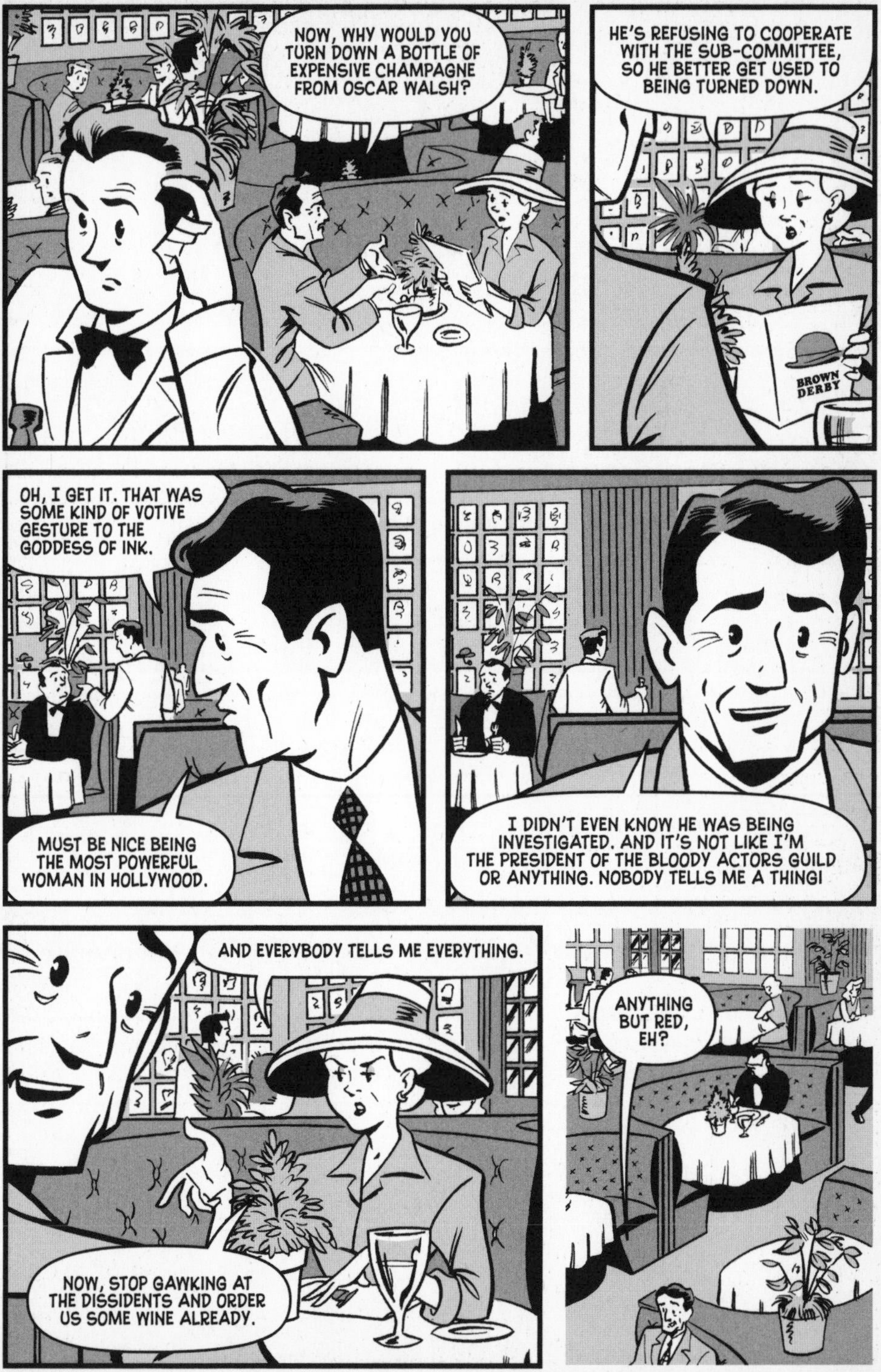
NOW, WHY WOULD YOU TURN DOWN A BOTTLE OF EXPENSIVE CHAMPAGNE FROM OSCAR WALSH?
HE'S REFUSING TO COOPERATE WITH THE SUB-COMMITTEE, SO HE BETTER GET USED TO BEING TURNED DOWN.
BROWN DERBY
OH, I GET IT. THAT WAS SOME KIND OF VOTIVE GESTURE TO THE GODDESS OF INK.
MUST BE NICE BEING THE MOST POWERFUL WOMAN IN HOLLYWOOD.
I DIDN'T EVEN KNOW HE WAS BEING INVESTIGATED. AND IT'S NOT LIKE I'M THE PRESIDENT OF THE BLOODY ACTORS GUILD OR ANYTHING. NOBODY TELLS ME A THING!
AND EVERYBODY TELLS ME EVERYTHING.
NOW, STOP GAWKING AT THE DISSIDENTS AND ORDER US SOME WINE ALREADY.
ANYTHING BUT RED, EH?

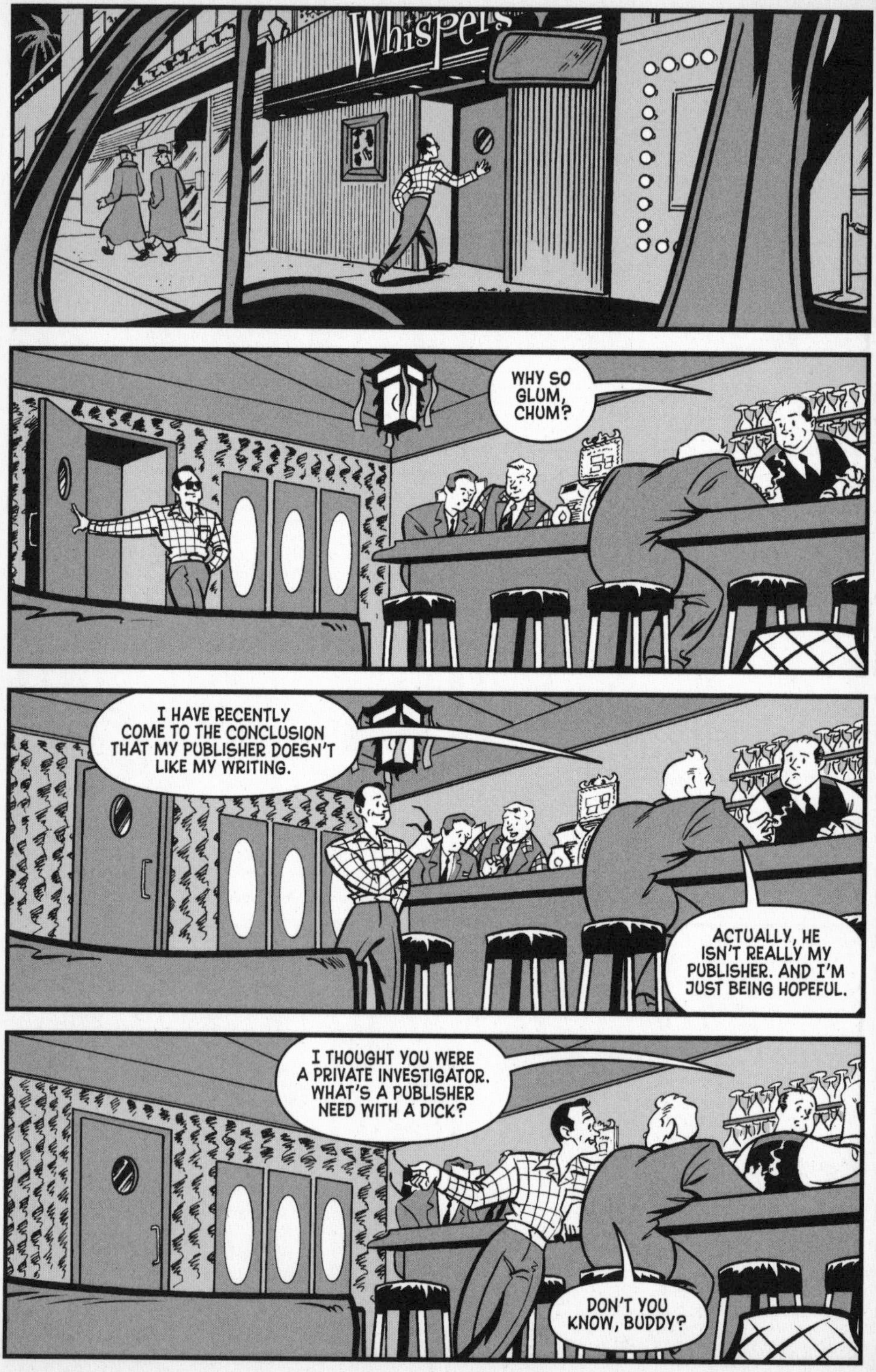
Whispers
WHY SO GLUM, CHUM?
I HAVE RECENTLY COME TO THE CONCLUSION THAT MY PUBLISHER DOESN'T LIKE MY WRITING.
ACTUALLY, HE ISN'T REALLY MY PUBLISHER. AND I'M JUST BEING HOPEFUL.
I THOUGHT YOU WERE A PRIVATE INVESTIGATOR. WHAT'S A PUBLISHER NEED WITH A DICK?
DON'T YOU KNOW, BUDDY?

HARRY HERE CATCHES MARRIED MEN WITH THEIR PANTS DOWN IN FRONT OF WOMEN WHO AREN'T THEIR WIVES.

FINDS OUT WHICH STARLETS POWDER THEIR NOSES WITH MORE THAN MAX FACTOR.

POINTS OUT THE COLORED FOLK IN THE CAST. YOU KNOW, WHICH ACTORS ARE RED AND WHICH ONES ARE PINK.

I'M NOT GETTIN' YA.

GIMME THAT RAG YOU GOT OVER THERE.

AND THEN GIMME THE USUAL.

SHE... WAS A

Innue

SHE SERVED HUBBY DIVORCE PAPERS FOR DINNER

WHERE DO YOU THINK A PUBLICATION BASED IN NEW YORK GETS ALL THESE HOLLYWOOD STORIES FROM?

THEY DON'T JUST MAKE THEM UP, YOU KNOW!

SHE... WAS A HE!

Innuendo

HE PUNCHED HIS PRODUCER FOR BEING TARDY!

SHE SERVED HUBBY DIVORCE PAPERS FOR DINNER!

HOLLYWOOD HUNK A WIFE-SWAPPER!

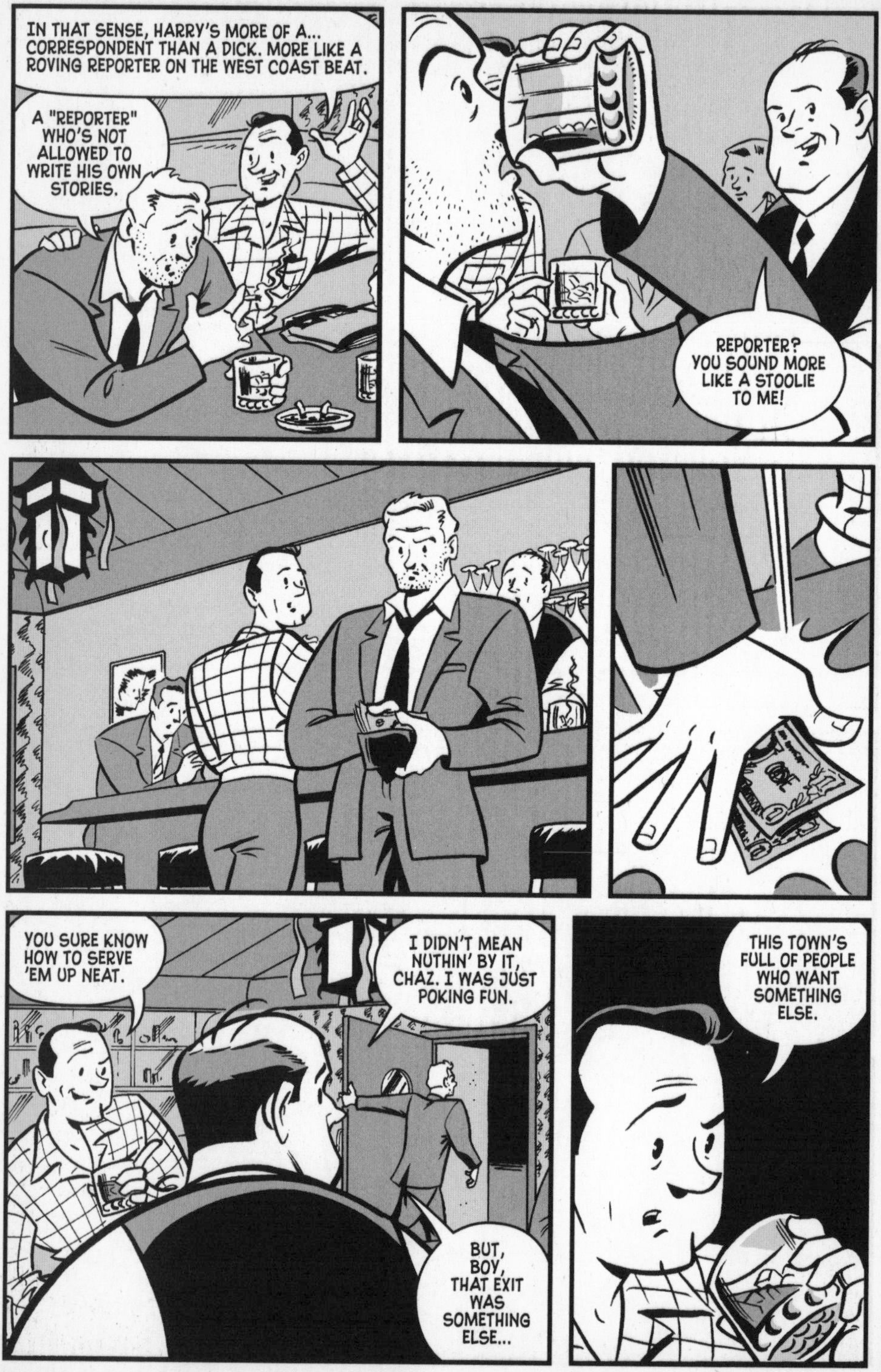
IN THAT SENSE, HARRY'S MORE OF A... CORRESPONDENT THAN A DICK. MORE LIKE A ROVING REPORTER ON THE WEST COAST BEAT.
A "REPORTER" WHO'S NOT ALLOWED TO WRITE HIS OWN STORIES.
REPORTER? YOU SOUND MORE LIKE A STOOLIE TO ME!
YOU SURE KNOW HOW TO SERVE 'EM UP NEAT.
I DIDN'T MEAN NUTHIN' BY IT, CHAZ. I WAS JUST POKING FUN.
BUT, BOY, THAT EXIT WAS SOMETHING ELSE...
THIS TOWN'S FULL OF PEOPLE WHO WANT SOMETHING ELSE.

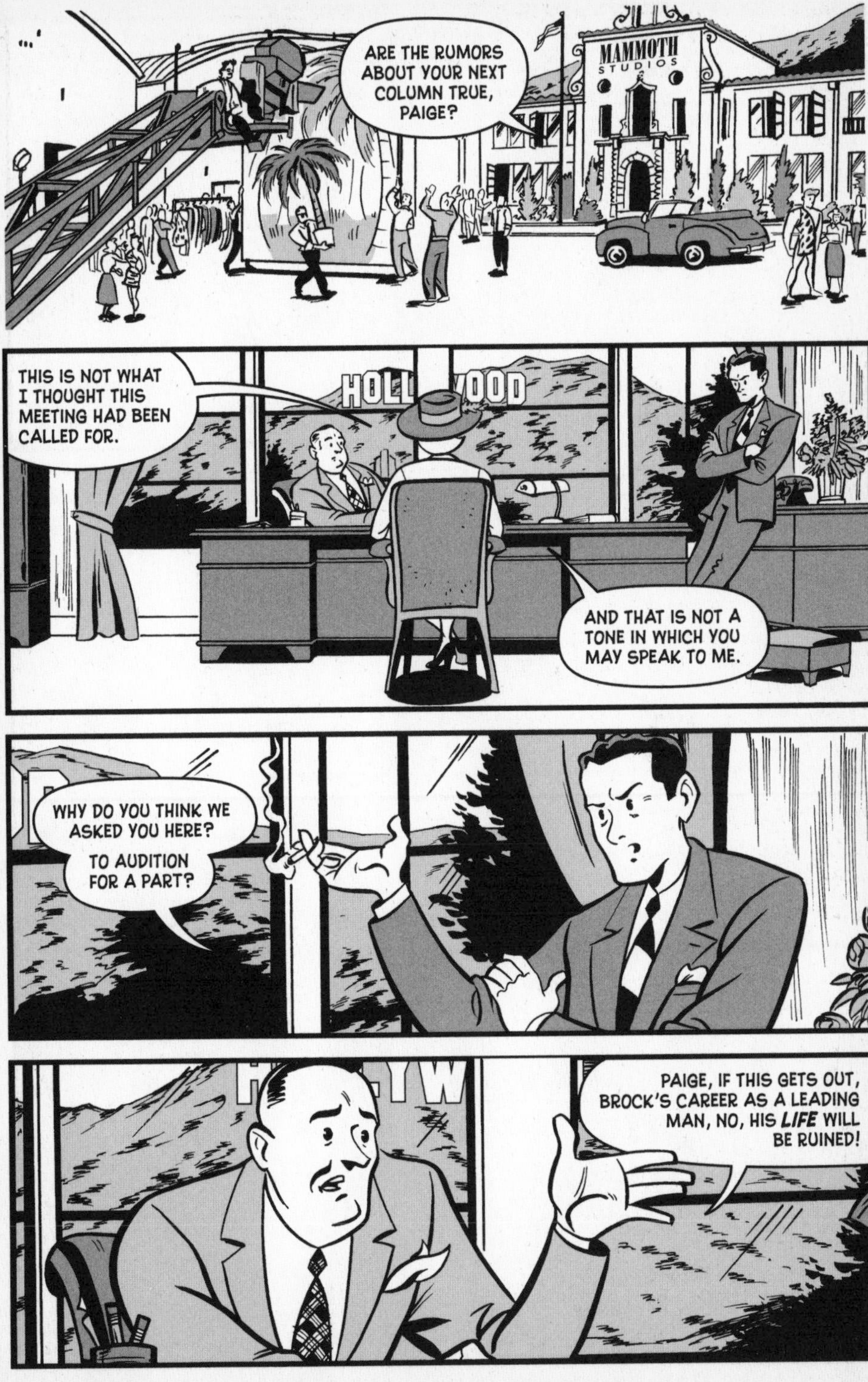

ARE THE RUMORS ABOUT YOUR NEXT COLUMN TRUE, PAIGE?
MAMMOTH STUDIOS
HOLLYWOOD
THIS IS NOT WHAT I THOUGHT THIS MEETING HAD BEEN CALLED FOR.
AND THAT IS NOT A TONE IN WHICH YOU MAY SPEAK TO ME.
WHY DO YOU THINK WE ASKED YOU HERE?
TO AUDITION FOR A PART?
PAIGE, IF THIS GETS OUT, BROCK'S CAREER AS A LEADING MAN, NO, HIS *LIFE* WILL BE RUINED!

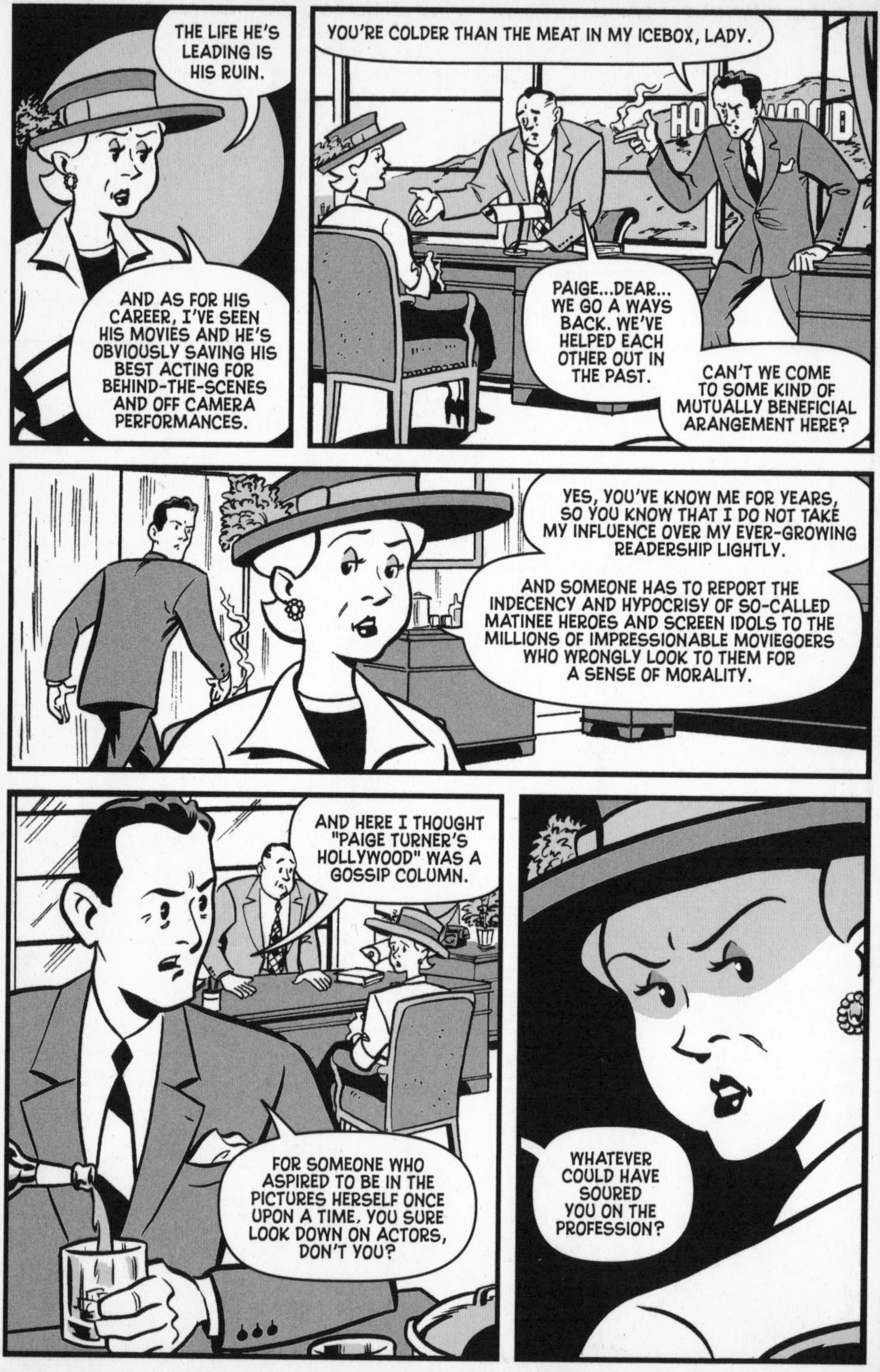
THE LIFE HE'S LEADING IS HIS RUIN.
AND AS FOR HIS CAREER, I'VE SEEN HIS MOVIES AND HE'S OBVIOUSLY SAVING HIS BEST ACTING FOR BEHIND-THE-SCENES AND OFF CAMERA PERFORMANCES.
YOU'RE COLDER THAN THE MEAT IN MY ICEBOX, LADY.
HOLLYWOOD
PAIGE...DEAR... WE GO A WAYS BACK. WE'VE HELPED EACH OTHER OUT IN THE PAST.
CAN'T WE COME TO SOME KIND OF MUTUALLY BENEFICIAL ARANGEMENT HERE?
YES, YOU'VE KNOW ME FOR YEARS, SO YOU KNOW THAT I DO NOT TAKE MY INFLUENCE OVER MY EVER-GROWING READERSHIP LIGHTLY.
AND SOMEONE HAS TO REPORT THE INDECENCY AND HYPOCRISY OF SO-CALLED MATINEE HEROES AND SCREEN IDOLS TO THE MILLIONS OF IMPRESSIONABLE MOVIEGOERS WHO WRONGLY LOOK TO THEM FOR A SENSE OF MORALITY.
AND HERE I THOUGHT "PAIGE TURNER'S HOLLYWOOD" WAS A GOSSIP COLUMN.
FOR SOMEONE WHO ASPIRED TO BE IN THE PICTURES HERSELF ONCE UPON A TIME, YOU SURE LOOK DOWN ON ACTORS, DON'T YOU?
WHATEVER COULD HAVE SOURED YOU ON THE PROFESSION?

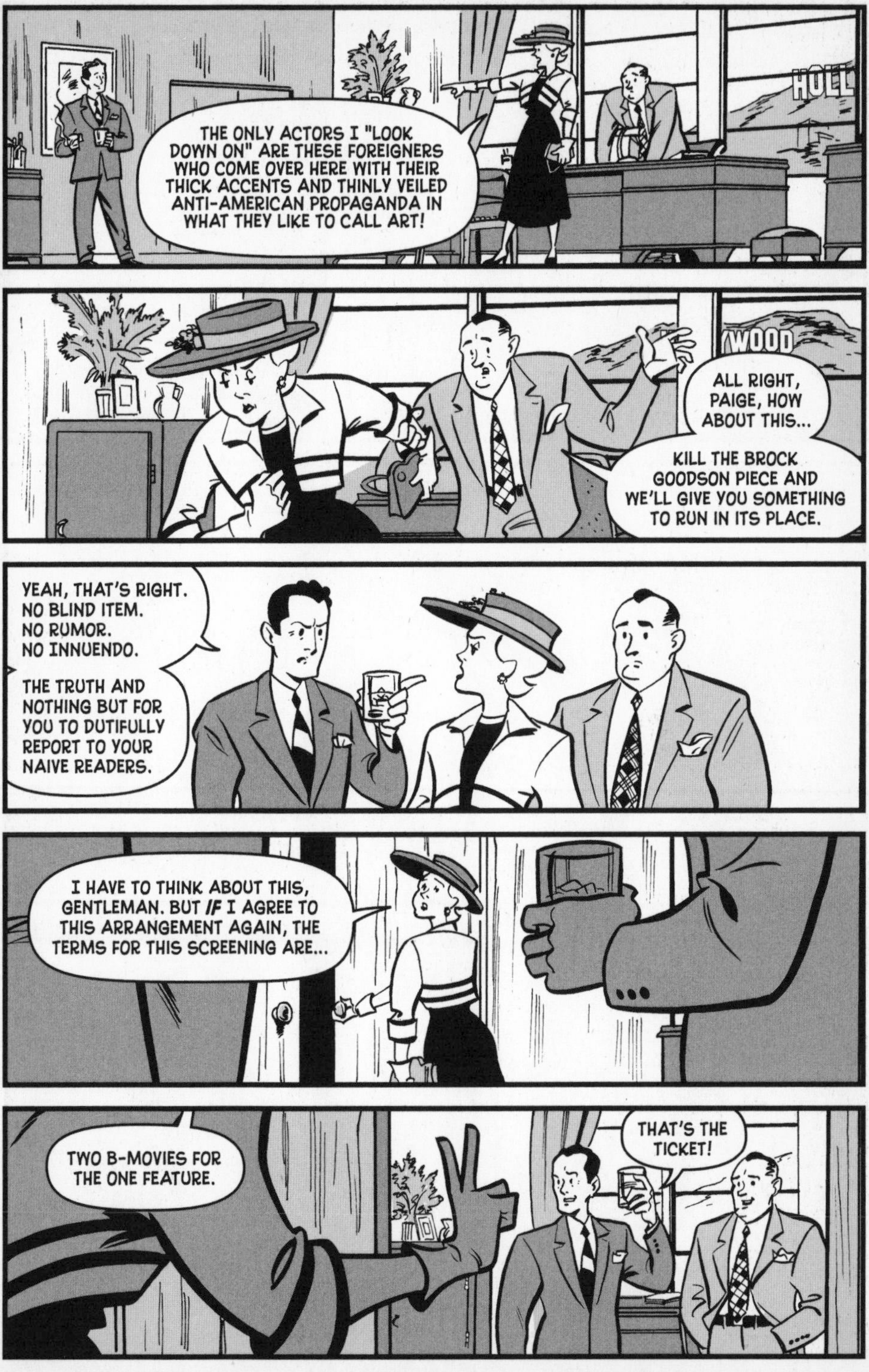
HOLL
THE ONLY ACTORS I "LOOK DOWN ON" ARE THESE FOREIGNERS WHO COME OVER HERE WITH THEIR THICK ACCENTS AND THINLY VEILED ANTI-AMERICAN PROPAGANDA IN WHAT THEY LIKE TO CALL ART!
WOOD
ALL RIGHT, PAIGE, HOW ABOUT THIS...
KILL THE BROCK GOODSON PIECE AND WE'LL GIVE YOU SOMETHING TO RUN IN ITS PLACE.
YEAH, THAT'S RIGHT. NO BLIND ITEM. NO RUMOR. NO INNUENDO.
THE TRUTH AND NOTHING BUT FOR YOU TO DUTIFULLY REPORT TO YOUR NAIVE READERS.
I HAVE TO THINK ABOUT THIS, GENTLEMAN. BUT *IF* I AGREE TO THIS ARRANGEMENT AGAIN, THE TERMS FOR THIS SCREENING ARE...
TWO B-MOVIES FOR THE ONE FEATURE.
THAT'S THE TICKET!

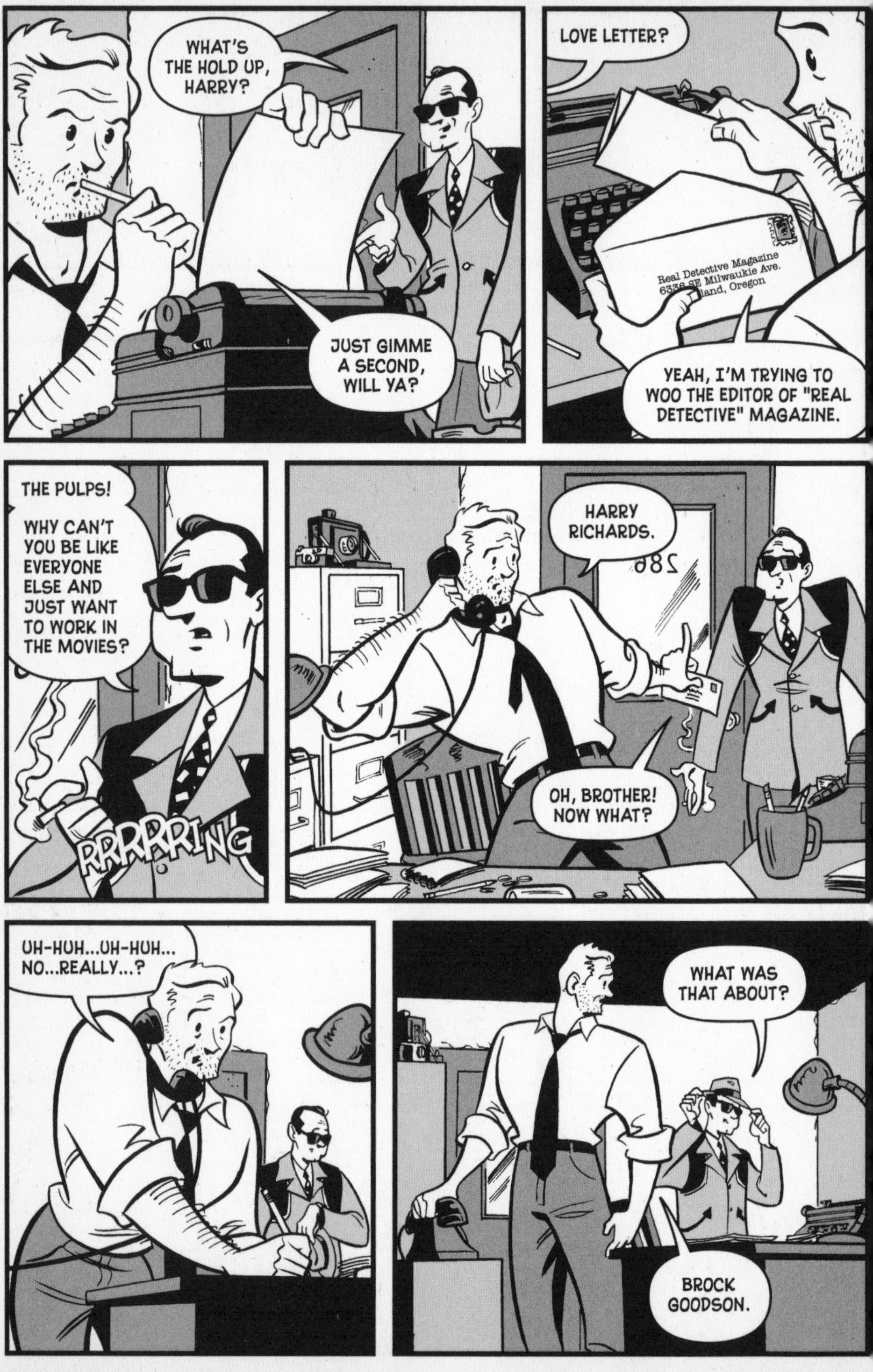
WHAT'S THE HOLD UP, HARRY?
JUST GIMME A SECOND, WILL YA?
LOVE LETTER?
Real Detective Magazine
6336 SE Milwaukie Ave.
land, Oregon
YEAH, I'M TRYING TO WOO THE EDITOR OF "REAL DETECTIVE" MAGAZINE.
THE PULPS!
WHY CAN'T YOU BE LIKE EVERYONE ELSE AND JUST WANT TO WORK IN THE MOVIES?
RRRRRING
HARRY RICHARDS.
OH, BROTHER! NOW WHAT?
UH-HUH...UH-HUH... NO...REALLY...?
WHAT WAS THAT ABOUT?
BROCK GOODSON.

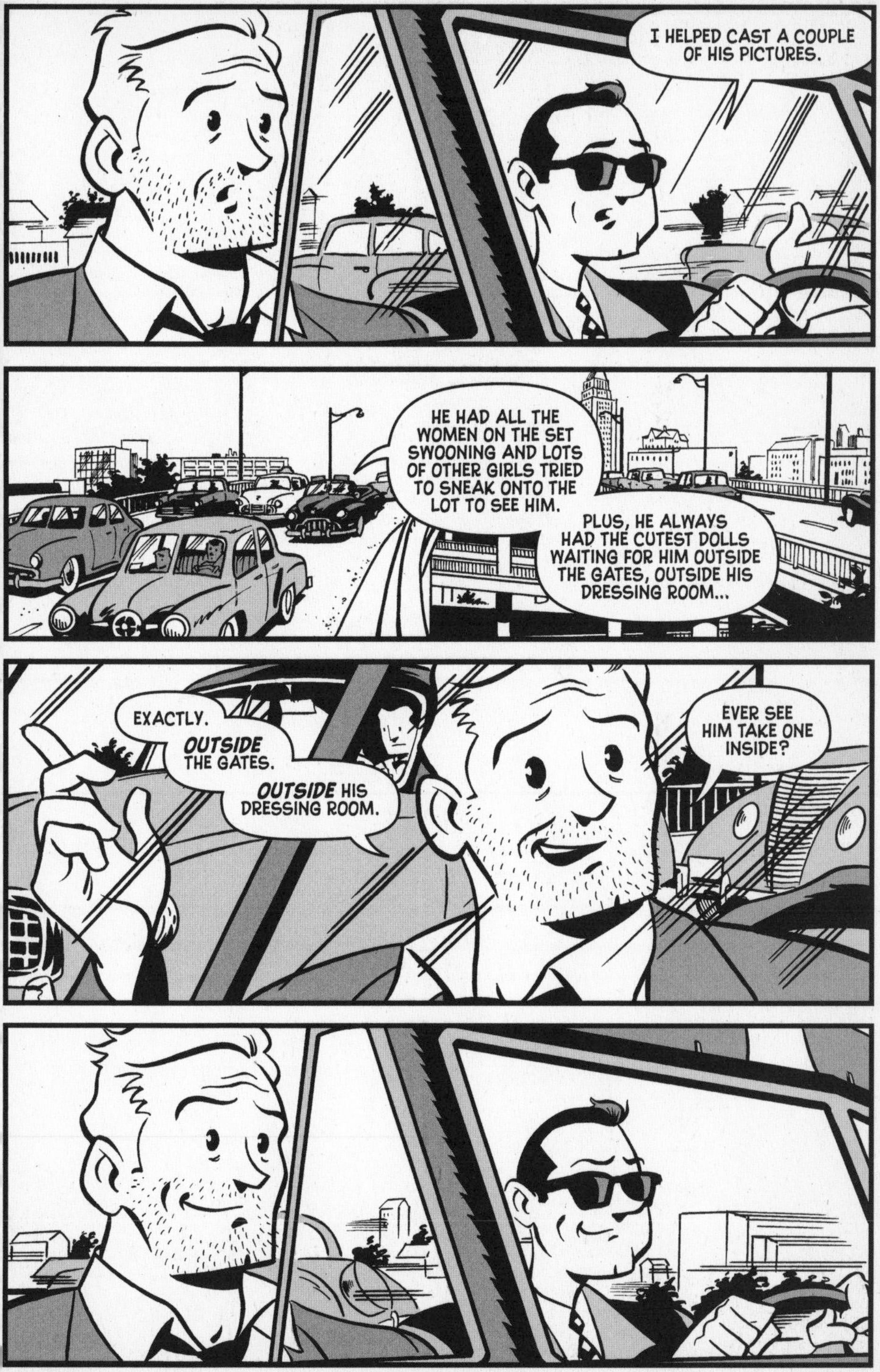

I HELPED CAST A COUPLE OF HIS PICTURES.
HE HAD ALL THE WOMEN ON THE SET SWOONING AND LOTS OF OTHER GIRLS TRIED TO SNEAK ONTO THE LOT TO SEE HIM.
PLUS, HE ALWAYS HAD THE CUTEST DOLLS WAITING FOR HIM OUTSIDE THE GATES, OUTSIDE HIS DRESSING ROOM...
EXACTLY.
OUTSIDE THE GATES.
OUTSIDE HIS DRESSING ROOM.
EVER SEE HIM TAKE ONE INSIDE?

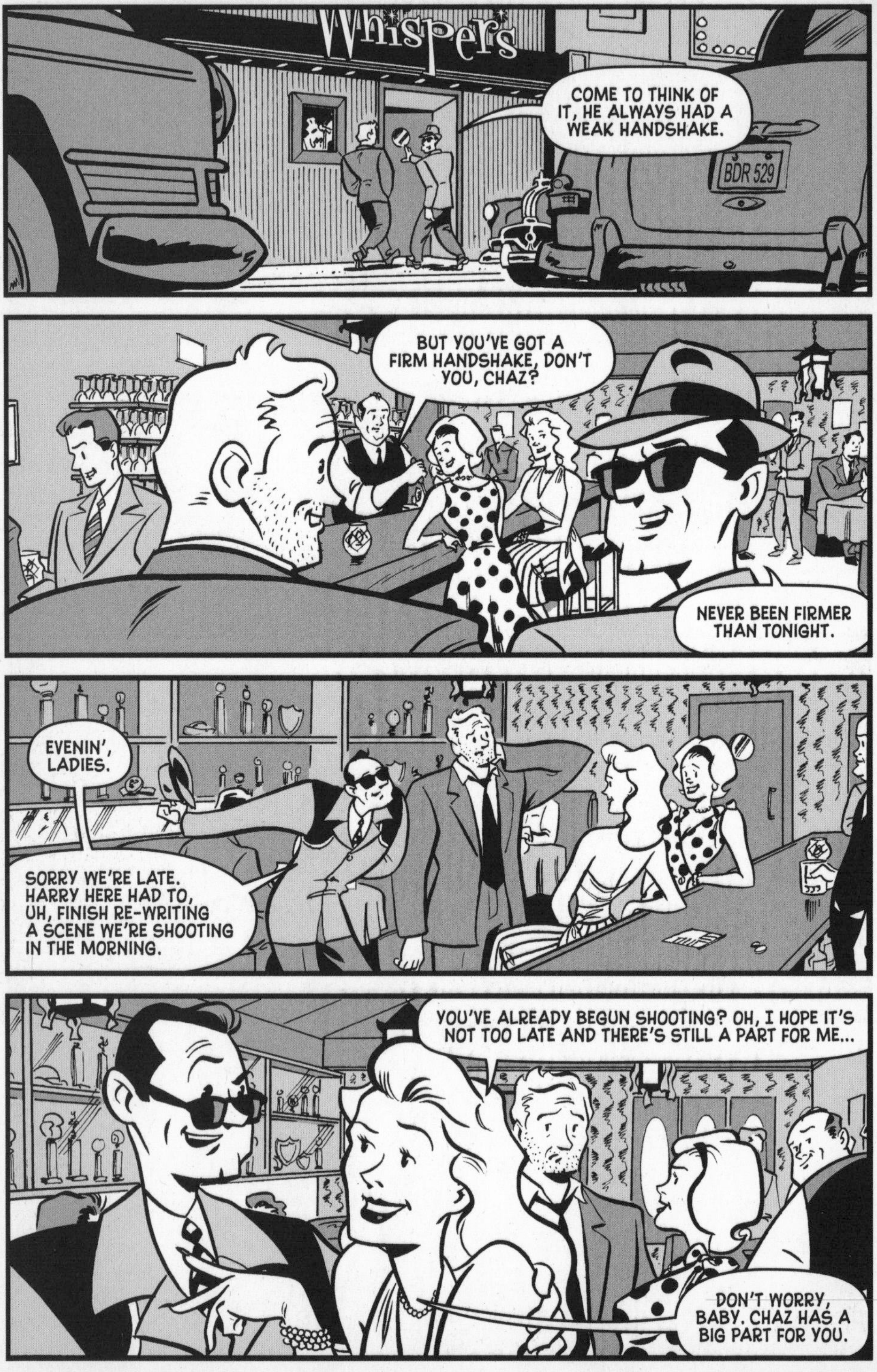

Whispers
COME TO THINK OF IT, HE ALWAYS HAD A WEAK HANDSHAKE.
BDR 529
BUT YOU'VE GOT A FIRM HANDSHAKE, DON'T YOU, CHAZ?
NEVER BEEN FIRMER THAN TONIGHT.
EVENIN', LADIES.
SORRY WE'RE LATE. HARRY HERE HAD TO, UH, FINISH RE-WRITING A SCENE WE'RE SHOOTING IN THE MORNING.
YOU'VE ALREADY BEGUN SHOOTING? OH, I HOPE IT'S NOT TOO LATE AND THERE'S STILL A PART FOR ME...
DON'T WORRY, BABY. CHAZ HAS A BIG PART FOR YOU.

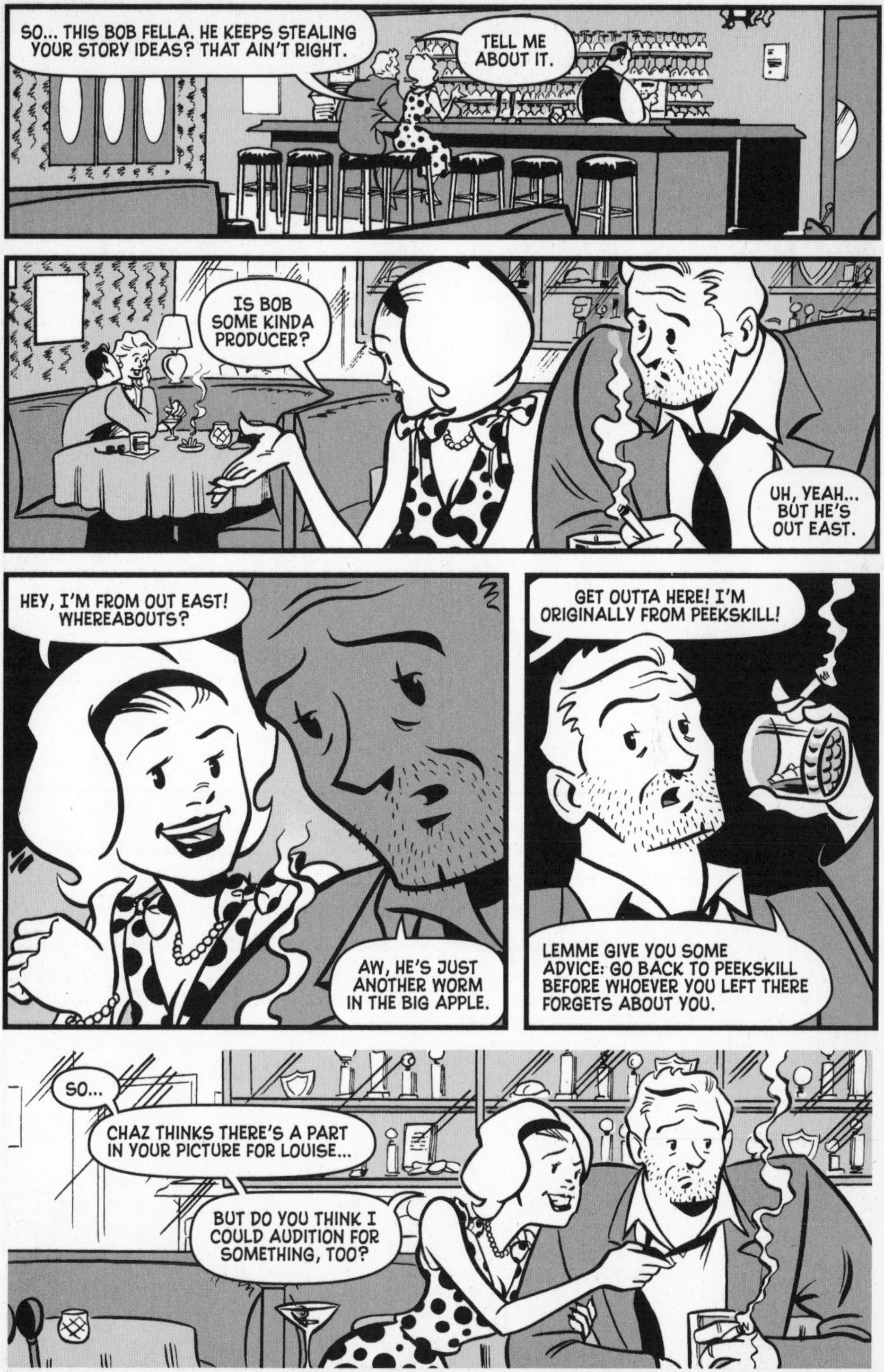
SO... THIS BOB FELLA, HE KEEPS STEALING YOUR STORY IDEAS? THAT AIN'T RIGHT.
TELL ME ABOUT IT.
IS BOB SOME KINDA PRODUCER?
UH, YEAH... BUT HE'S OUT EAST.
HEY, I'M FROM OUT EAST! WHEREABOUTS?
AW, HE'S JUST ANOTHER WORM IN THE BIG APPLE.
GET OUTTA HERE! I'M ORIGINALLY FROM PEEKSKILL!
LEMME GIVE YOU SOME ADVICE: GO BACK TO PEEKSKILL BEFORE WHOEVER YOU LEFT THERE FORGETS ABOUT YOU.
SO...
CHAZ THINKS THERE'S A PART IN YOUR PICTURE FOR LOUISE...
BUT DO YOU THINK I COULD AUDITION FOR SOMETHING, TOO?

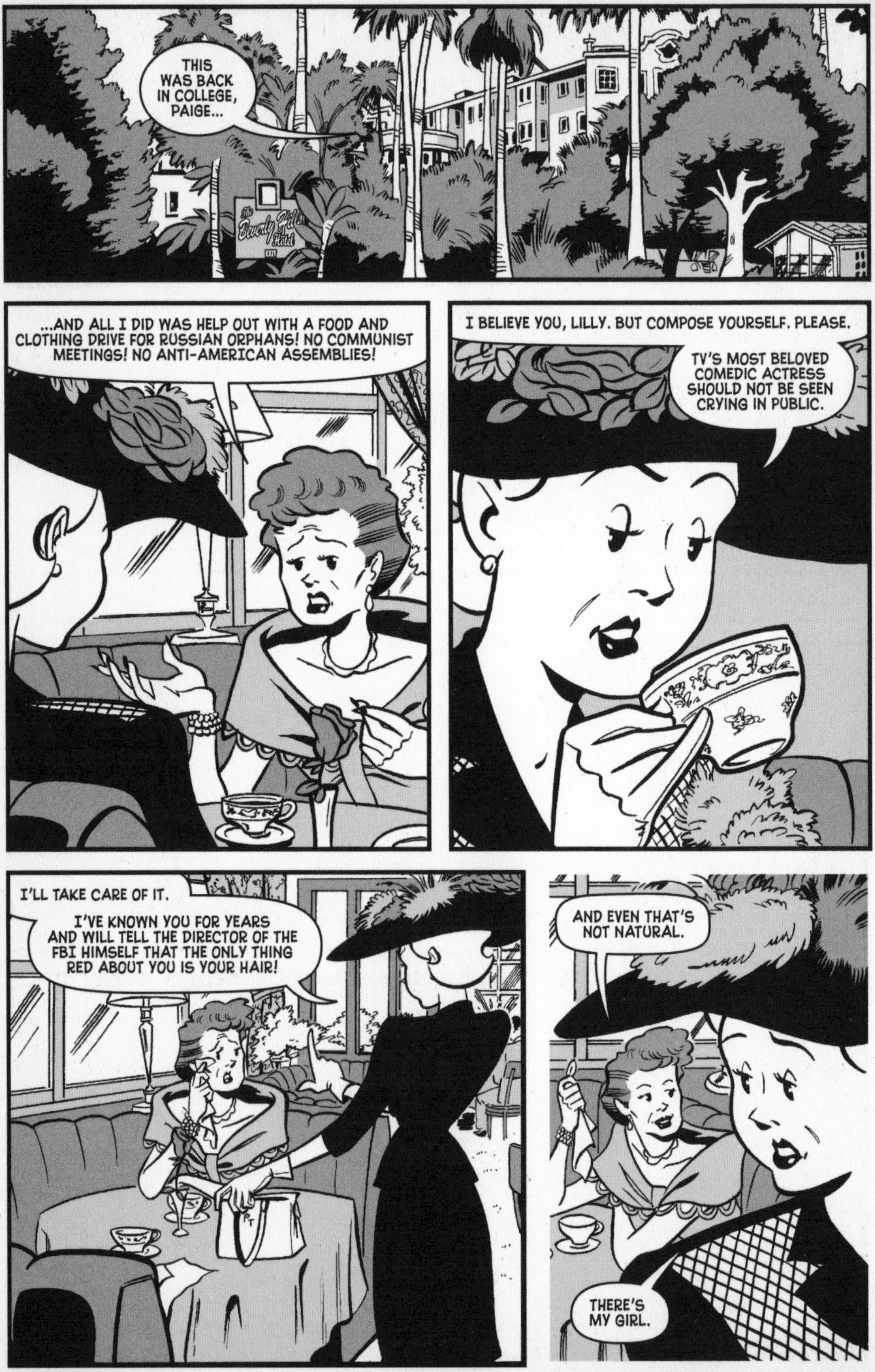
THIS WAS BACK IN COLLEGE, PAIGE...
...AND ALL I DID WAS HELP OUT WITH A FOOD AND CLOTHING DRIVE FOR RUSSIAN ORPHANS! NO COMMUNIST MEETINGS! NO ANTI-AMERICAN ASSEMBLIES!
I BELIEVE YOU, LILLY. BUT COMPOSE YOURSELF. PLEASE.
TV'S MOST BELOVED COMEDIC ACTRESS SHOULD NOT BE SEEN CRYING IN PUBLIC.
I'LL TAKE CARE OF IT.
I'VE KNOWN YOU FOR YEARS AND WILL TELL THE DIRECTOR OF THE FBI HIMSELF THAT THE ONLY THING RED ABOUT YOU IS YOUR HAIR!
AND EVEN THAT'S NOT NATURAL.
THERE'S MY GIRL.

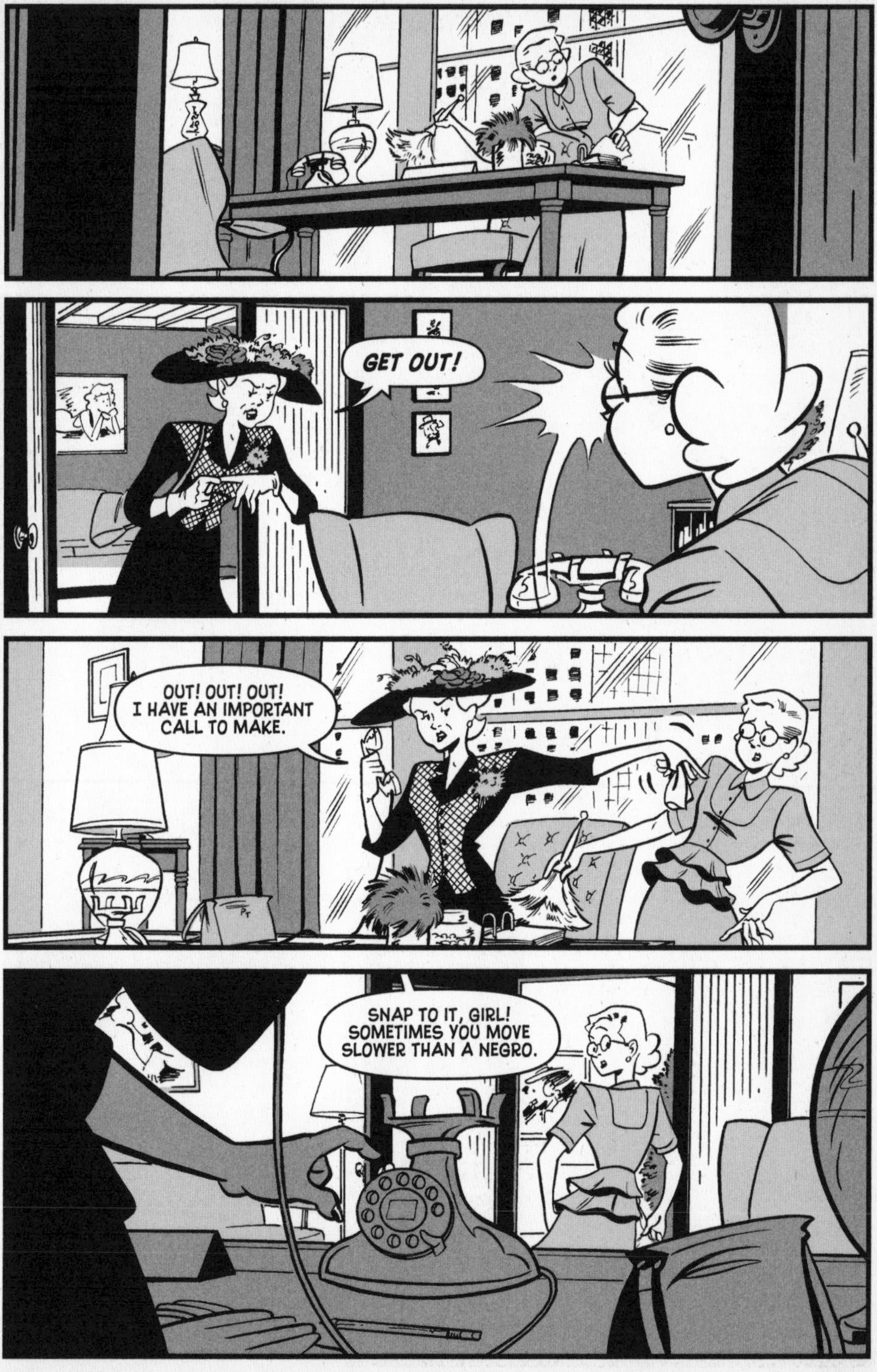
GET OUT!
OUT! OUT! OUT! I HAVE AN IMPORTANT CALL TO MAKE.
SNAP TO IT, GIRL! SOMETIMES YOU MOVE SLOWER THAN A NEGRO.

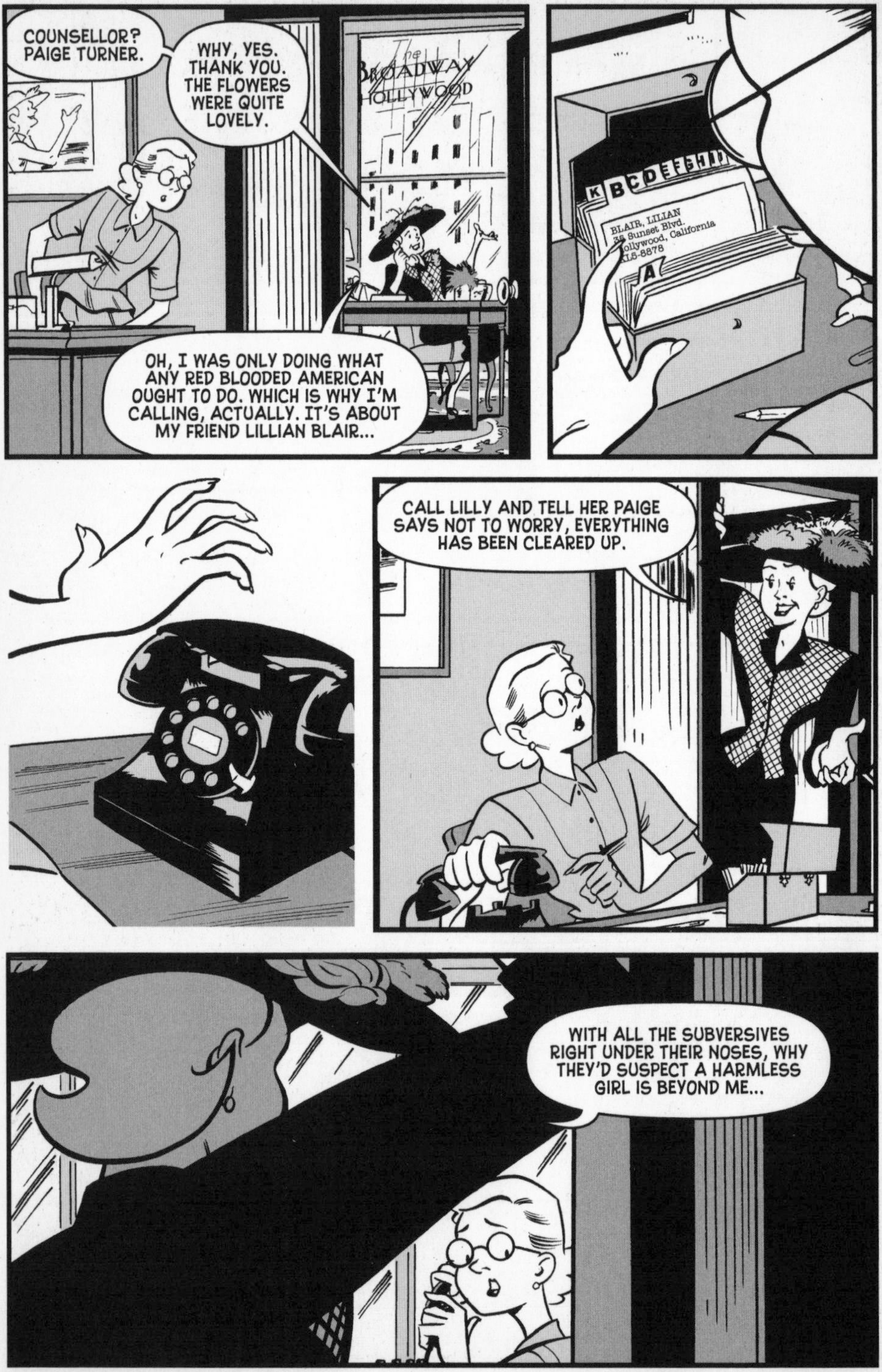
COUNSELLOR? PAIGE TURNER.
WHY, YES. THANK YOU. THE FLOWERS WERE QUITE LOVELY.
The BROADWAY HOLLYWOOD
OH, I WAS ONLY DOING WHAT ANY RED BLOODED AMERICAN OUGHT TO DO. WHICH IS WHY I'M CALLING, ACTUALLY. IT'S ABOUT MY FRIEND LILLIAN BLAIR...
K B C D E F G H I J
BLAIR, LILIAN
Sunset Blvd.
ollywood, California
A
CALL LILLY AND TELL HER PAIGE SAYS NOT TO WORRY, EVERYTHING HAS BEEN CLEARED UP.
WITH ALL THE SUBVERSIVES RIGHT UNDER THEIR NOSES, WHY THEY'D SUSPECT A HARMLESS GIRL IS BEYOND ME...

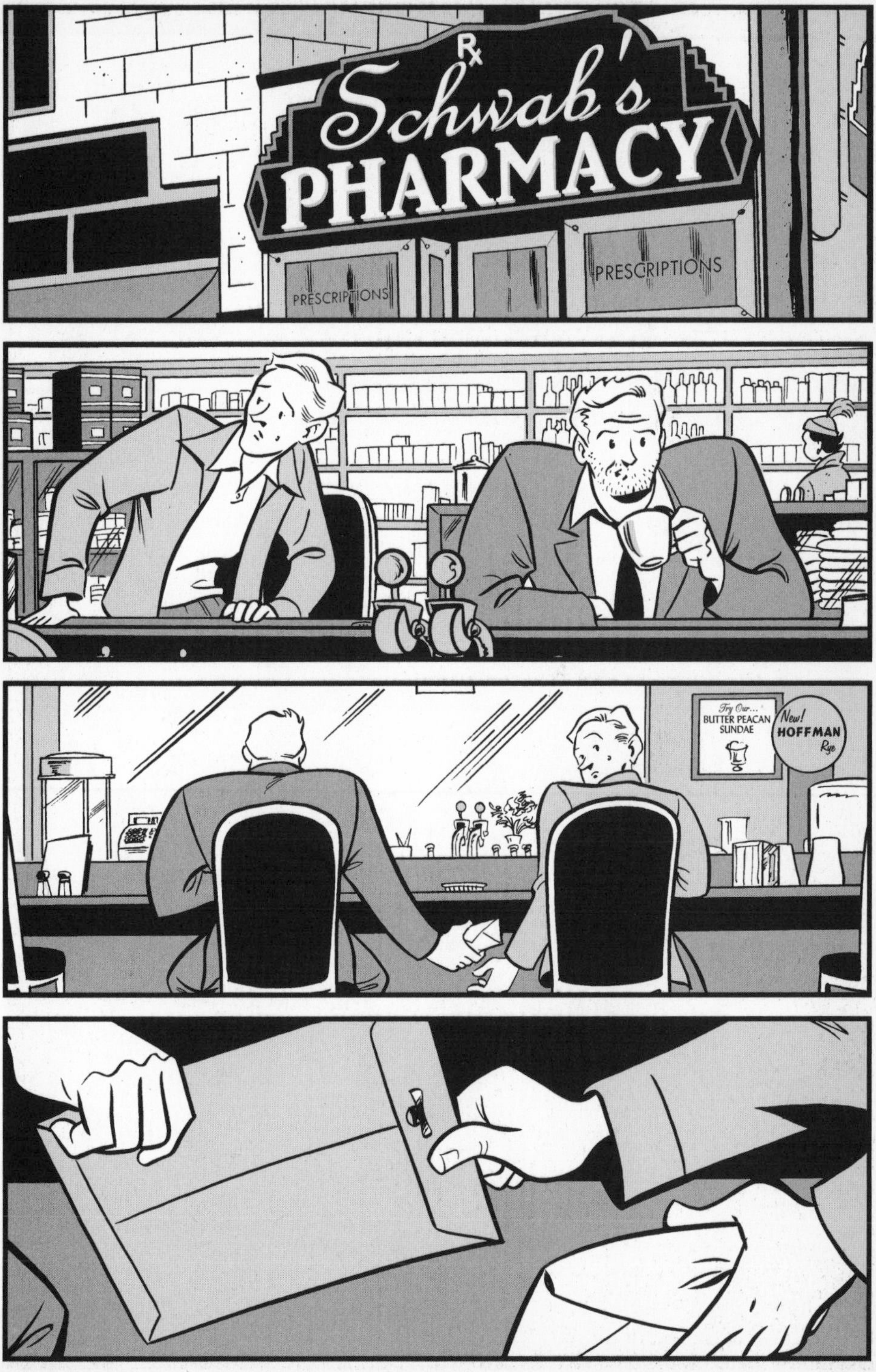
Rx
Schwab's
PHARMACY
PRESCRIPTIONS
PRESCRIPTIONS
Try Our...
BUTTER PEACAN
SUNDAE
New!
HOFFMAN
Rye

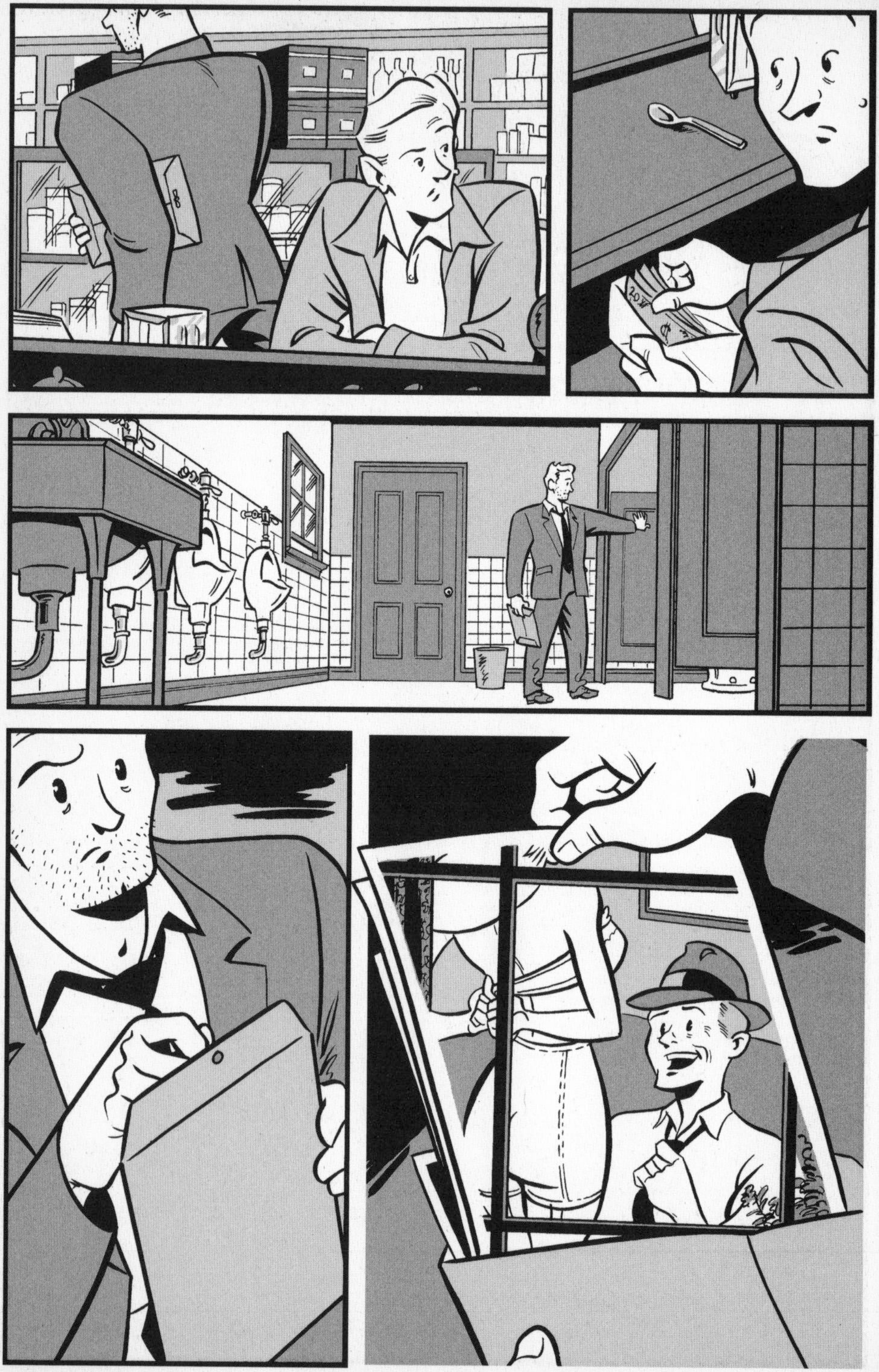

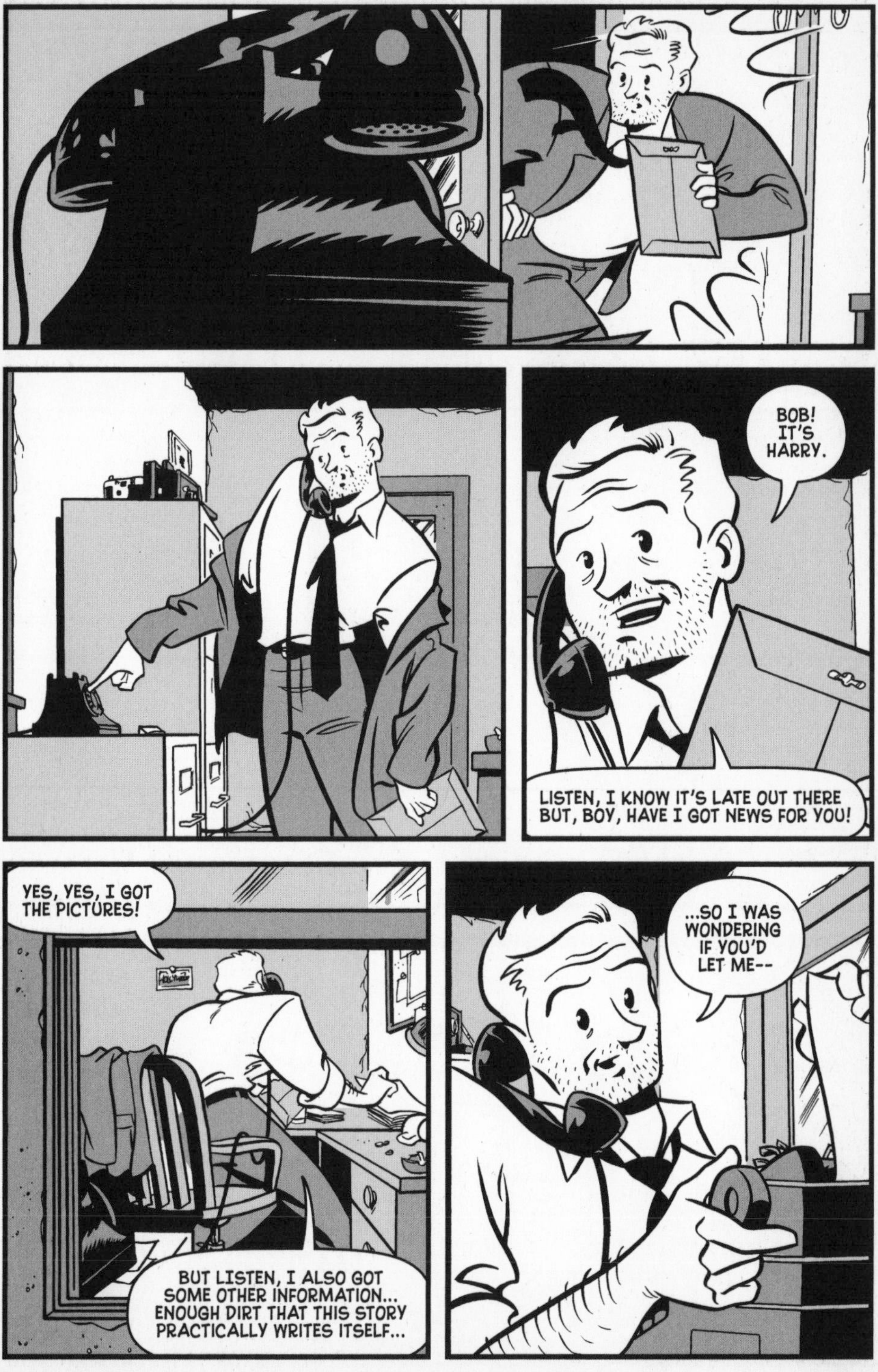
BOB! IT'S HARRY.
LISTEN, I KNOW IT'S LATE OUT THERE BUT, BOY, HAVE I GOT NEWS FOR YOU!
YES, YES, I GOT THE PICTURES!
BUT LISTEN, I ALSO GOT SOME OTHER INFORMATION... ENOUGH DIRT THAT THIS STORY PRACTICALLY WRITES ITSELF...
...SO I WAS WONDERING IF YOU'D LET ME--

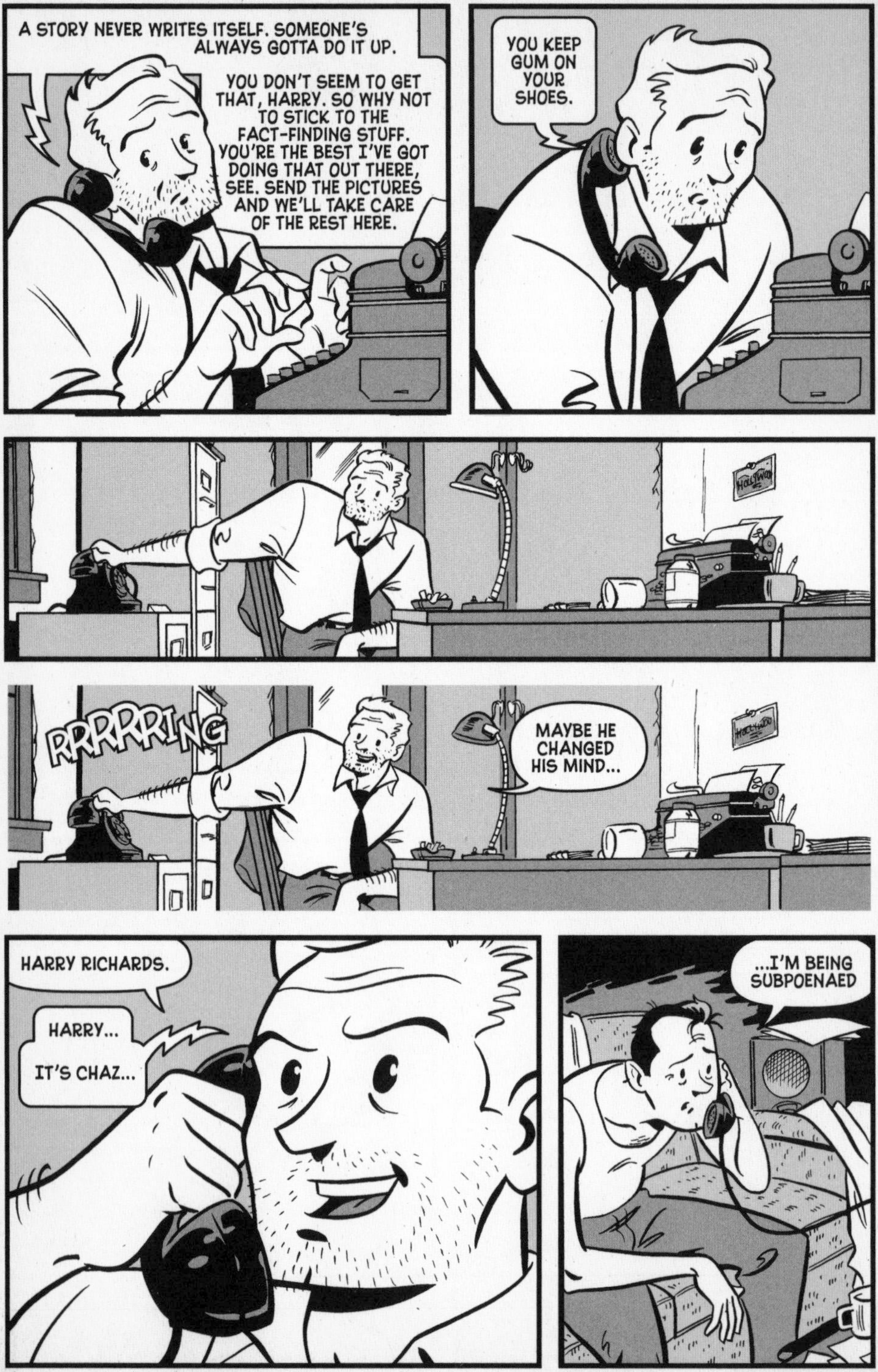
A STORY NEVER WRITES ITSELF. SOMEONE'S ALWAYS GOTTA DO IT UP.
YOU DON'T SEEM TO GET THAT, HARRY. SO WHY NOT TO STICK TO THE FACT-FINDING STUFF. YOU'RE THE BEST I'VE GOT DOING THAT OUT THERE, SEE. SEND THE PICTURES AND WE'LL TAKE CARE OF THE REST HERE.
YOU KEEP GUM ON YOUR SHOES.
RRRRRING
MAYBE HE CHANGED HIS MIND...
HARRY RICHARDS.
HARRY...
IT'S CHAZ...
...I'M BEING SUBPOENAED

Act II

"Everybody reads it, but
they say the cook brought
it into the house."
- Humphrey Bogart

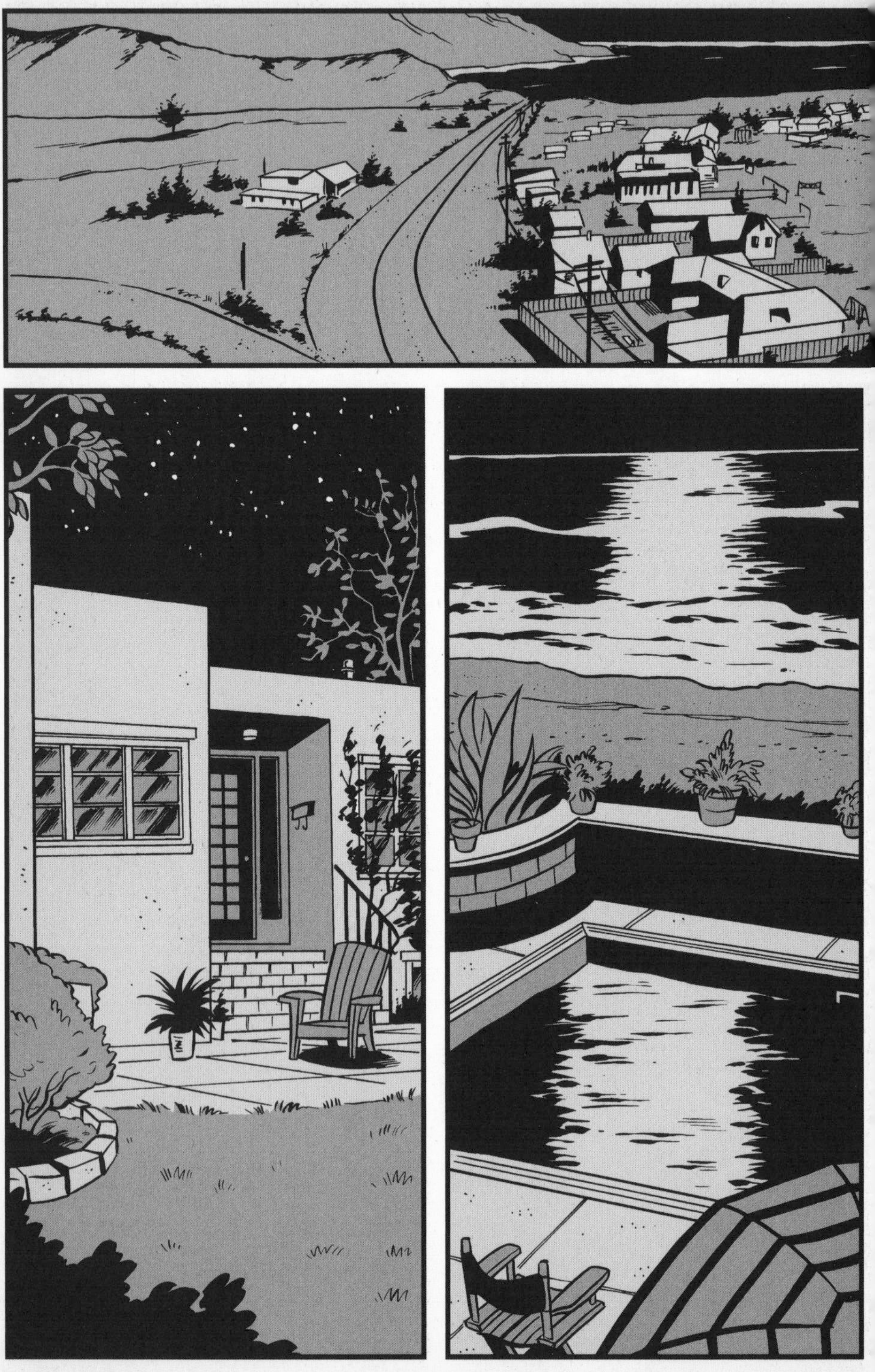

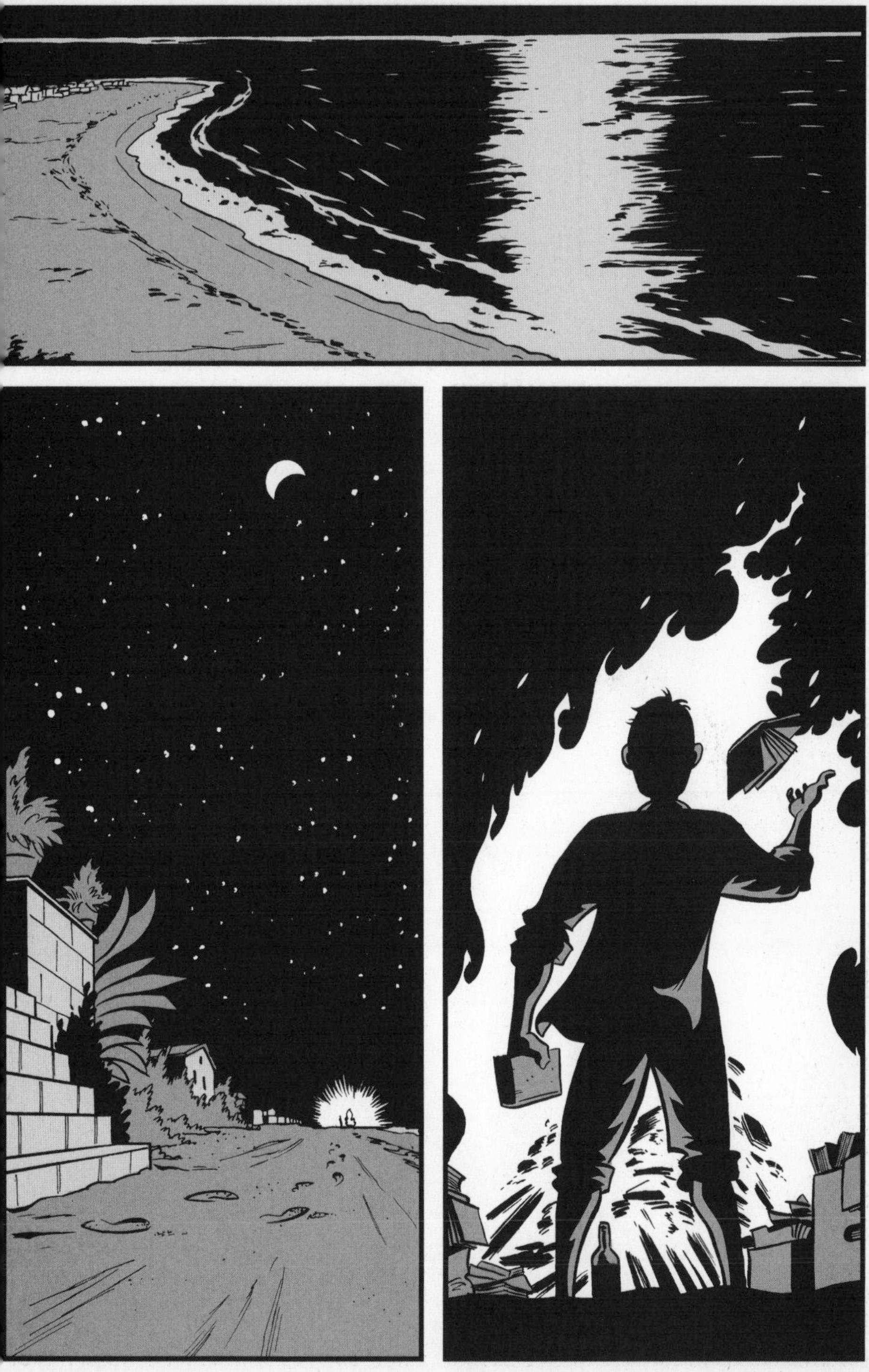

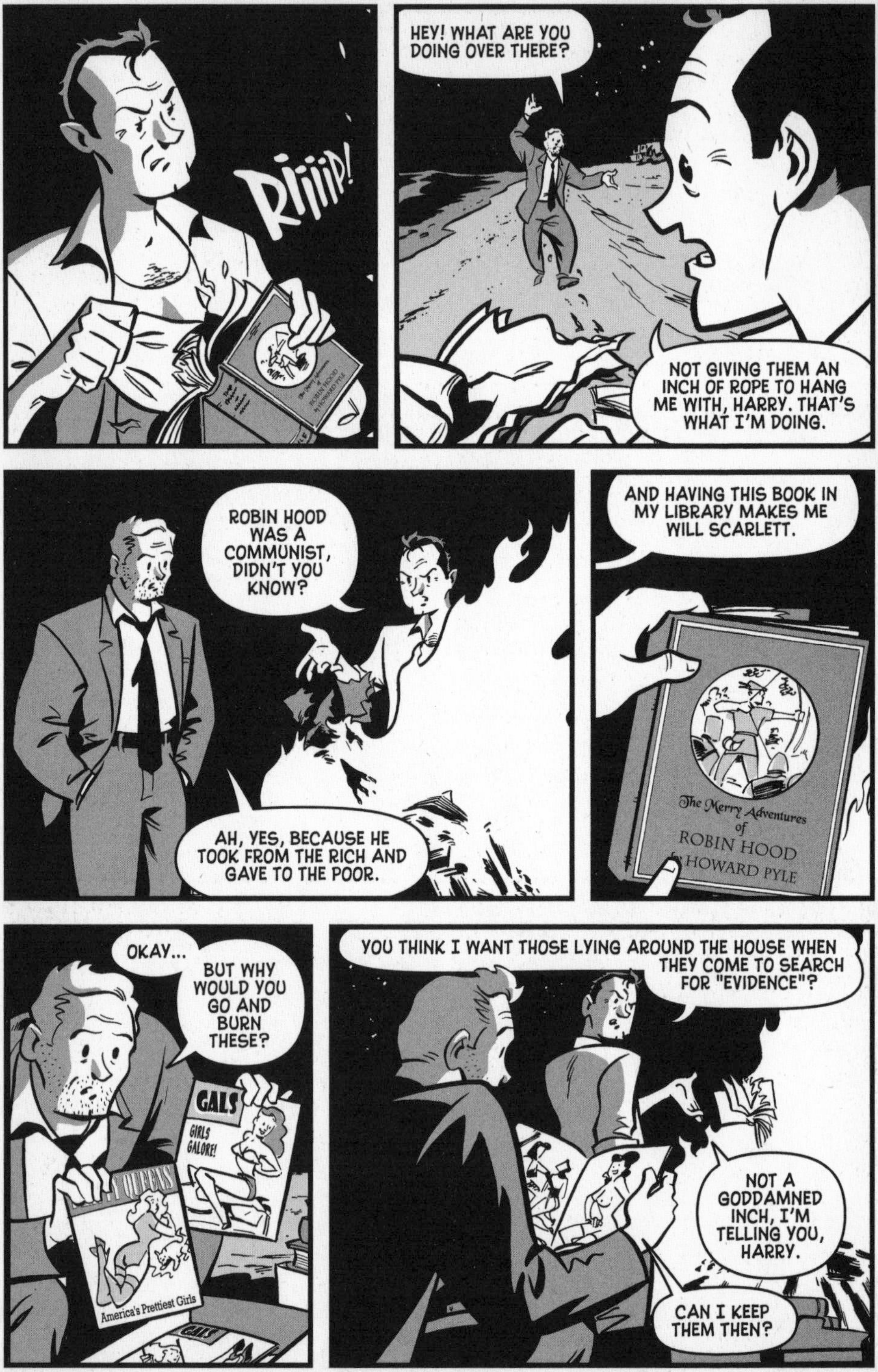

RIIIIP!
HEY! WHAT ARE YOU DOING OVER THERE?
NOT GIVING THEM AN INCH OF ROPE TO HANG ME WITH, HARRY. THAT'S WHAT I'M DOING.
ROBIN HOOD WAS A COMMUNIST, DIDN'T YOU KNOW?
AH, YES, BECAUSE HE TOOK FROM THE RICH AND GAVE TO THE POOR.
AND HAVING THIS BOOK IN MY LIBRARY MAKES ME WILL SCARLETT.
The Merry Adventures of ROBIN HOOD by HOWARD PYLE
OKAY...
BUT WHY WOULD YOU GO AND BURN THESE?
GALS
GIRLS GALORE!
America's Prettiest Girls
YOU THINK I WANT THOSE LYING AROUND THE HOUSE WHEN THEY COME TO SEARCH FOR "EVIDENCE"?
NOT A GODDAMNED INCH, I'M TELLING YOU, HARRY.
CAN I KEEP THEM THEN?

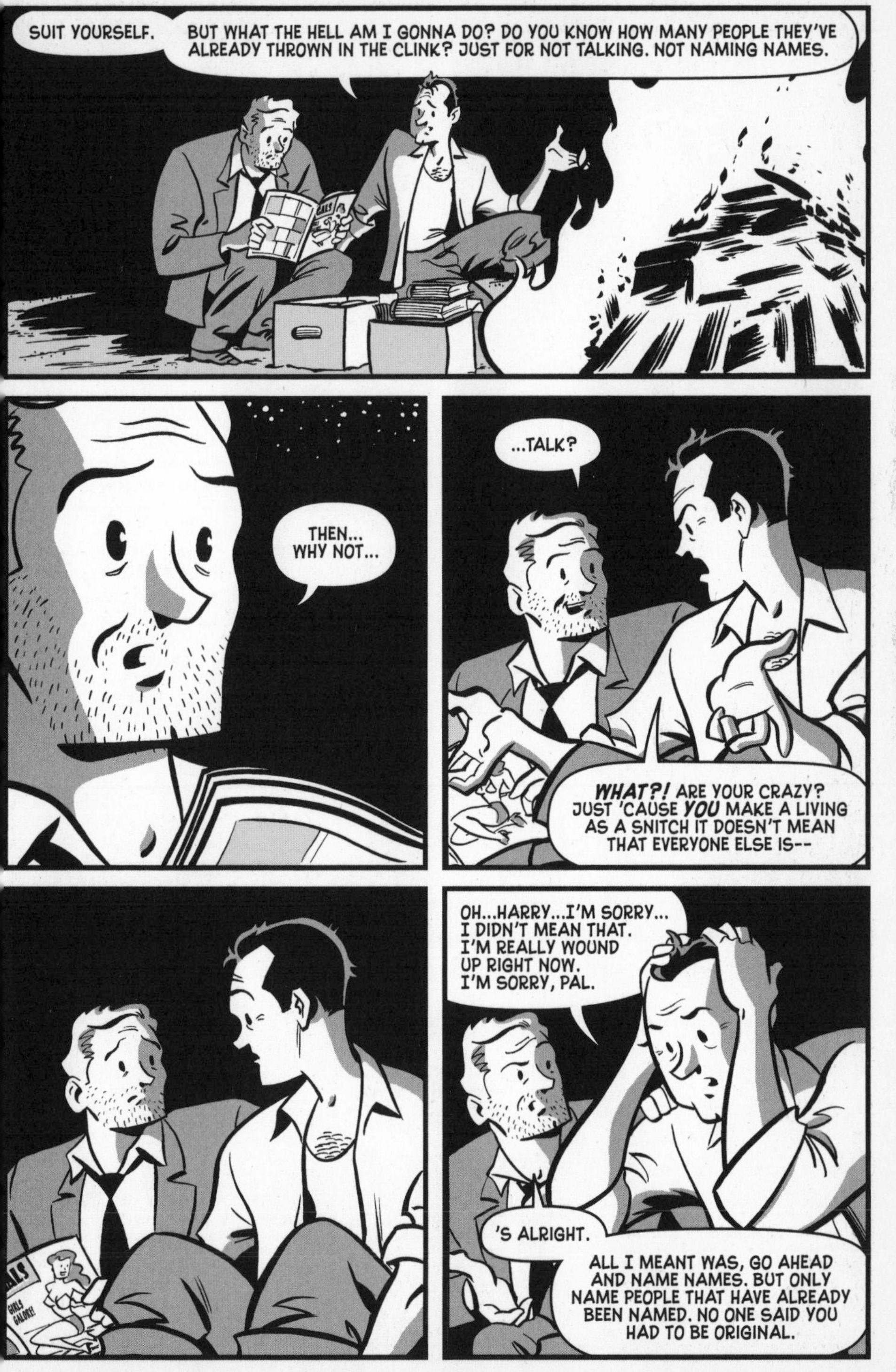
SUIT YOURSELF.
BUT WHAT THE HELL AM I GONNA DO? DO YOU KNOW HOW MANY PEOPLE THEY'VE ALREADY THROWN IN THE CLINK? JUST FOR NOT TALKING. NOT NAMING NAMES.
THEN... WHY NOT...
...TALK?
WHAT?! ARE YOUR CRAZY? JUST 'CAUSE YOU MAKE A LIVING AS A SNITCH IT DOESN'T MEAN THAT EVERYONE ELSE IS--
OH...HARRY...I'M SORRY... I DIDN'T MEAN THAT. I'M REALLY WOUND UP RIGHT NOW. I'M SORRY, PAL.
'S ALRIGHT.
ALL I MEANT WAS, GO AHEAD AND NAME NAMES. BUT ONLY NAME PEOPLE THAT HAVE ALREADY BEEN NAMED. NO ONE SAID YOU HAD TO BE ORIGINAL.

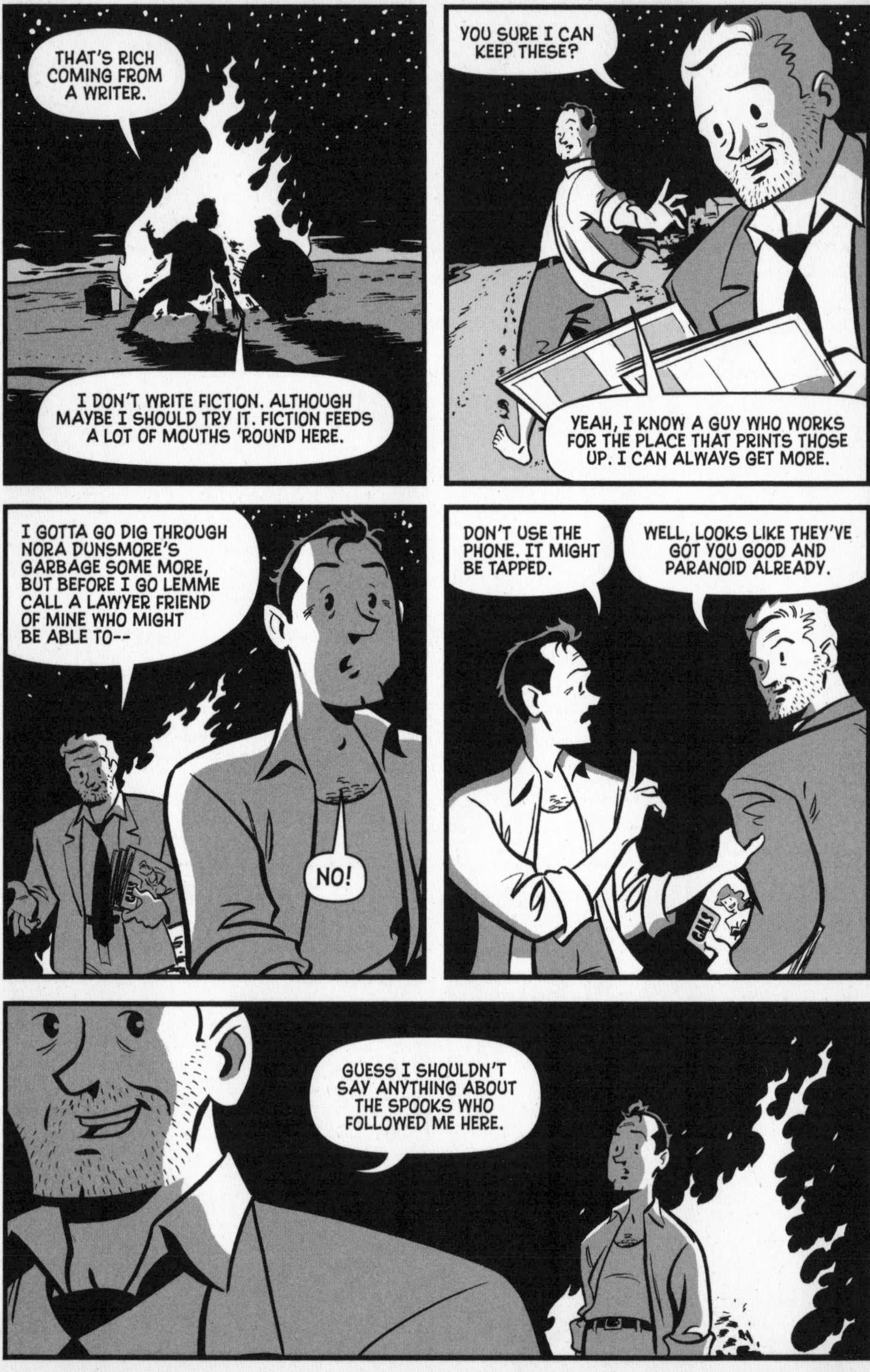
THAT'S RICH COMING FROM A WRITER.
I DON'T WRITE FICTION. ALTHOUGH MAYBE I SHOULD TRY IT. FICTION FEEDS A LOT OF MOUTHS 'ROUND HERE.
YOU SURE I CAN KEEP THESE?
YEAH, I KNOW A GUY WHO WORKS FOR THE PLACE THAT PRINTS THOSE UP. I CAN ALWAYS GET MORE.
I GOTTA GO DIG THROUGH NORA DUNSMORE'S GARBAGE SOME MORE, BUT BEFORE I GO LEMME CALL A LAWYER FRIEND OF MINE WHO MIGHT BE ABLE TO--
NO!
DON'T USE THE PHONE. IT MIGHT BE TAPPED.
WELL, LOOKS LIKE THEY'VE GOT YOU GOOD AND PARANOID ALREADY.
GALS
GUESS I SHOULDN'T SAY ANYTHING ABOUT THE SPOOKS WHO FOLLOWED ME HERE.

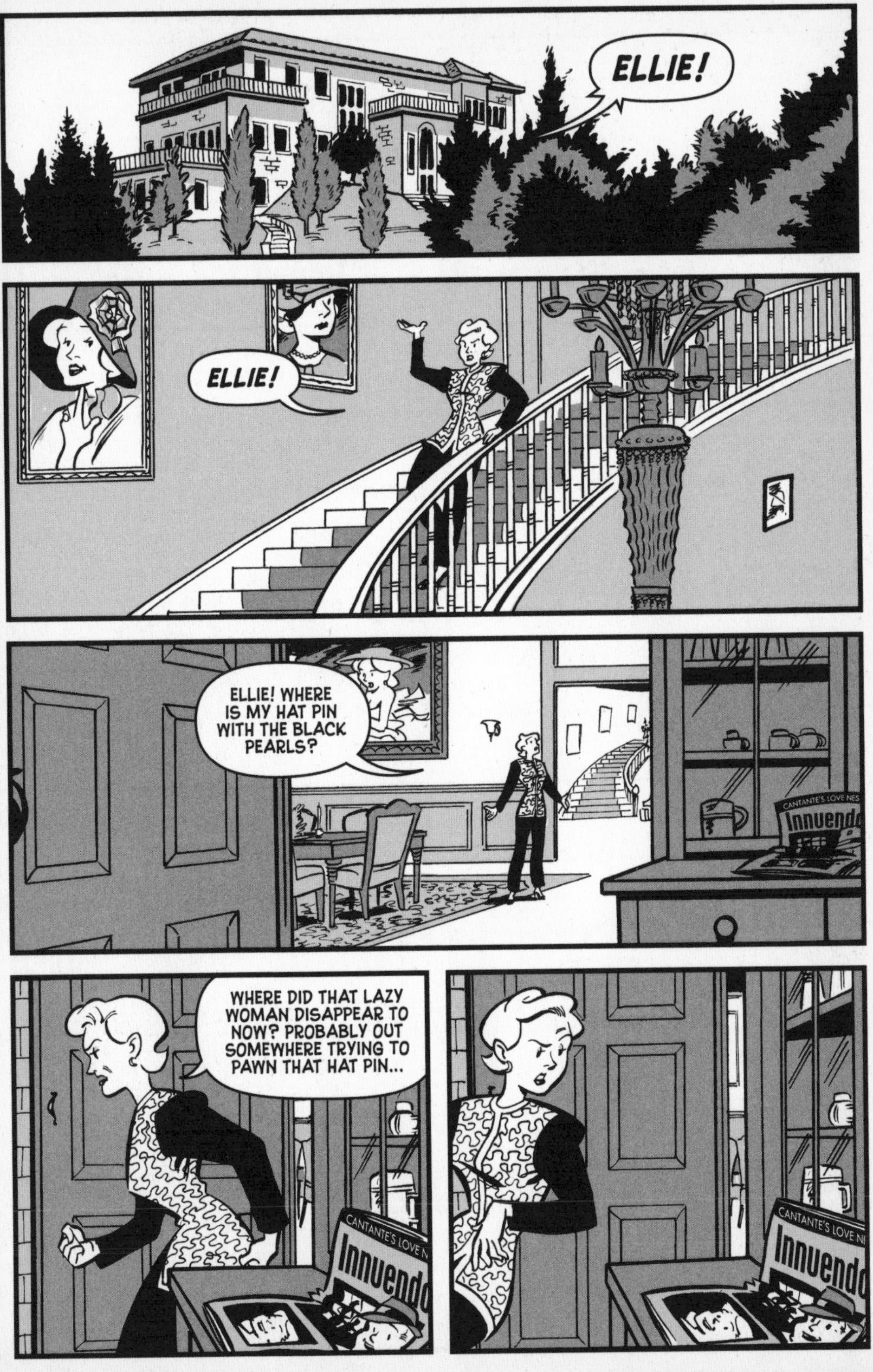
ELLIE!
ELLIE!
ELLIE! WHERE IS MY HAT PIN WITH THE BLACK PEARLS?
CANTANTE'S LOVE NES
Innuendo
WHERE DID THAT LAZY WOMAN DISAPPEAR TO NOW? PROBABLY OUT SOMEWHERE TRYING TO PAWN THAT HAT PIN...
CANTANTE'S LOVE N
Innuendo
CANTANTE'S LOVE NE
Innuendo

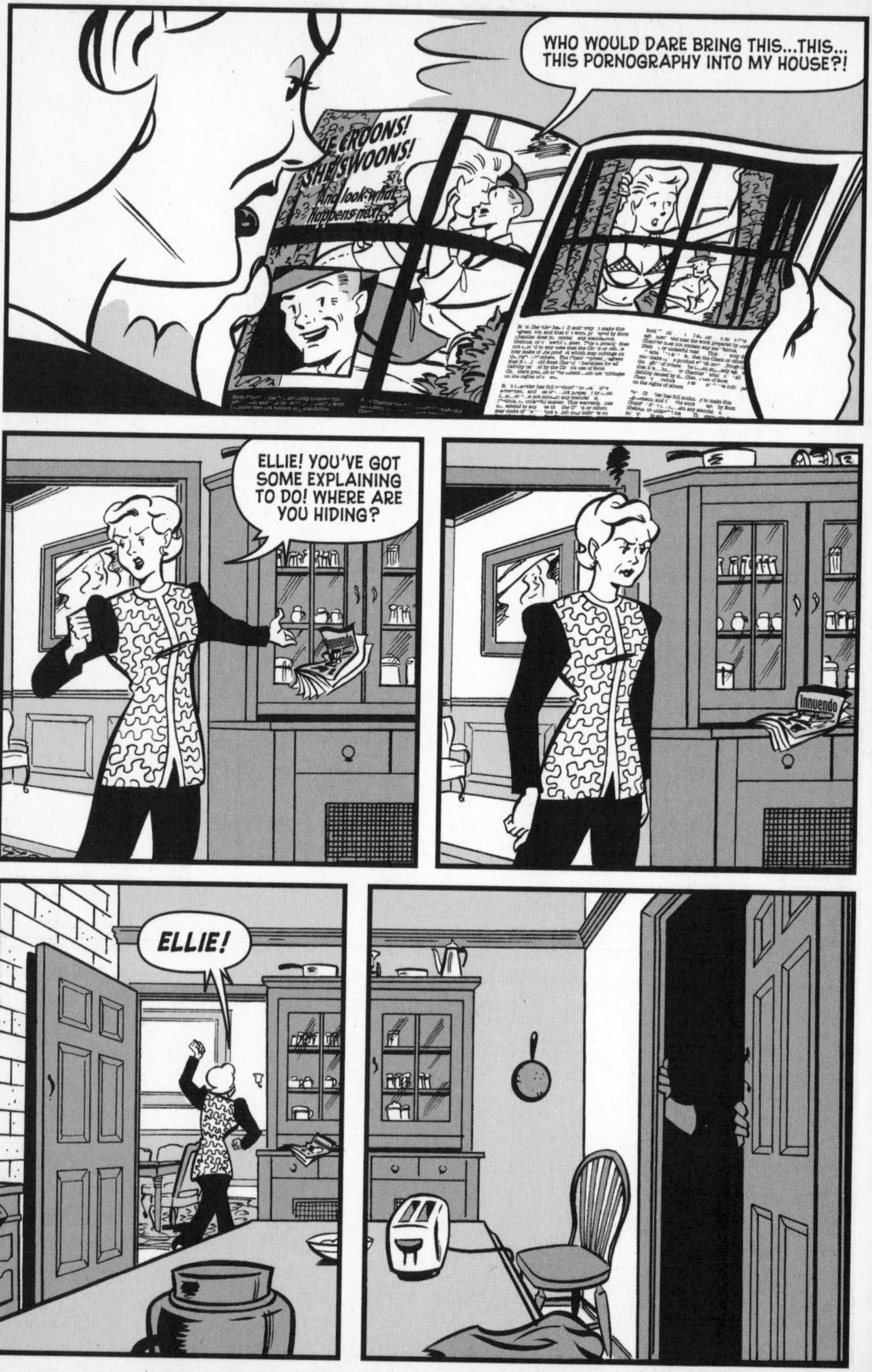
WHO WOULD DARE BRING THIS...THIS... THIS PORNOGRAPHY INTO MY HOUSE?!
ELLIE! YOU'VE GOT SOME EXPLAINING TO DO! WHERE ARE YOU HIDING?
Innuendo
ELLIE!

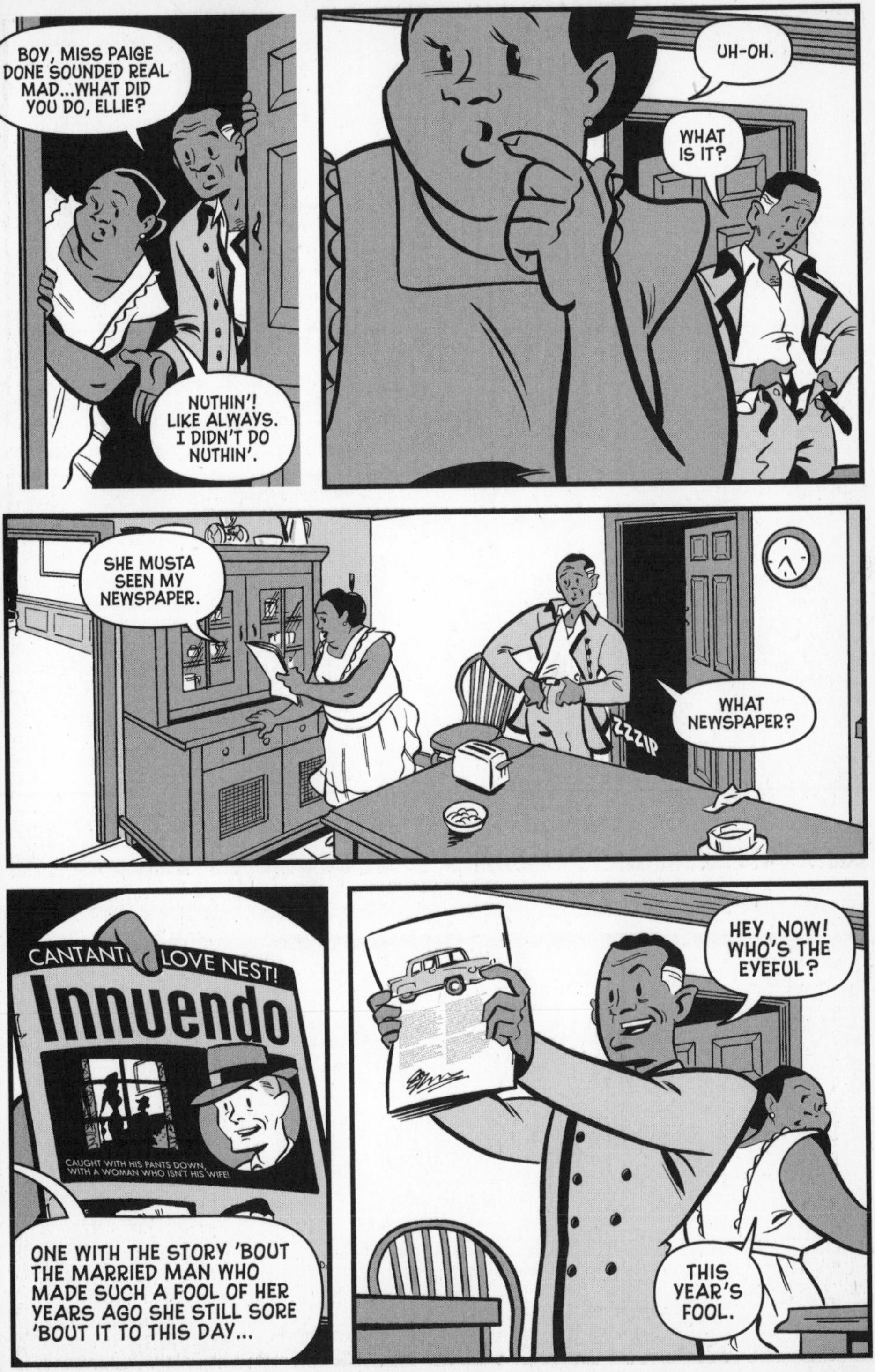
BOY, MISS PAIGE DONE SOUNDED REAL MAD...WHAT DID YOU DO, ELLIE?
NUTHIN'! LIKE ALWAYS. I DIDN'T DO NUTHIN'.
UH-OH.
WHAT IS IT?
SHE MUSTA SEEN MY NEWSPAPER.
WHAT NEWSPAPER?
ZZZIP
CANTANTI LOVE NEST!
Innuendo
CAUGHT WITH HIS PANTS DOWN, WITH A WOMAN WHO ISN'T HIS WIFE!
ONE WITH THE STORY 'BOUT THE MARRIED MAN WHO MADE SUCH A FOOL OF HER YEARS AGO SHE STILL SORE 'BOUT IT TO THIS DAY...
HEY, NOW! WHO'S THE EYEFUL?
THIS YEAR'S FOOL.

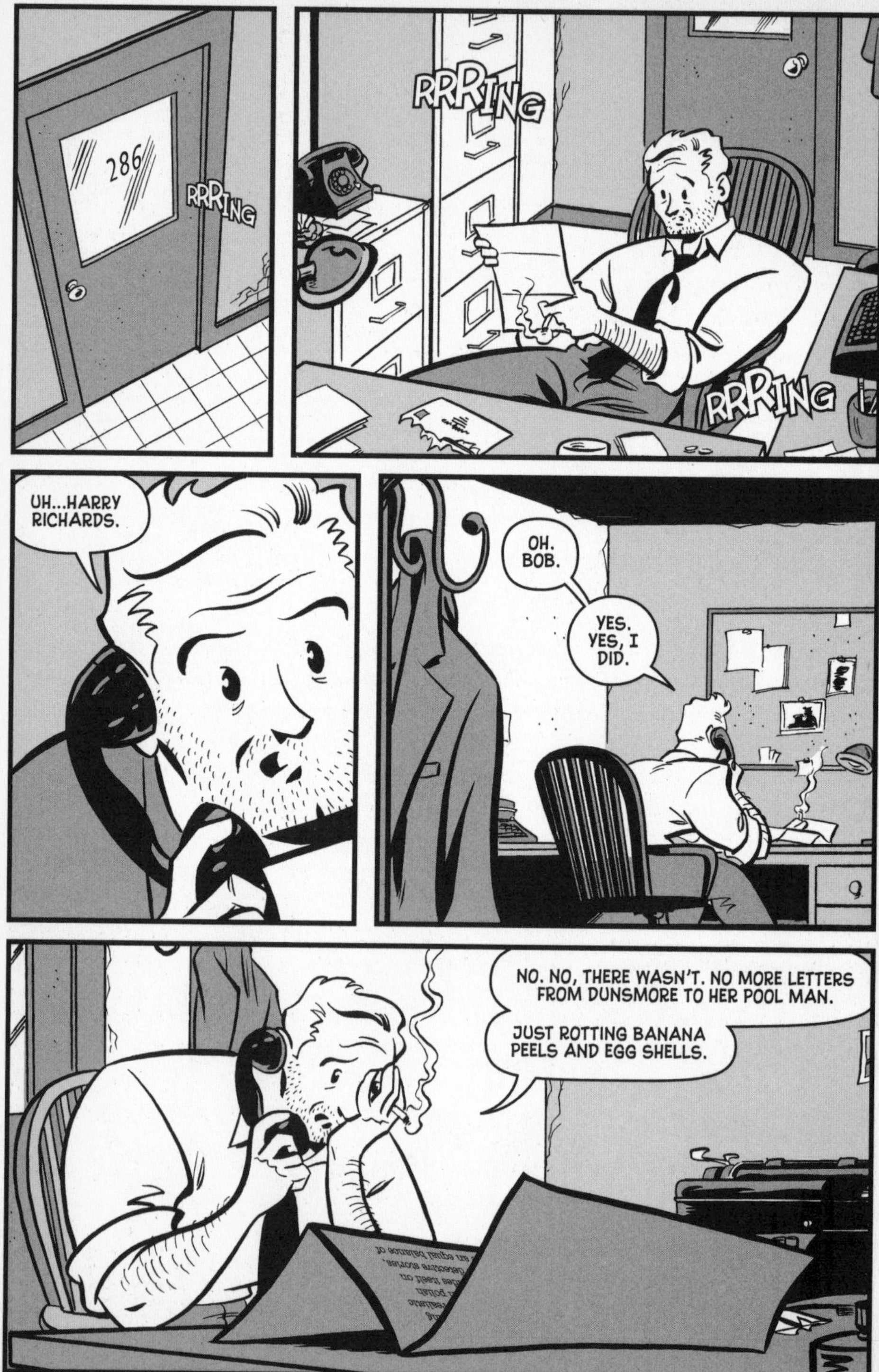
286
RRRING
RRRING
RRRING
UH...HARRY RICHARDS.
OH. BOB.
YES. YES, I DID.
NO. NO, THERE WASN'T. NO MORE LETTERS FROM DUNSMORE TO HER POOL MAN.
JUST ROTTING BANANA PEELS AND EGG SHELLS.

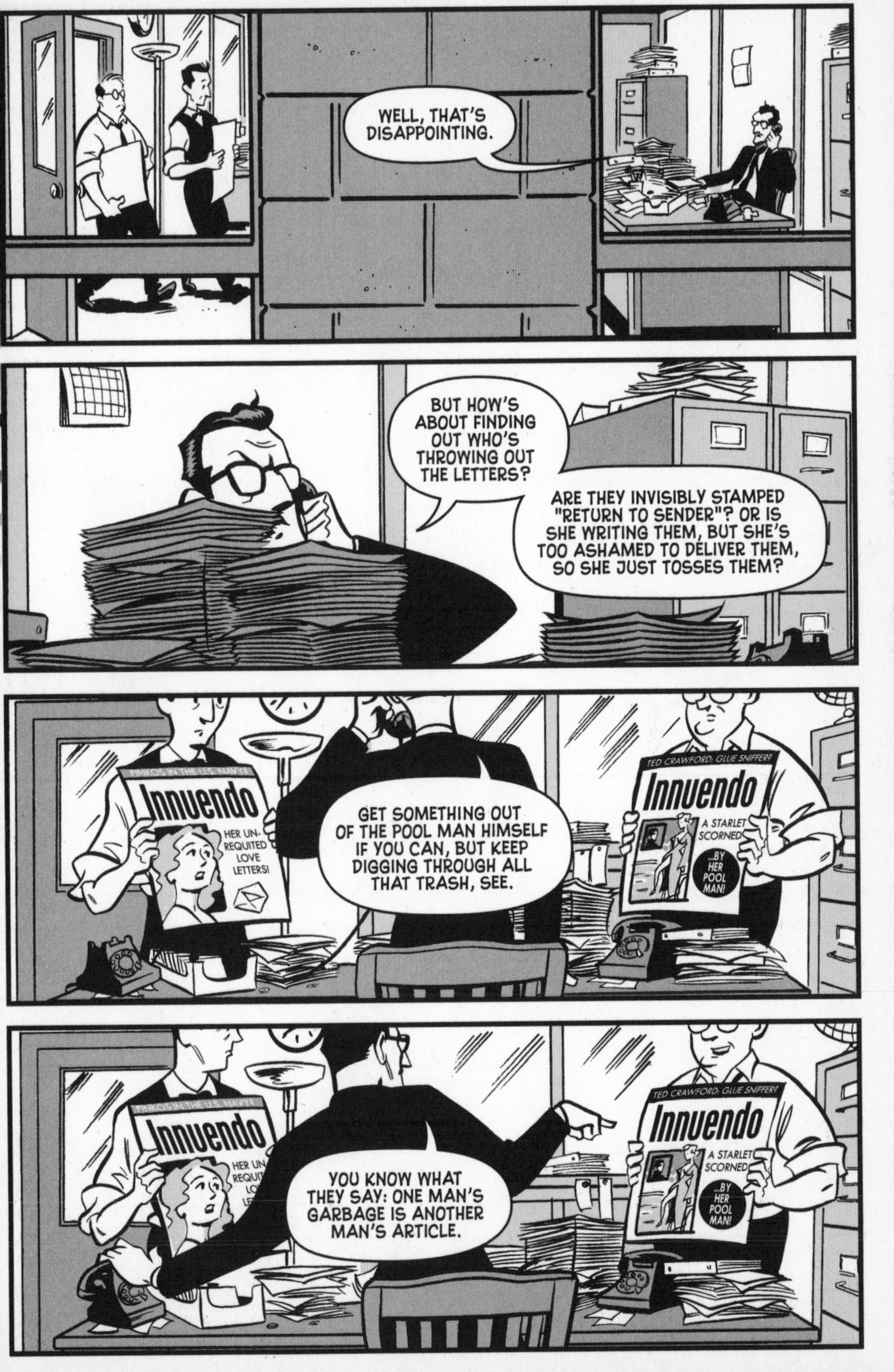

WELL, THAT'S DISAPPOINTING.
BUT HOW'S ABOUT FINDING OUT WHO'S THROWING OUT THE LETTERS?
ARE THEY INVISIBLY STAMPED "RETURN TO SENDER"? OR IS SHE WRITING THEM, BUT SHE'S TOO ASHAMED TO DELIVER THEM, SO SHE JUST TOSSES THEM?
PINKOS IN THE U.S. NAVY?
Innuendo
HER UN-REQUITED LOVE LETTERS!
TED CRAWFORD: GLUE SNIFFER?
Innuendo
A STARLET SCORNED
...BY HER POOL MAN!
GET SOMETHING OUT OF THE POOL MAN HIMSELF IF YOU CAN, BUT KEEP DIGGING THROUGH ALL THAT TRASH, SEE.
TED CRAWFORD: GLUE SNIFFER?
Innuendo
A STARLET SCORNED
...BY HER POOL MAN!
YOU KNOW WHAT THEY SAY: ONE MAN'S GARBAGE IS ANOTHER MAN'S ARTICLE.

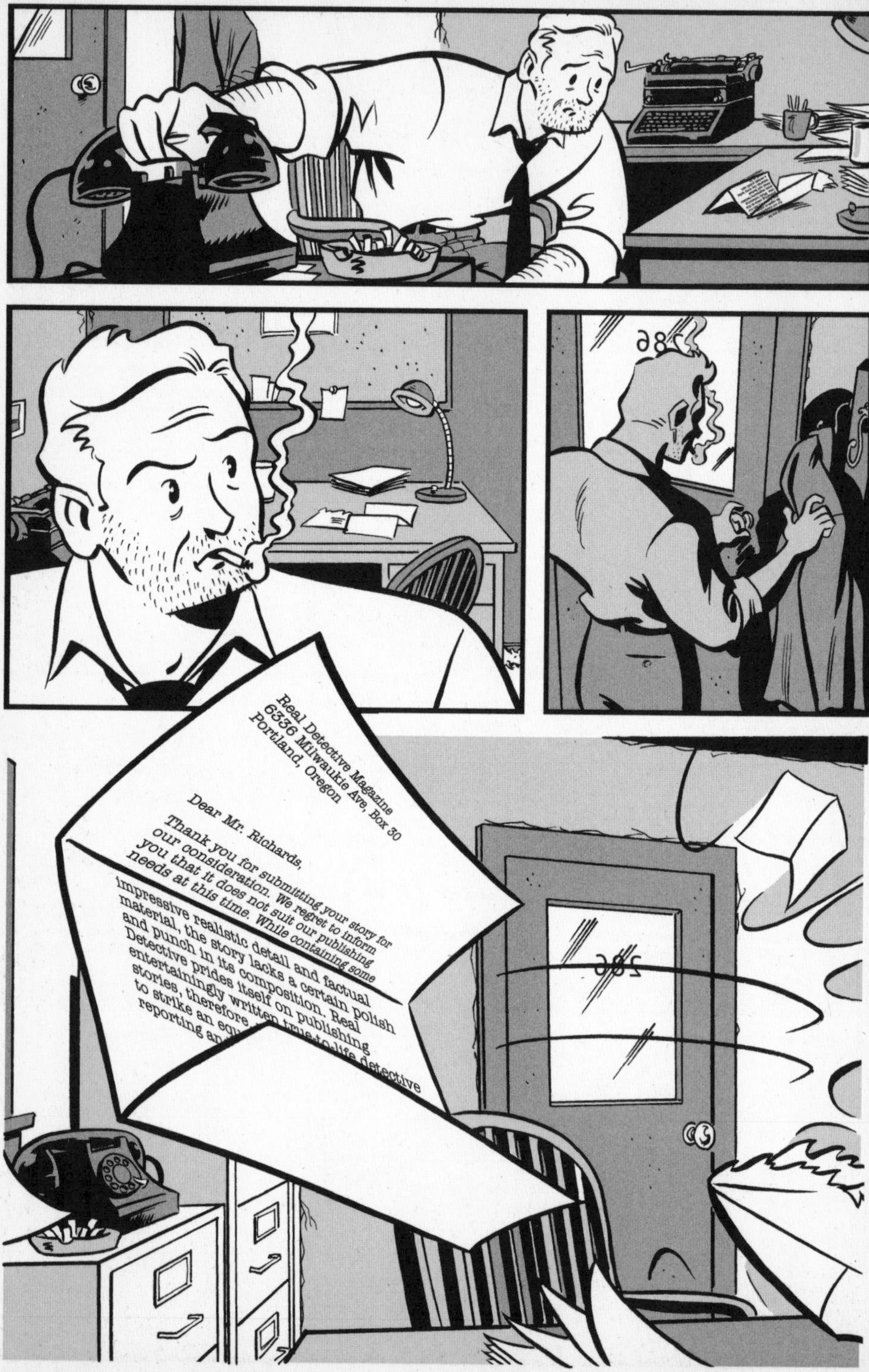
Real Detective Magazine
6336 Milwaukie Ave, Box 30
Portland, Oregon
Dear Mr. Richards,
Thank you for submitting your story for our consideration. We regret to inform you that it does not suit our publishing needs at this time. While containing some impressive realistic detail and factual material, the story lacks a certain polish and punch in its composition. Real Detective prides itself on publishing entertainingly written true-to-life detective stories, therefore
to strike an equ
reporting an

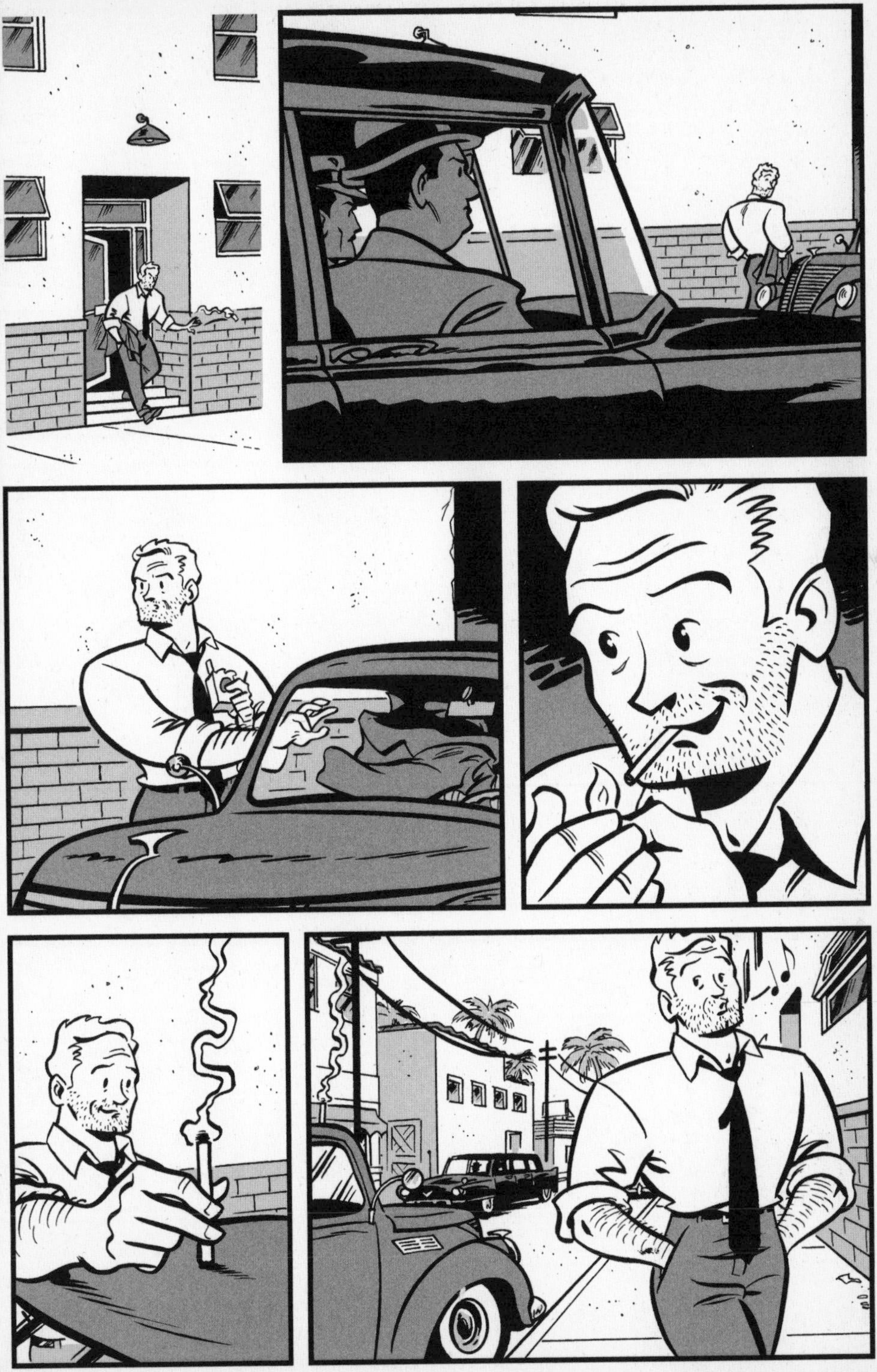

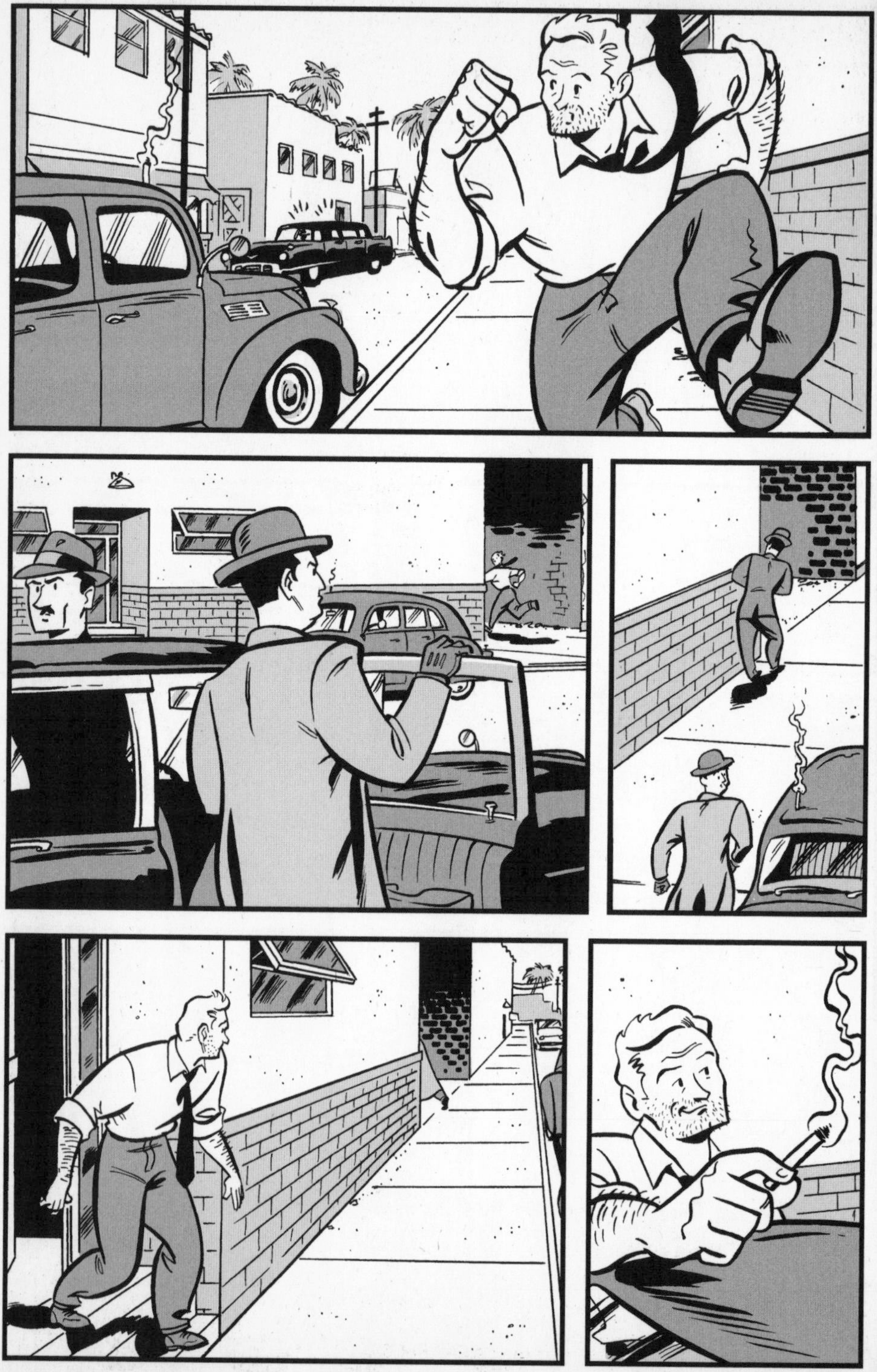

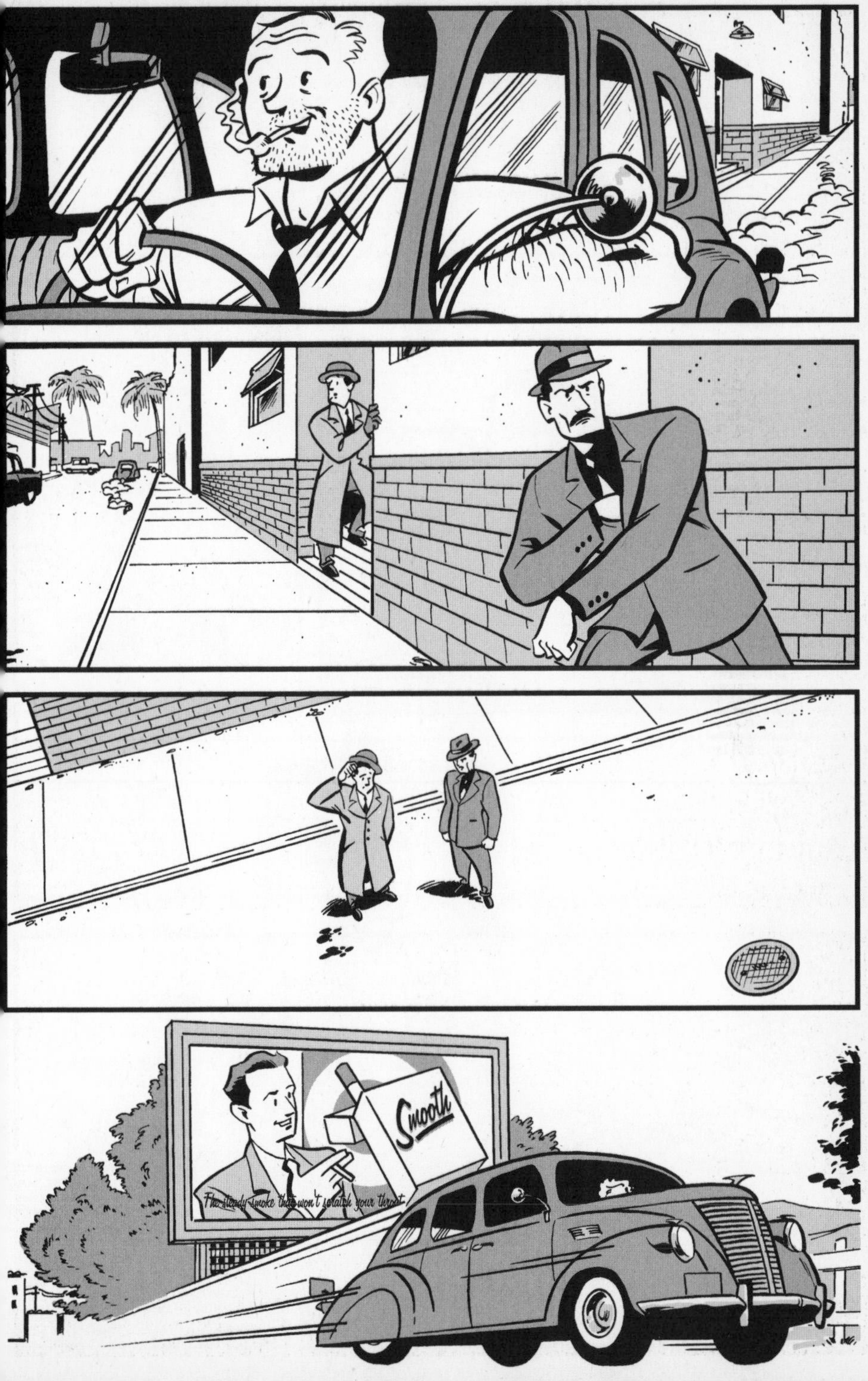

Smooth
The steady smoke that won't scratch your throat

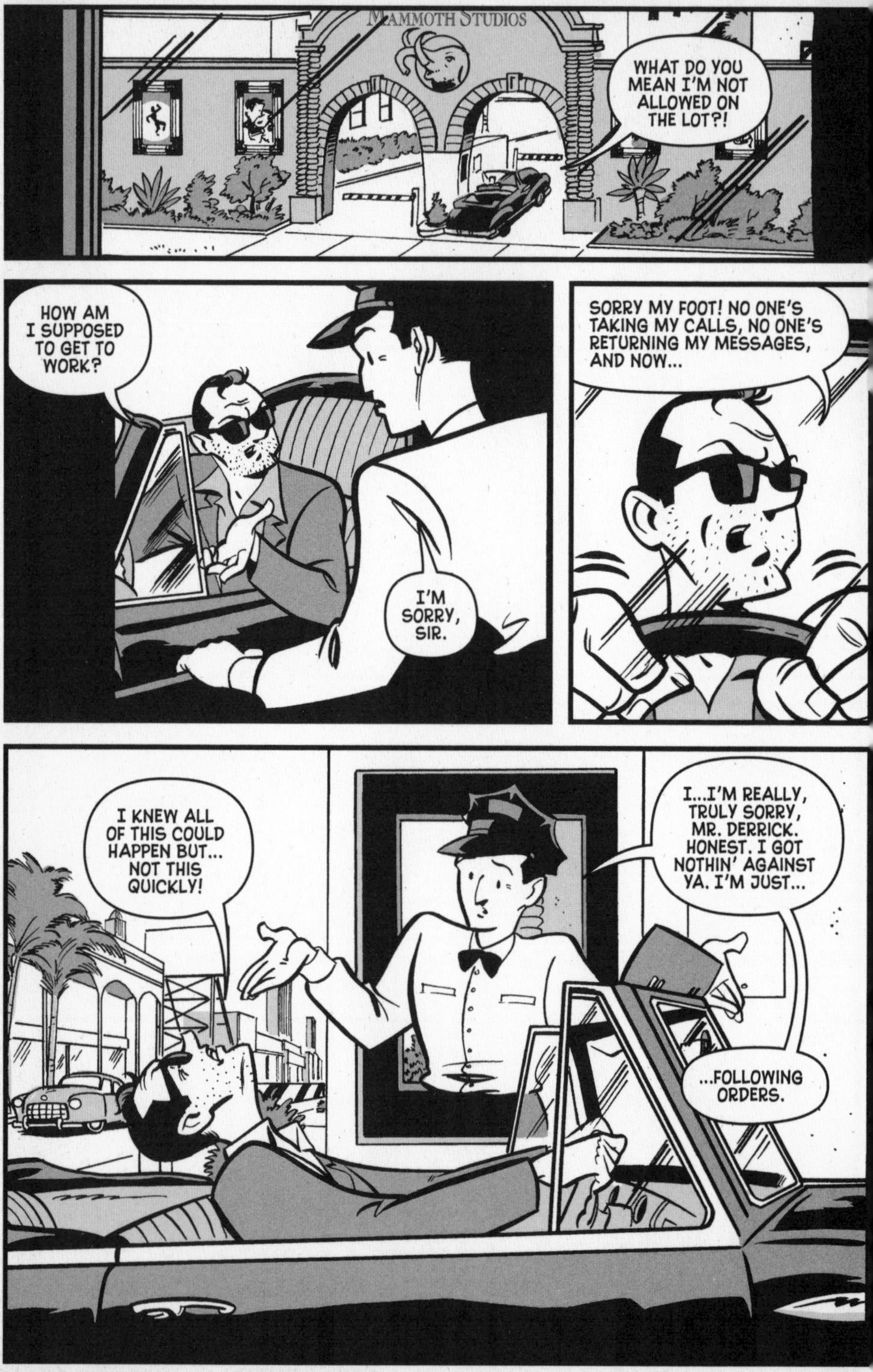
MAMMOTH STUDIOS
WHAT DO YOU MEAN I'M NOT ALLOWED ON THE LOT?!
HOW AM I SUPPOSED TO GET TO WORK?
I'M SORRY, SIR.
SORRY MY FOOT! NO ONE'S TAKING MY CALLS, NO ONE'S RETURNING MY MESSAGES, AND NOW...
I KNEW ALL OF THIS COULD HAPPEN BUT... NOT THIS QUICKLY!
I...I'M REALLY, TRULY SORRY, MR. DERRICK. HONEST. I GOT NOTHIN' AGAINST YA. I'M JUST...
...FOLLOWING ORDERS.

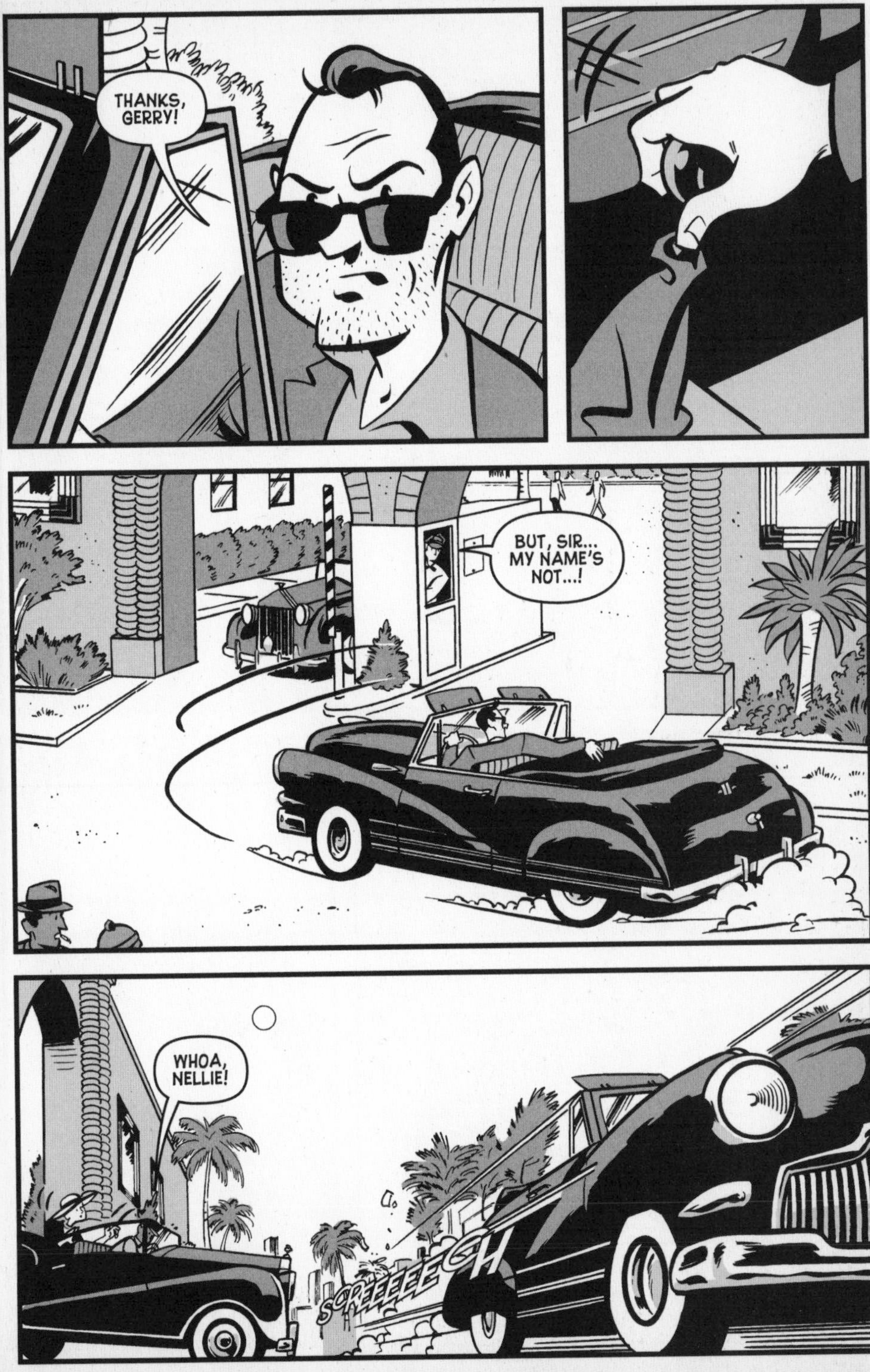
THANKS, GERRY!
BUT, SIR... MY NAME'S NOT...!
WHOA, NELLIE!
SCREEEEEECH

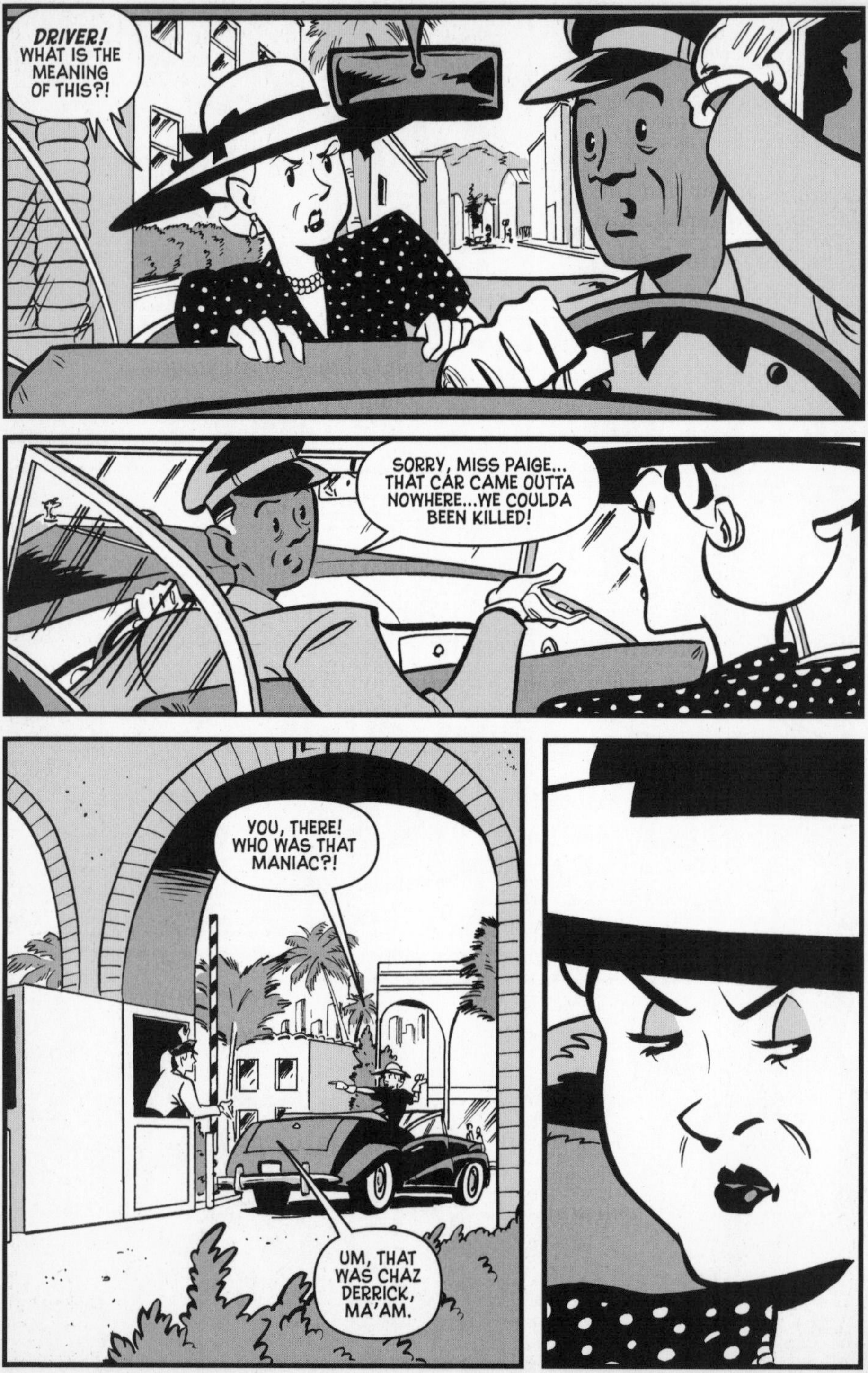
DRIVER! WHAT IS THE MEANING OF THIS?!
SORRY, MISS PAIGE... THAT CAR CAME OUTTA NOWHERE...WE COULDA BEEN KILLED!
YOU, THERE! WHO WAS THAT MANIAC?!
UM, THAT WAS CHAZ DERRICK, MA'AM.

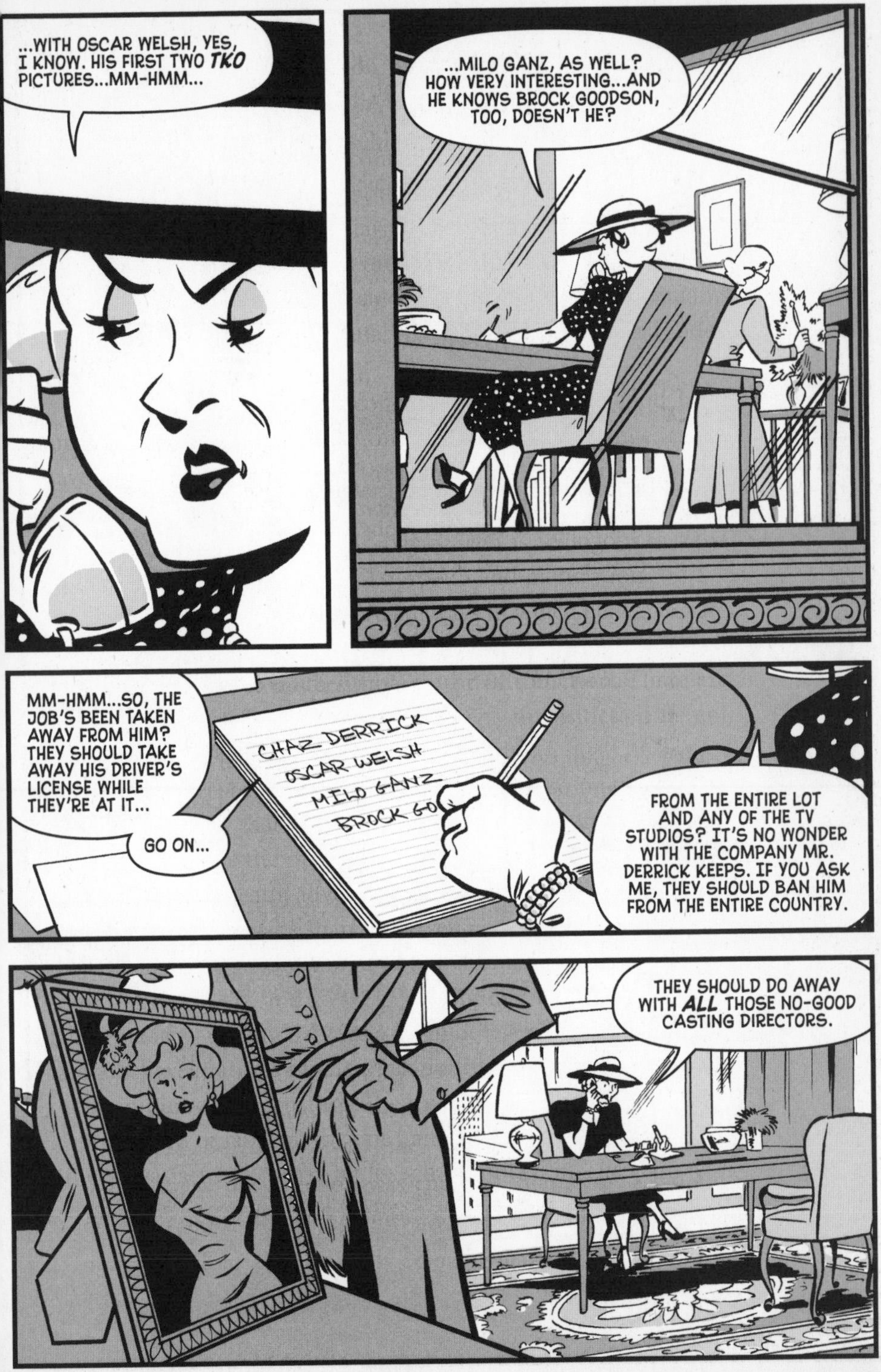
...WITH OSCAR WELSH, YES, I KNOW. HIS FIRST TWO TKO PICTURES...MM-HMM...
...MILO GANZ, AS WELL? HOW VERY INTERESTING...AND HE KNOWS BROCK GOODSON, TOO, DOESN'T HE?
MM-HMM...SO, THE JOB'S BEEN TAKEN AWAY FROM HIM? THEY SHOULD TAKE AWAY HIS DRIVER'S LICENSE WHILE THEY'RE AT IT...
GO ON...
CHAZ DERRICK
OSCAR WELSH
MILO GANZ
BROCK GO
FROM THE ENTIRE LOT AND ANY OF THE TV STUDIOS? IT'S NO WONDER WITH THE COMPANY MR. DERRICK KEEPS. IF YOU ASK ME, THEY SHOULD BAN HIM FROM THE ENTIRE COUNTRY.
THEY SHOULD DO AWAY WITH ALL THOSE NO-GOOD CASTING DIRECTORS.

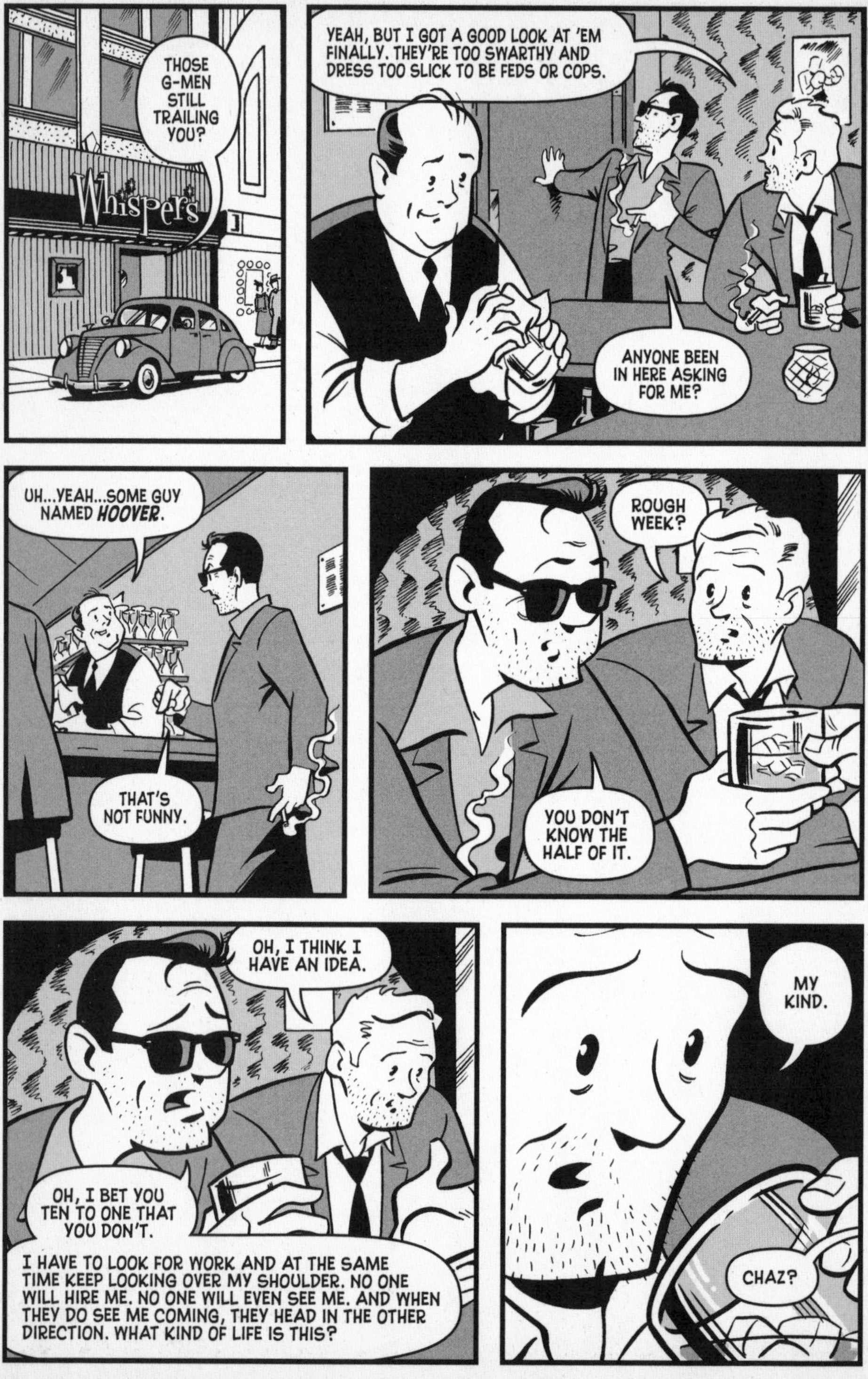
Whispers
THOSE G-MEN STILL TRAILING YOU?
YEAH, BUT I GOT A GOOD LOOK AT 'EM FINALLY. THEY'RE TOO SWARTHY AND DRESS TOO SLICK TO BE FEDS OR COPS.
ANYONE BEEN IN HERE ASKING FOR ME?
UH...YEAH...SOME GUY NAMED HOOVER.
THAT'S NOT FUNNY.
ROUGH WEEK?
YOU DON'T KNOW THE HALF OF IT.
OH, I THINK I HAVE AN IDEA.
OH, I BET YOU TEN TO ONE THAT YOU DON'T.
I HAVE TO LOOK FOR WORK AND AT THE SAME TIME KEEP LOOKING OVER MY SHOULDER. NO ONE WILL HIRE ME. NO ONE WILL EVEN SEE ME. AND WHEN THEY DO SEE ME COMING, THEY HEAD IN THE OTHER DIRECTION. WHAT KIND OF LIFE IS THIS?
MY KIND.
CHAZ?

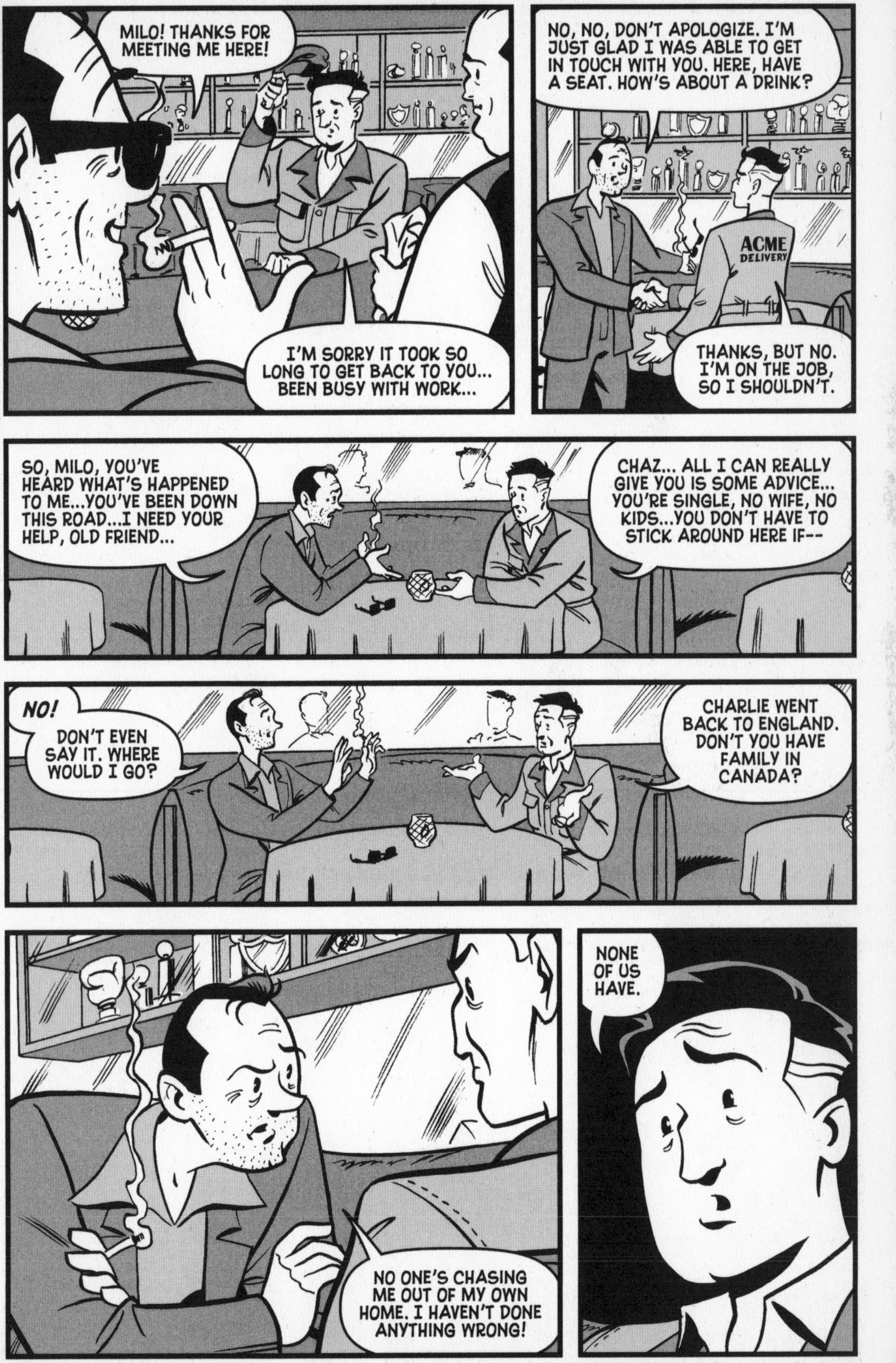
MILO! THANKS FOR MEETING ME HERE!
I'M SORRY IT TOOK SO LONG TO GET BACK TO YOU... BEEN BUSY WITH WORK...
NO, NO, DON'T APOLOGIZE. I'M JUST GLAD I WAS ABLE TO GET IN TOUCH WITH YOU. HERE, HAVE A SEAT. HOW'S ABOUT A DRINK?
ACME DELIVERY
THANKS, BUT NO. I'M ON THE JOB, SO I SHOULDN'T.
SO, MILO, YOU'VE HEARD WHAT'S HAPPENED TO ME...YOU'VE BEEN DOWN THIS ROAD...I NEED YOUR HELP, OLD FRIEND...
CHAZ... ALL I CAN REALLY GIVE YOU IS SOME ADVICE... YOU'RE SINGLE, NO WIFE, NO KIDS...YOU DON'T HAVE TO STICK AROUND HERE IF--
NO! DON'T EVEN SAY IT. WHERE WOULD I GO?
CHARLIE WENT BACK TO ENGLAND. DON'T YOU HAVE FAMILY IN CANADA?
NO ONE'S CHASING ME OUT OF MY OWN HOME. I HAVEN'T DONE ANYTHING WRONG!
NONE OF US HAVE.

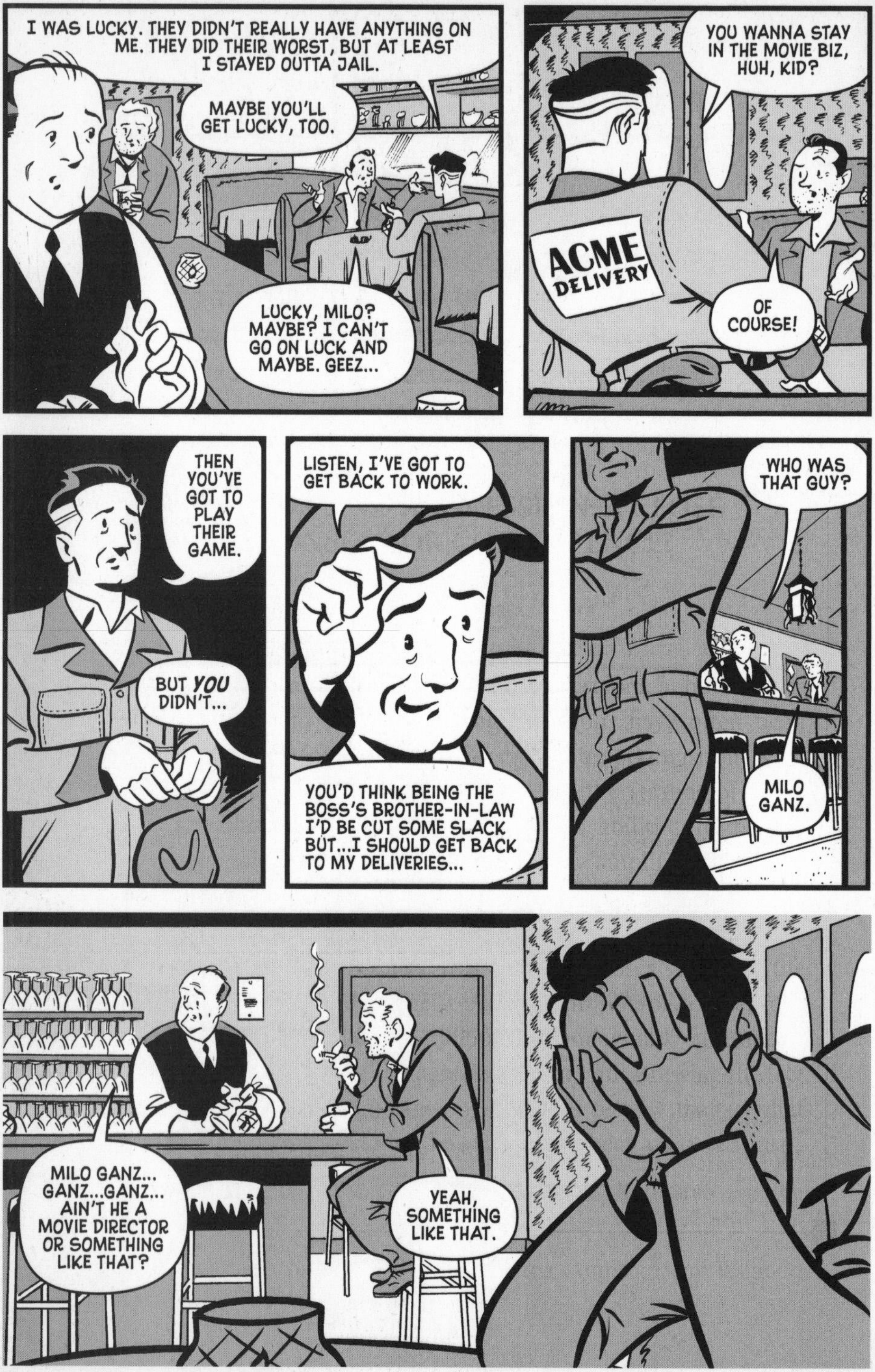
I WAS LUCKY. THEY DIDN'T REALLY HAVE ANYTHING ON ME. THEY DID THEIR WORST, BUT AT LEAST I STAYED OUTTA JAIL.
MAYBE YOU'LL GET LUCKY, TOO.
LUCKY, MILO? MAYBE? I CAN'T GO ON LUCK AND MAYBE. GEEZ...
YOU WANNA STAY IN THE MOVIE BIZ, HUH, KID?
ACME DELIVERY
OF COURSE!
THEN YOU'VE GOT TO PLAY THEIR GAME.
BUT *YOU* DIDN'T...
LISTEN, I'VE GOT TO GET BACK TO WORK.
YOU'D THINK BEING THE BOSS'S BROTHER-IN-LAW I'D BE CUT SOME SLACK BUT...I SHOULD GET BACK TO MY DELIVERIES...
WHO WAS THAT GUY?
MILO GANZ.
MILO GANZ... GANZ...GANZ... AIN'T HE A MOVIE DIRECTOR OR SOMETHING LIKE THAT?
YEAH, SOMETHING LIKE THAT.

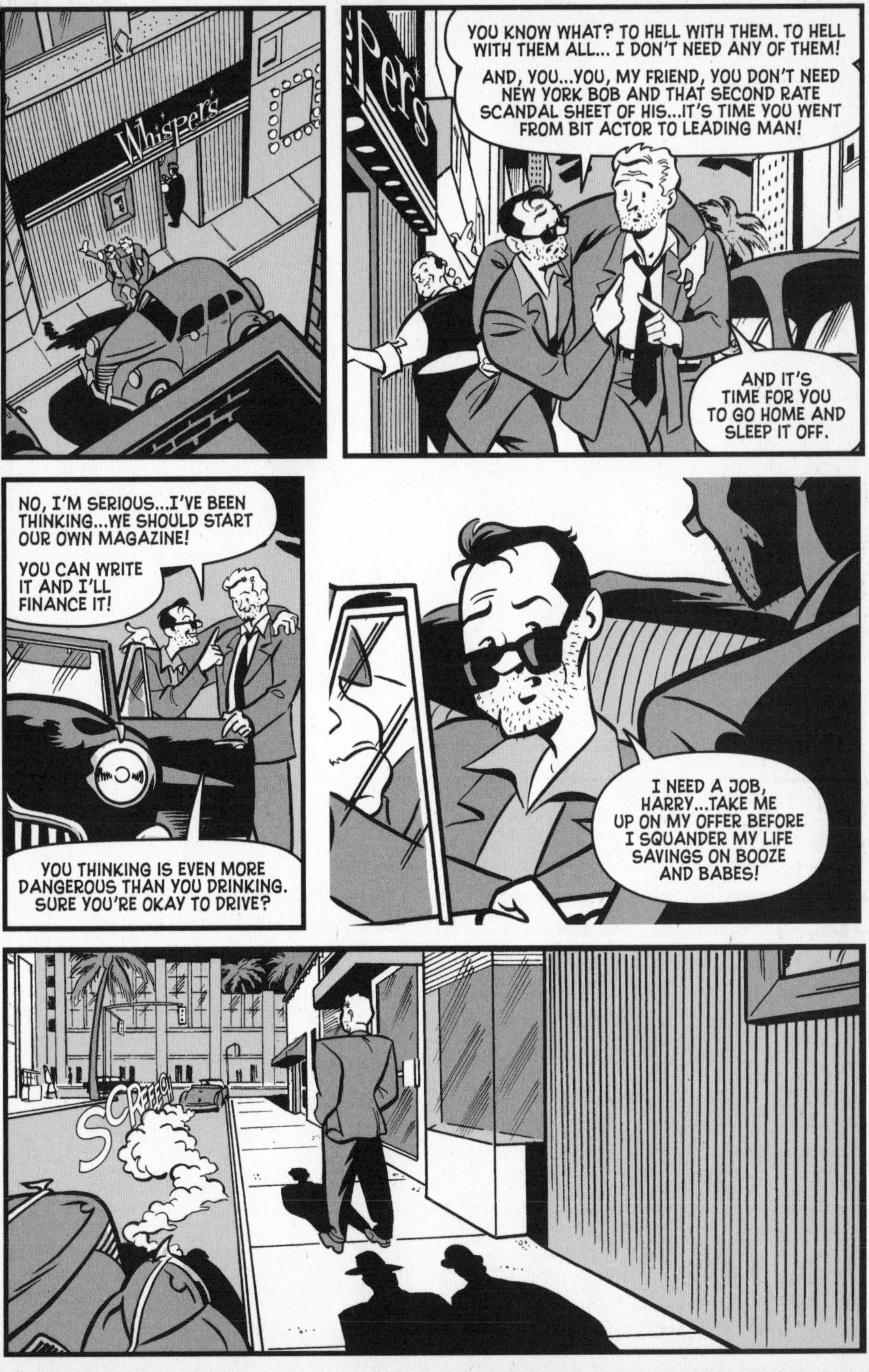
Whispers
YOU KNOW WHAT? TO HELL WITH THEM. TO HELL WITH THEM ALL... I DON'T NEED ANY OF THEM!
AND, YOU...YOU, MY FRIEND, YOU DON'T NEED NEW YORK BOB AND THAT SECOND RATE SCANDAL SHEET OF HIS...IT'S TIME YOU WENT FROM BIT ACTOR TO LEADING MAN!
AND IT'S TIME FOR YOU TO GO HOME AND SLEEP IT OFF.
NO, I'M SERIOUS...I'VE BEEN THINKING...WE SHOULD START OUR OWN MAGAZINE!
YOU CAN WRITE IT AND I'LL FINANCE IT!
YOU THINKING IS EVEN MORE DANGEROUS THAN YOU DRINKING. SURE YOU'RE OKAY TO DRIVE?
I NEED A JOB, HARRY...TAKE ME UP ON MY OFFER BEFORE I SQUANDER MY LIFE SAVINGS ON BOOZE AND BABES!
SCREEECH

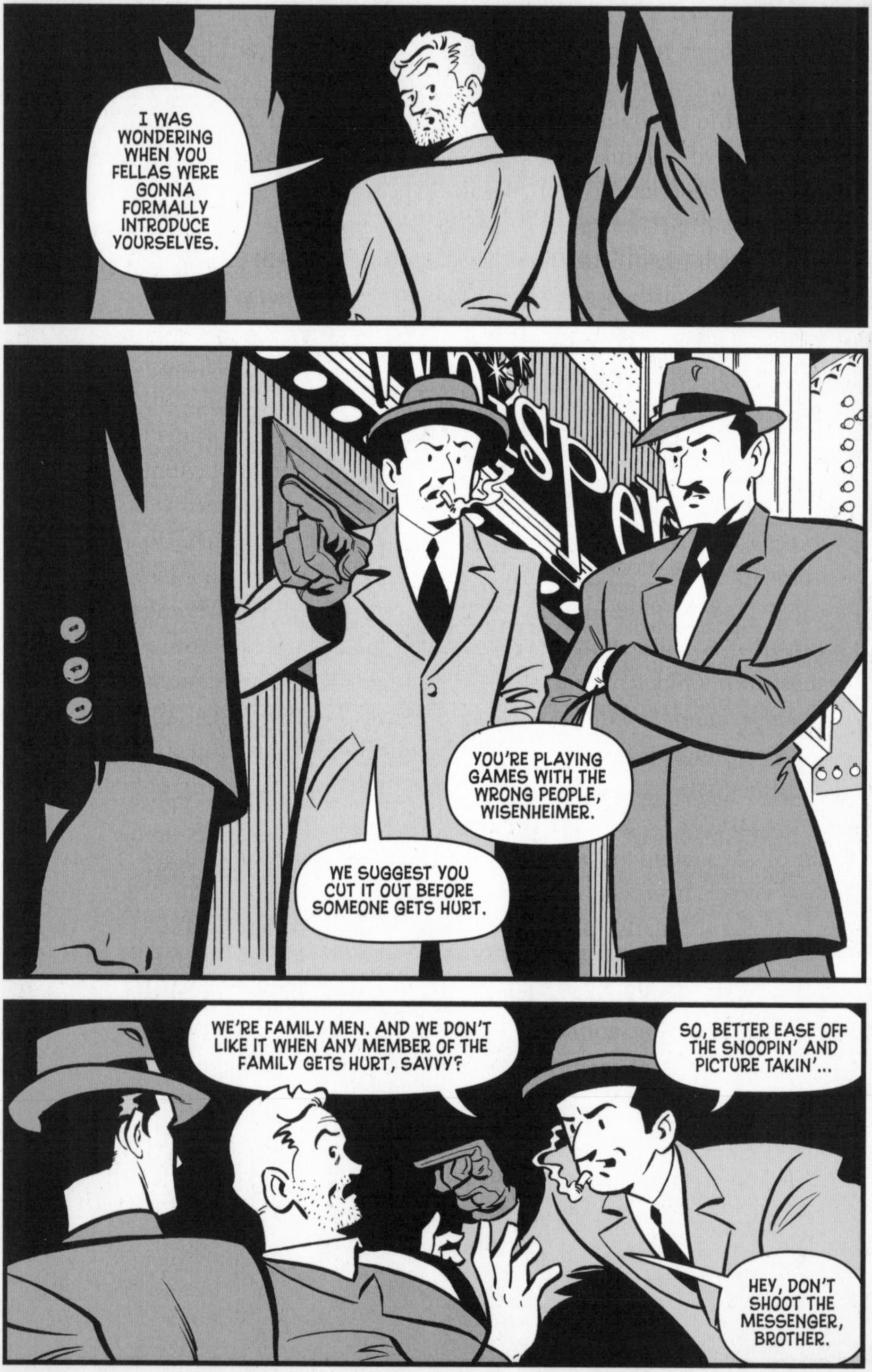
I WAS WONDERING WHEN YOU FELLAS WERE GONNA FORMALLY INTRODUCE YOURSELVES.
YOU'RE PLAYING GAMES WITH THE WRONG PEOPLE, WISENHEIMER.
WE SUGGEST YOU CUT IT OUT BEFORE SOMEONE GETS HURT.
WE'RE FAMILY MEN. AND WE DON'T LIKE IT WHEN ANY MEMBER OF THE FAMILY GETS HURT, SAVVY?
SO, BETTER EASE OFF THE SNOOPIN' AND PICTURE TAKIN'...
HEY, DON'T SHOOT THE MESSENGER, BROTHER.

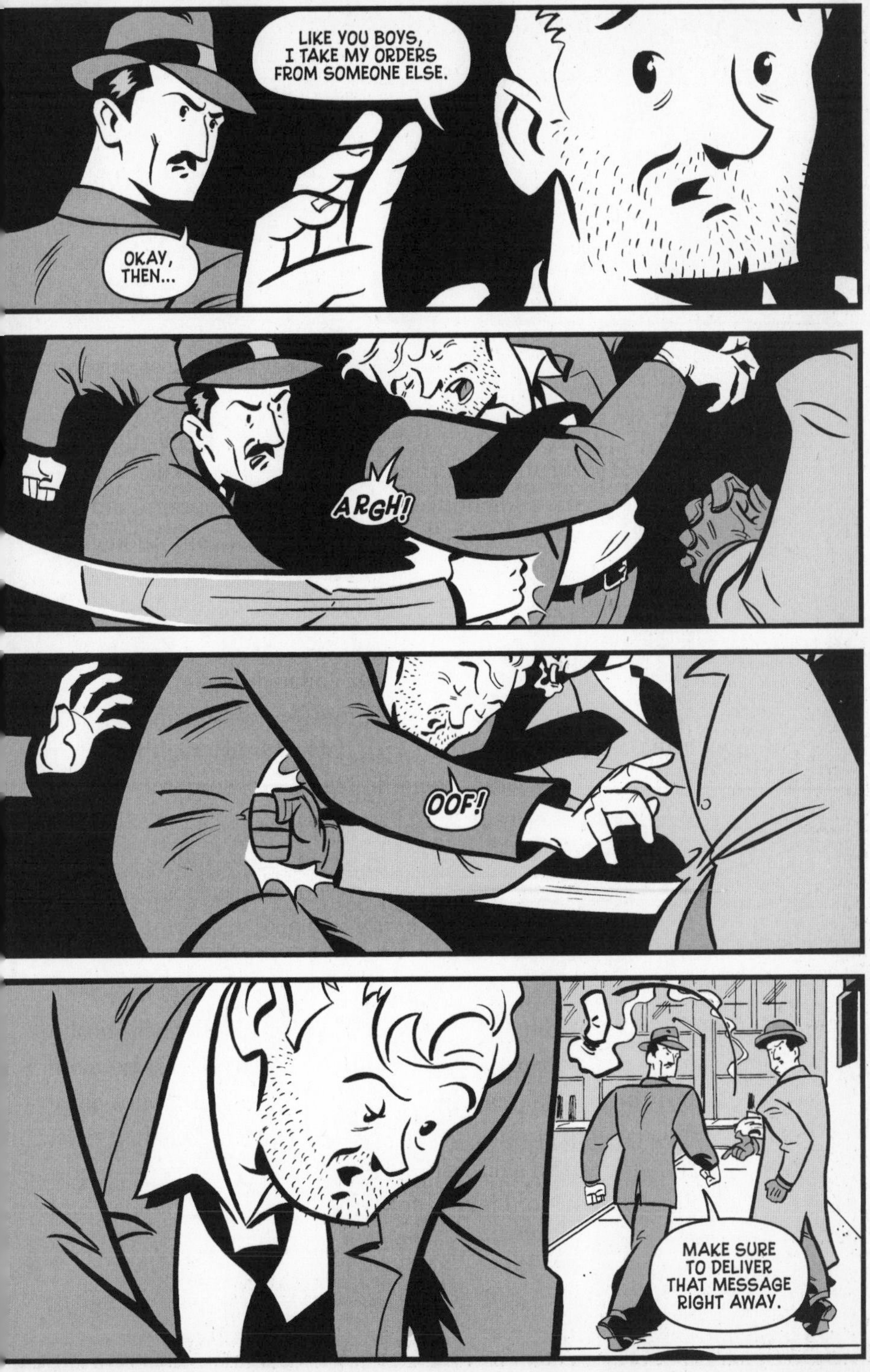

LIKE YOU BOYS, I TAKE MY ORDERS FROM SOMEONE ELSE.
OKAY, THEN...
ARGH!
OOF!
MAKE SURE TO DELIVER THAT MESSAGE RIGHT AWAY.

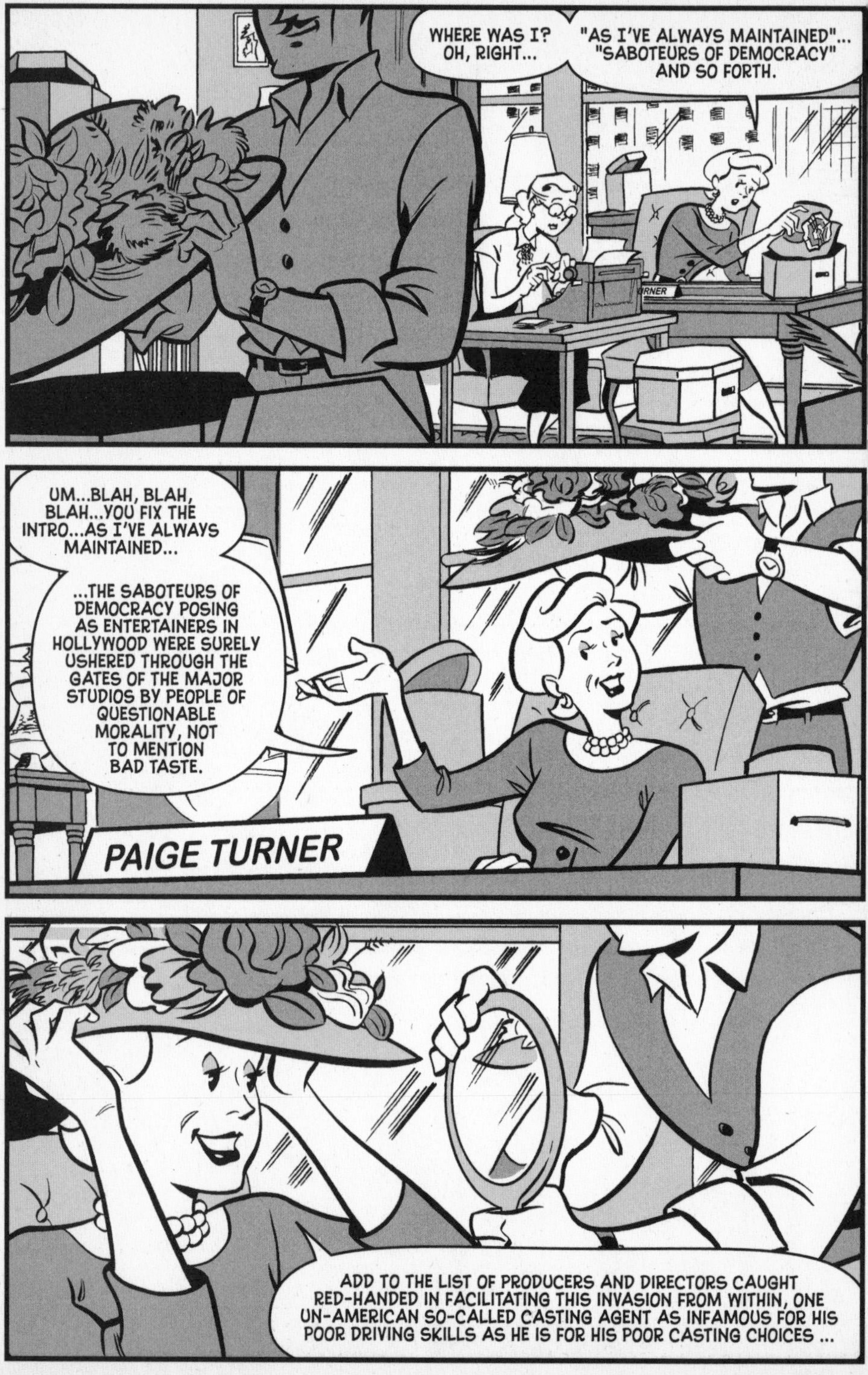
WHERE WAS I? OH, RIGHT...
"AS I'VE ALWAYS MAINTAINED"... "SABOTEURS OF DEMOCRACY" AND SO FORTH.
RNER
UM...BLAH, BLAH, BLAH...YOU FIX THE INTRO...AS I'VE ALWAYS MAINTAINED...
...THE SABOTEURS OF DEMOCRACY POSING AS ENTERTAINERS IN HOLLYWOOD WERE SURELY USHERED THROUGH THE GATES OF THE MAJOR STUDIOS BY PEOPLE OF QUESTIONABLE MORALITY, NOT TO MENTION BAD TASTE.
PAIGE TURNER
ADD TO THE LIST OF PRODUCERS AND DIRECTORS CAUGHT RED-HANDED IN FACILITATING THIS INVASION FROM WITHIN, ONE UN-AMERICAN SO-CALLED CASTING AGENT AS INFAMOUS FOR HIS POOR DRIVING SKILLS AS HE IS FOR HIS POOR CASTING CHOICES ...

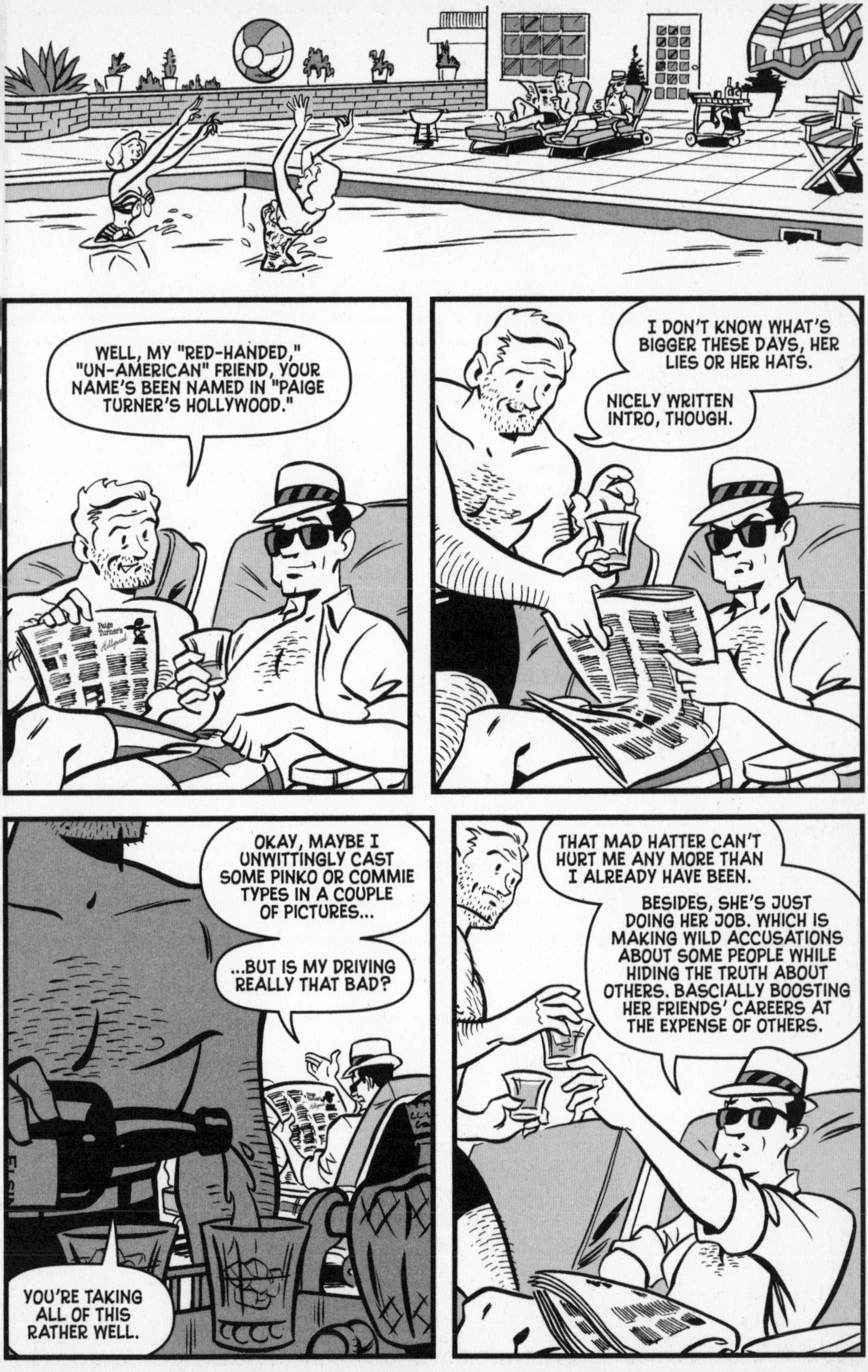
WELL, MY "RED-HANDED," "UN-AMERICAN" FRIEND, YOUR NAME'S BEEN NAMED IN "PAIGE TURNER'S HOLLYWOOD."
Paige Turner's Hollywood
I DON'T KNOW WHAT'S BIGGER THESE DAYS, HER LIES OR HER HATS.
NICELY WRITTEN INTRO, THOUGH.
OKAY, MAYBE I UNWITTINGLY CAST SOME PINKO OR COMMIE TYPES IN A COUPLE OF PICTURES...
...BUT IS MY DRIVING REALLY THAT BAD?
YOU'RE TAKING ALL OF THIS RATHER WELL.
THAT MAD HATTER CAN'T HURT ME ANY MORE THAN I ALREADY HAVE BEEN.
BESIDES, SHE'S JUST DOING HER JOB. WHICH IS MAKING WILD ACCUSATIONS ABOUT SOME PEOPLE WHILE HIDING THE TRUTH ABOUT OTHERS. BASCIALLY BOOSTING HER FRIENDS' CAREERS AT THE EXPENSE OF OTHERS.

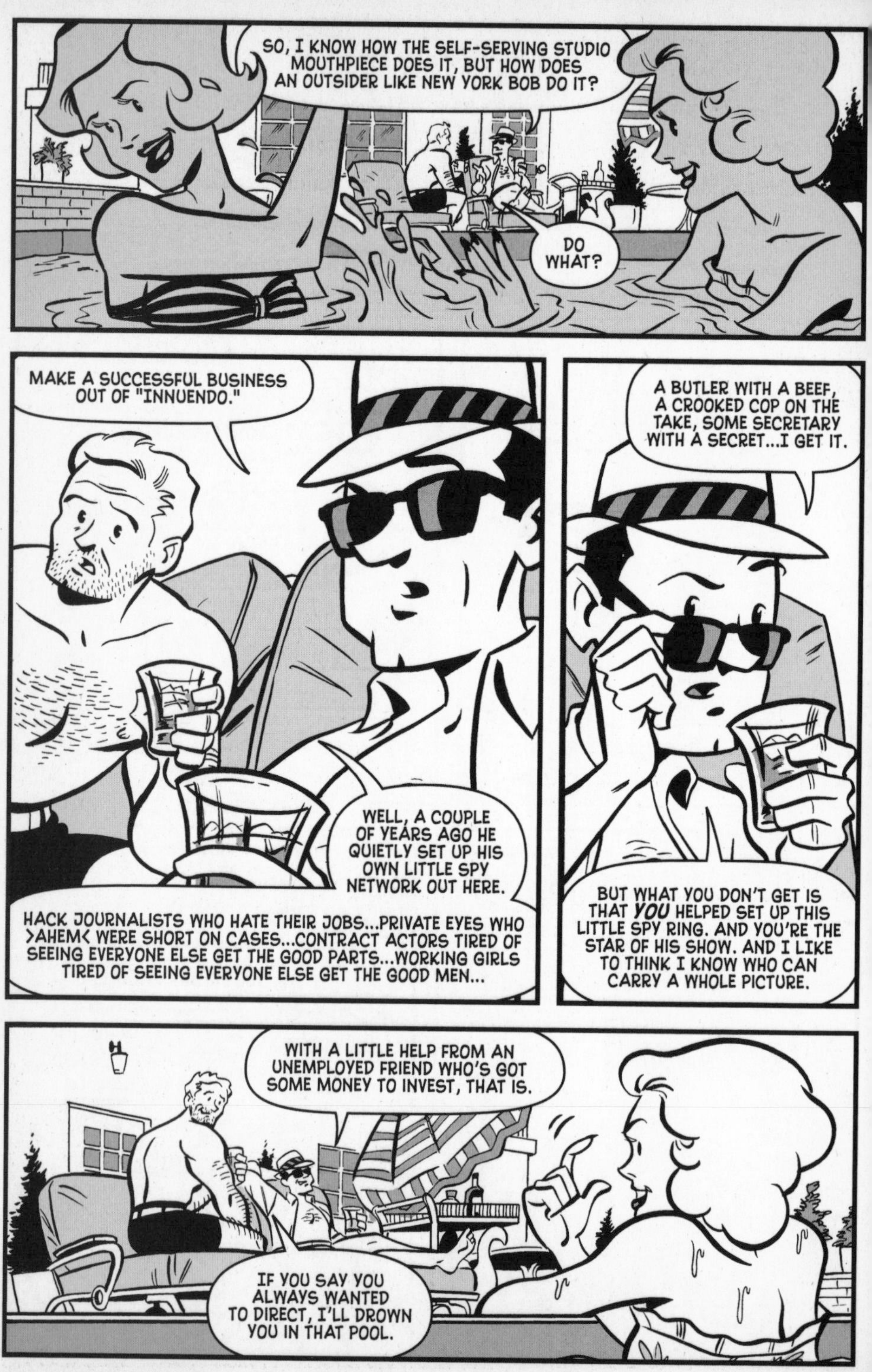
SO, I KNOW HOW THE SELF-SERVING STUDIO MOUTHPIECE DOES IT, BUT HOW DOES AN OUTSIDER LIKE NEW YORK BOB DO IT?
DO WHAT?
MAKE A SUCCESSFUL BUSINESS OUT OF "INNUENDO."
WELL, A COUPLE OF YEARS AGO HE QUIETLY SET UP HIS OWN LITTLE SPY NETWORK OUT HERE.
HACK JOURNALISTS WHO HATE THEIR JOBS...PRIVATE EYES WHO >AHEM< WERE SHORT ON CASES...CONTRACT ACTORS TIRED OF SEEING EVERYONE ELSE GET THE GOOD PARTS...WORKING GIRLS TIRED OF SEEING EVERYONE ELSE GET THE GOOD MEN...
A BUTLER WITH A BEEF, A CROOKED COP ON THE TAKE, SOME SECRETARY WITH A SECRET...I GET IT.
BUT WHAT YOU DON'T GET IS THAT *YOU* HELPED SET UP THIS LITTLE SPY RING. AND YOU'RE THE STAR OF HIS SHOW. AND I LIKE TO THINK I KNOW WHO CAN CARRY A WHOLE PICTURE.
WITH A LITTLE HELP FROM AN UNEMPLOYED FRIEND WHO'S GOT SOME MONEY TO INVEST, THAT IS.
IF YOU SAY YOU ALWAYS WANTED TO DIRECT, I'LL DROWN YOU IN THAT POOL.

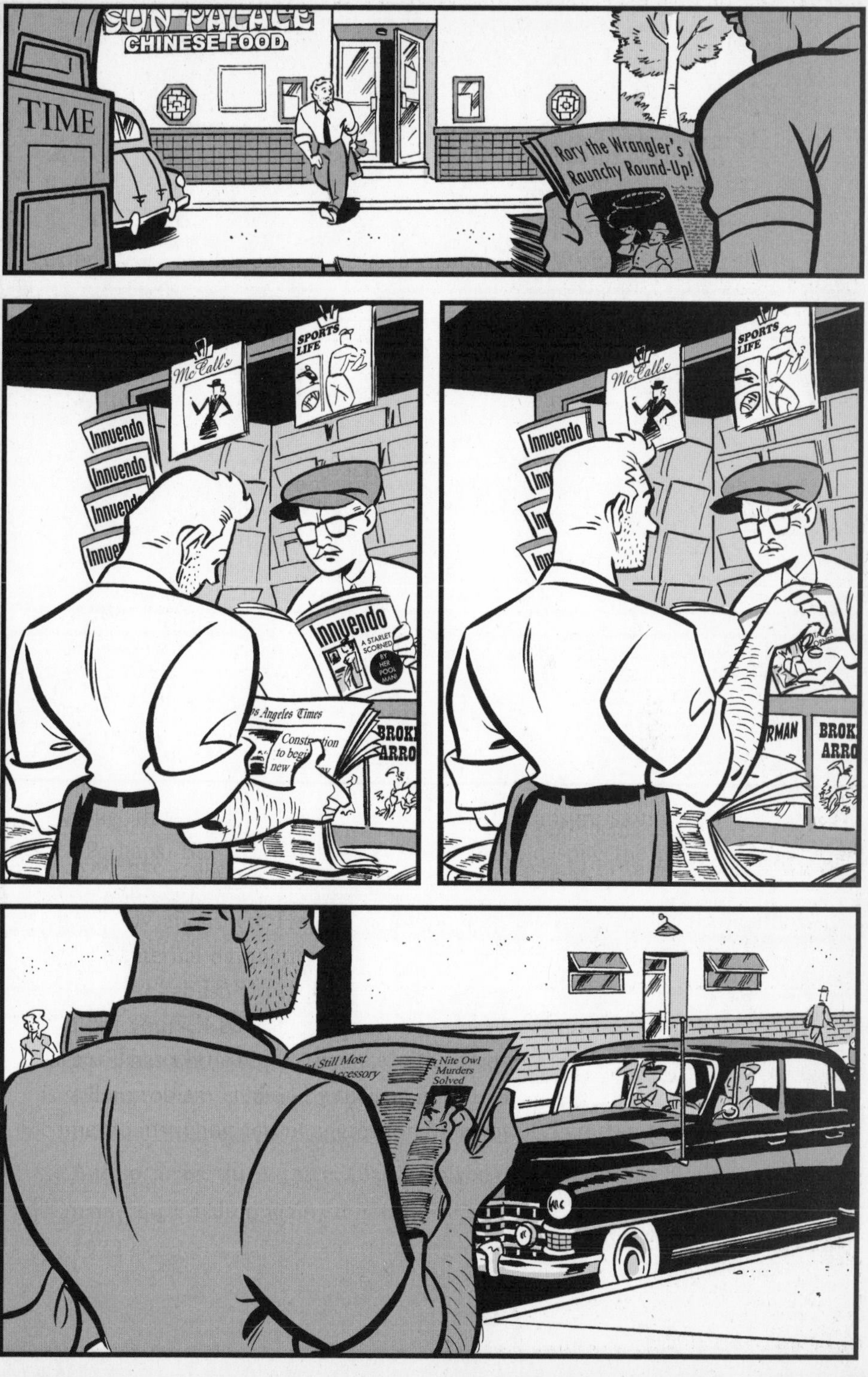
SUN PALACE
CHINESE FOOD
TIME
Rory the Wrangler's Raunchy Round-Up!
McCall's
SPORTS LIFE
Innuendo
Innuendo
A STARLET SCORNED BY HER POOL MAN!
Nite Owl Murders Solved

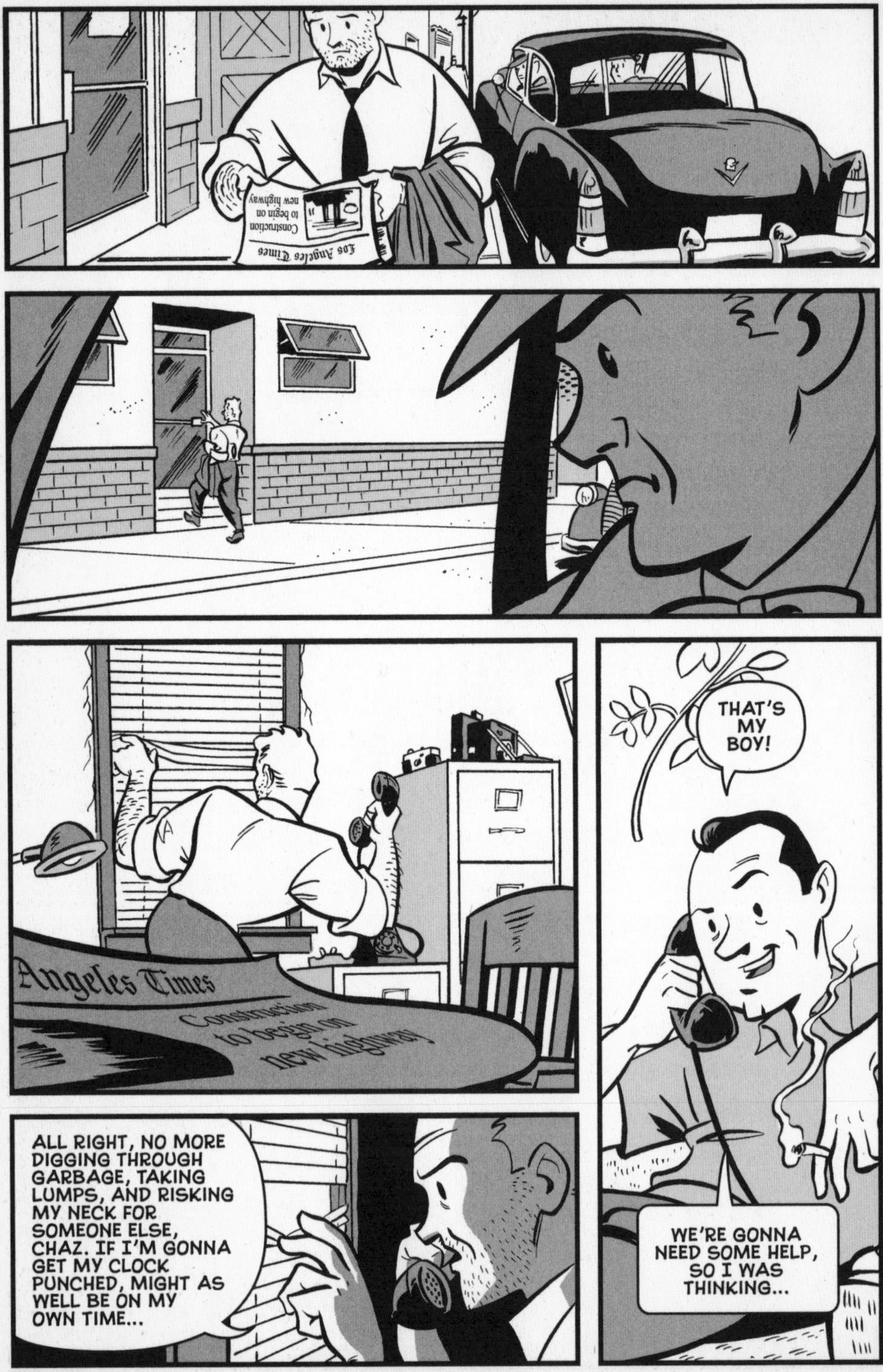
Los Angeles Times
Construction to begin on new highway
Angeles Times
Construction to begin on new highway
THAT'S MY BOY!
ALL RIGHT, NO MORE DIGGING THROUGH GARBAGE, TAKING LUMPS, AND RISKING MY NECK FOR SOMEONE ELSE, CHAZ. IF I'M GONNA GET MY CLOCK PUNCHED, MIGHT AS WELL BE ON MY OWN TIME...
WE'RE GONNA NEED SOME HELP, SO I WAS THINKING...

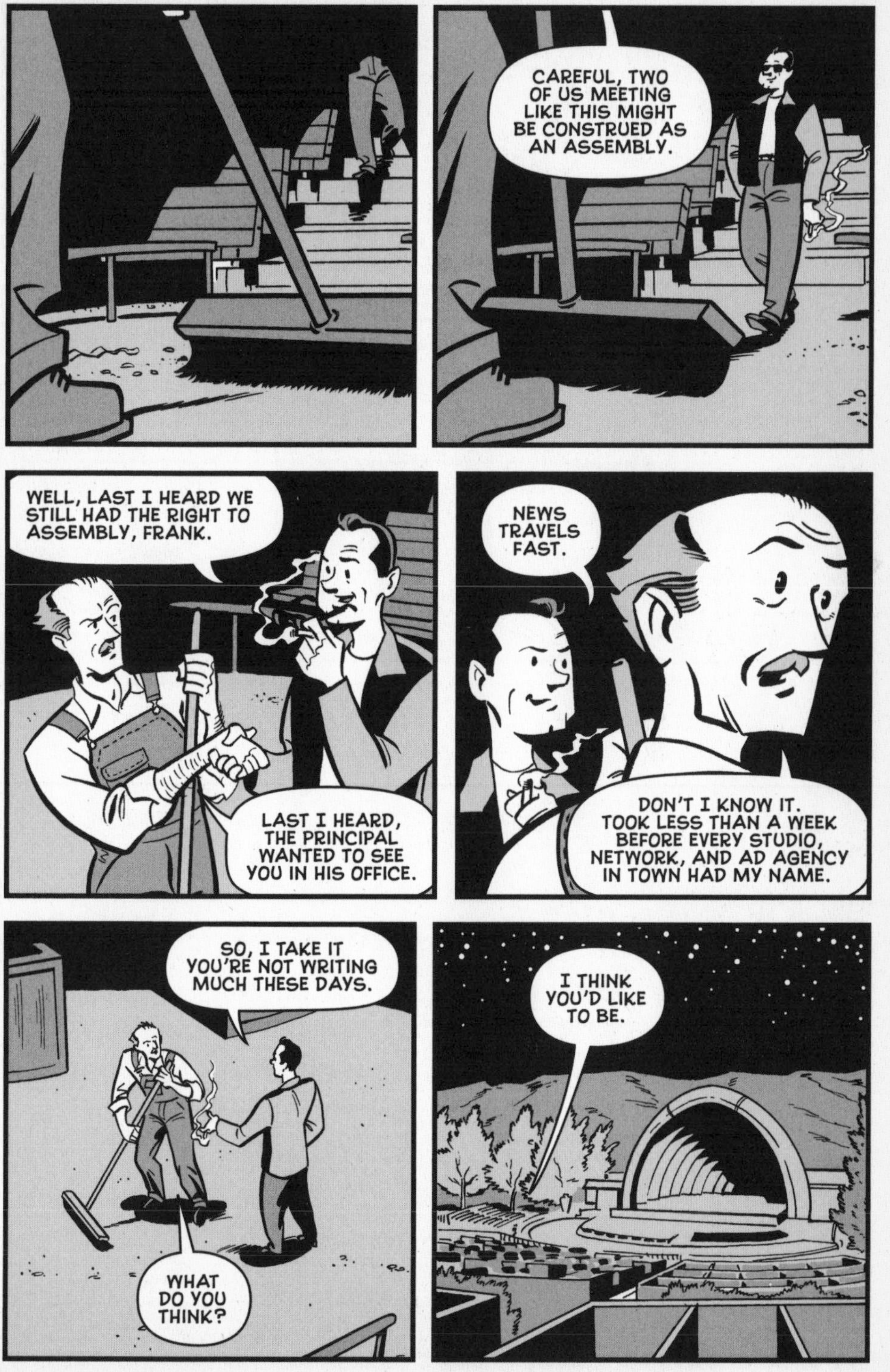
CAREFUL, TWO OF US MEETING LIKE THIS MIGHT BE CONSTRUED AS AN ASSEMBLY.
WELL, LAST I HEARD WE STILL HAD THE RIGHT TO ASSEMBLY, FRANK.
LAST I HEARD, THE PRINCIPAL WANTED TO SEE YOU IN HIS OFFICE.
NEWS TRAVELS FAST.
DON'T I KNOW IT. TOOK LESS THAN A WEEK BEFORE EVERY STUDIO, NETWORK, AND AD AGENCY IN TOWN HAD MY NAME.
SO, I TAKE IT YOU'RE NOT WRITING MUCH THESE DAYS.
WHAT DO YOU THINK?
I THINK YOU'D LIKE TO BE.

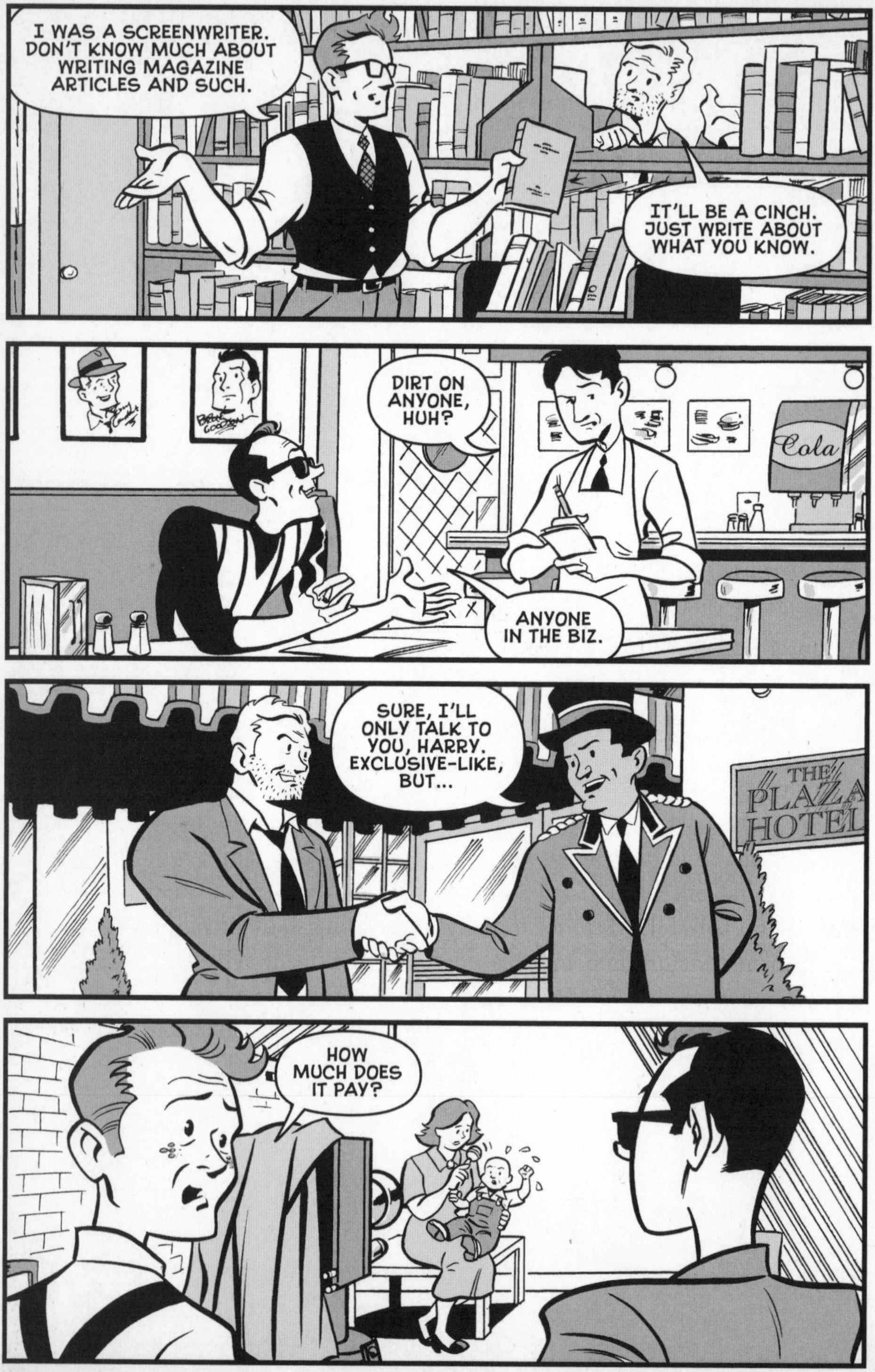
I WAS A SCREENWRITER. DON'T KNOW MUCH ABOUT WRITING MAGAZINE ARTICLES AND SUCH.
IT'LL BE A CINCH. JUST WRITE ABOUT WHAT YOU KNOW.
DIRT ON ANYONE, HUH?
Cola
ANYONE IN THE BIZ.
SURE, I'LL ONLY TALK TO YOU, HARRY. EXCLUSIVE-LIKE, BUT...
THE
HOW MUCH DOES IT PAY?

Act III

"Nobody's interested in
sweetness and light."
- Hedda Hopper.

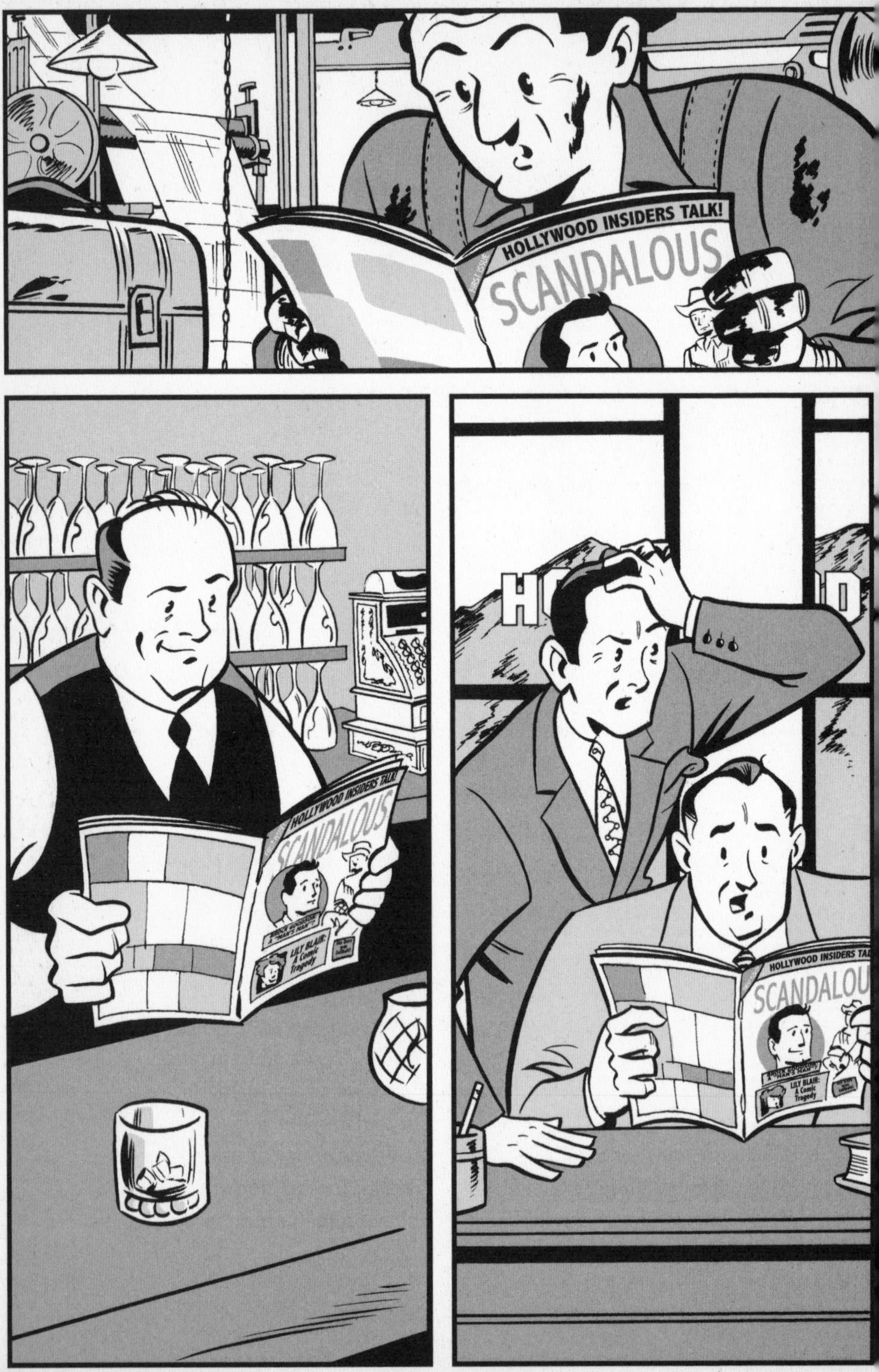

HOLLYWOOD INSIDERS TALK!
SCANDALOUS
HOLLYWOOD INSIDERS TALK!
SCANDALOUS
LILY BLAIR:
A Comic
Tragedy
HOLLYWOOD INSIDERS TAL
SCANDALOU
LILY BLAIR:
A Comic
Tragedy

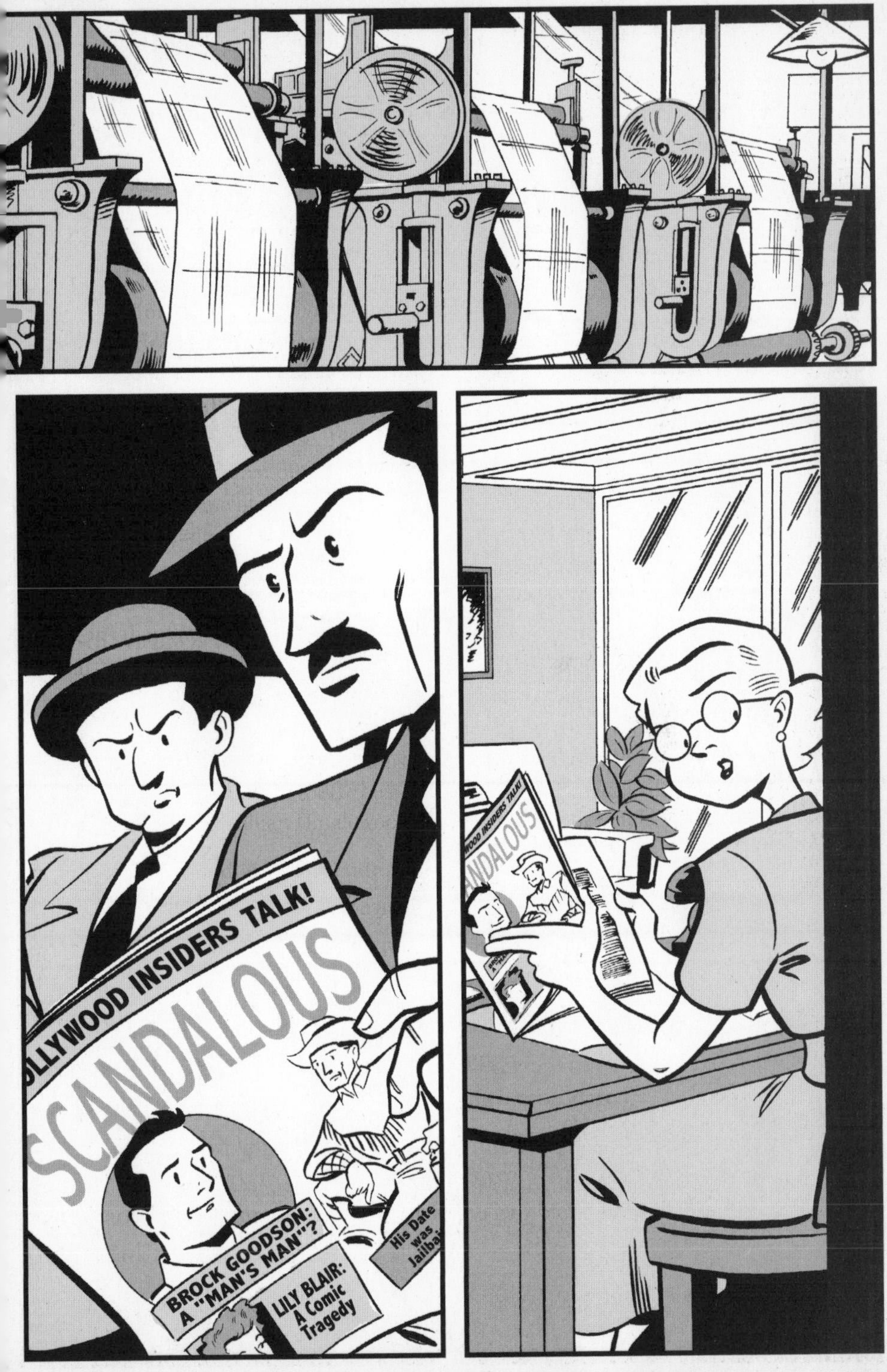
LLYWOOD INSIDERS TALK!
SCANDALOUS
BROCK GOODSON: A "MAN'S MAN"?
LILY BLAIR: A Comic Tragedy
His Date was

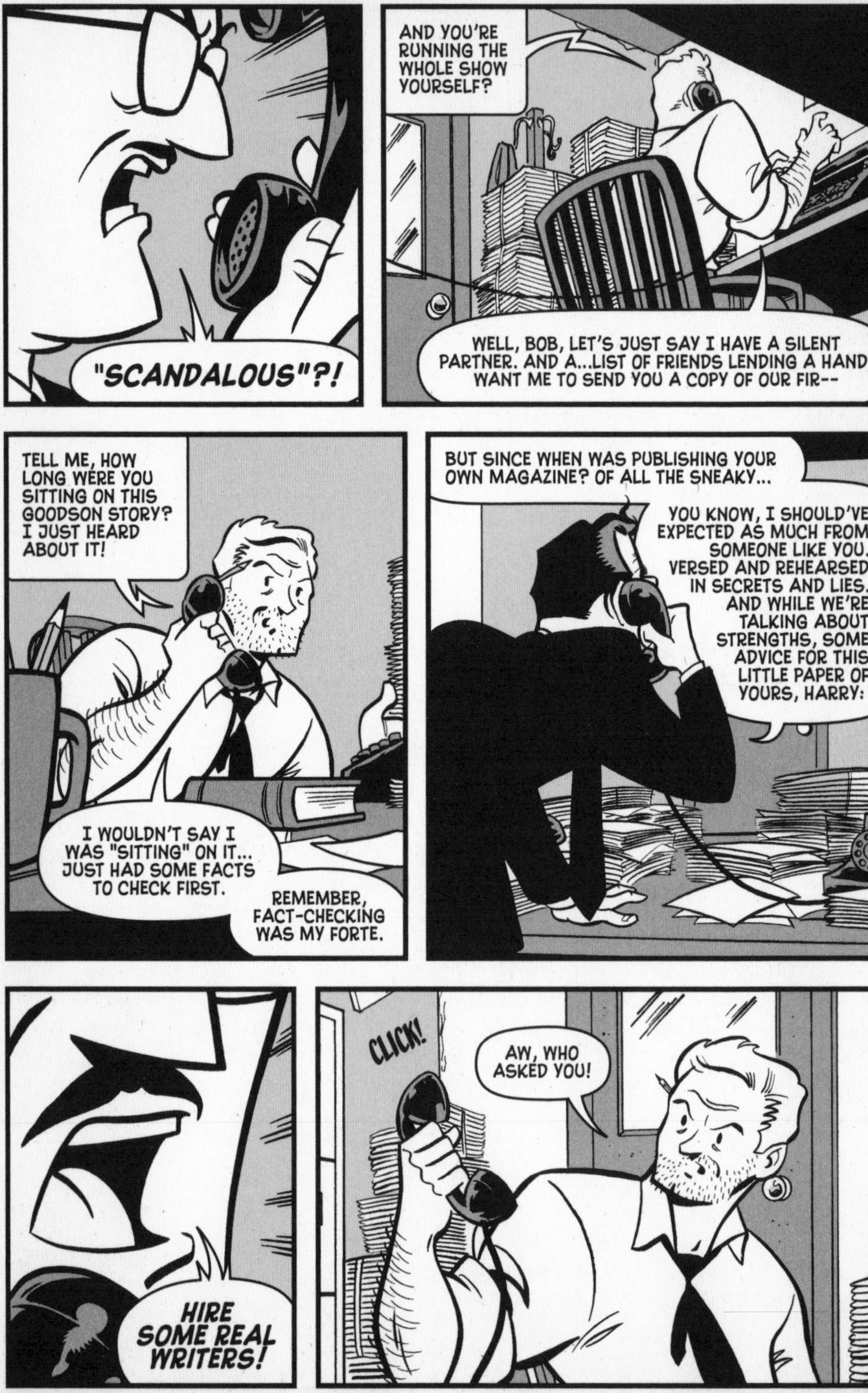
"SCANDALOUS"?!
AND YOU'RE RUNNING THE WHOLE SHOW YOURSELF?
WELL, BOB, LET'S JUST SAY I HAVE A SILENT PARTNER. AND A...LIST OF FRIENDS LENDING A HAND. WANT ME TO SEND YOU A COPY OF OUR FIR--
TELL ME, HOW LONG WERE YOU SITTING ON THIS GOODSON STORY? I JUST HEARD ABOUT IT!
I WOULDN'T SAY I WAS "SITTING" ON IT... JUST HAD SOME FACTS TO CHECK FIRST.
REMEMBER, FACT-CHECKING WAS MY FORTE.
BUT SINCE WHEN WAS PUBLISHING YOUR OWN MAGAZINE? OF ALL THE SNEAKY...
YOU KNOW, I SHOULD'VE EXPECTED AS MUCH FROM SOMEONE LIKE YOU. VERSED AND REHEARSED IN SECRETS AND LIES. AND WHILE WE'RE TALKING ABOUT STRENGTHS, SOME ADVICE FOR THIS LITTLE PAPER OF YOURS, HARRY:
HIRE SOME REAL WRITERS!
CLICK!
AW, WHO ASKED YOU!

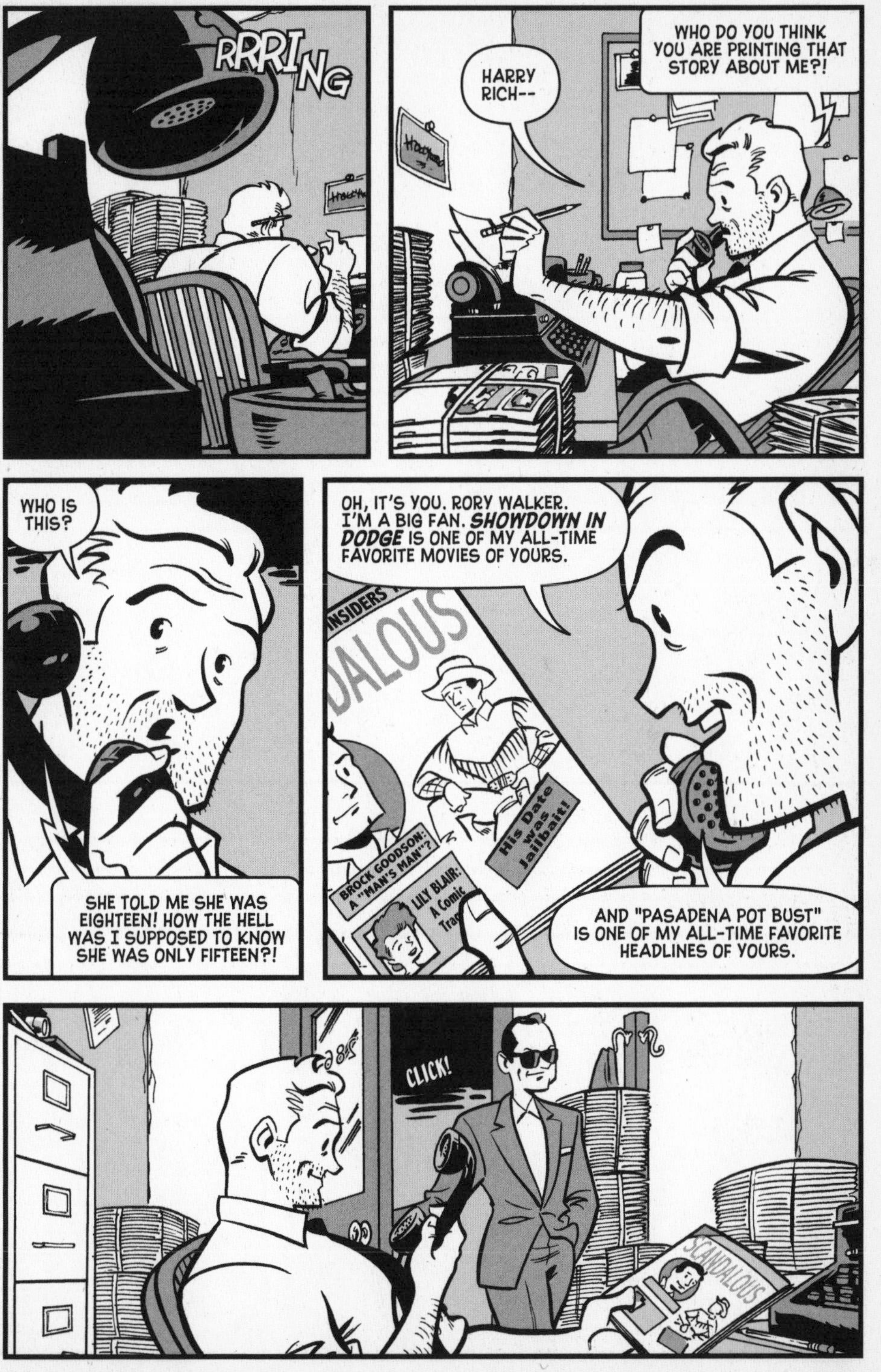
RRRING
HARRY RICH--
WHO DO YOU THINK YOU ARE PRINTING THAT STORY ABOUT ME?!
WHO IS THIS?
SHE TOLD ME SHE WAS EIGHTEEN! HOW THE HELL WAS I SUPPOSED TO KNOW SHE WAS ONLY FIFTEEN?!
OH, IT'S YOU. RORY WALKER. I'M A BIG FAN. SHOWDOWN IN DODGE IS ONE OF MY ALL-TIME FAVORITE MOVIES OF YOURS.
INSIDERS
DALOUS
His Date was Jailbait!
BROCK GOODSON: A "MAN'S MAN"?
LILY BLAIR: A Comic
AND "PASADENA POT BUST" IS ONE OF MY ALL-TIME FAVORITE HEADLINES OF YOURS.
CLICK!
SCANDALOUS

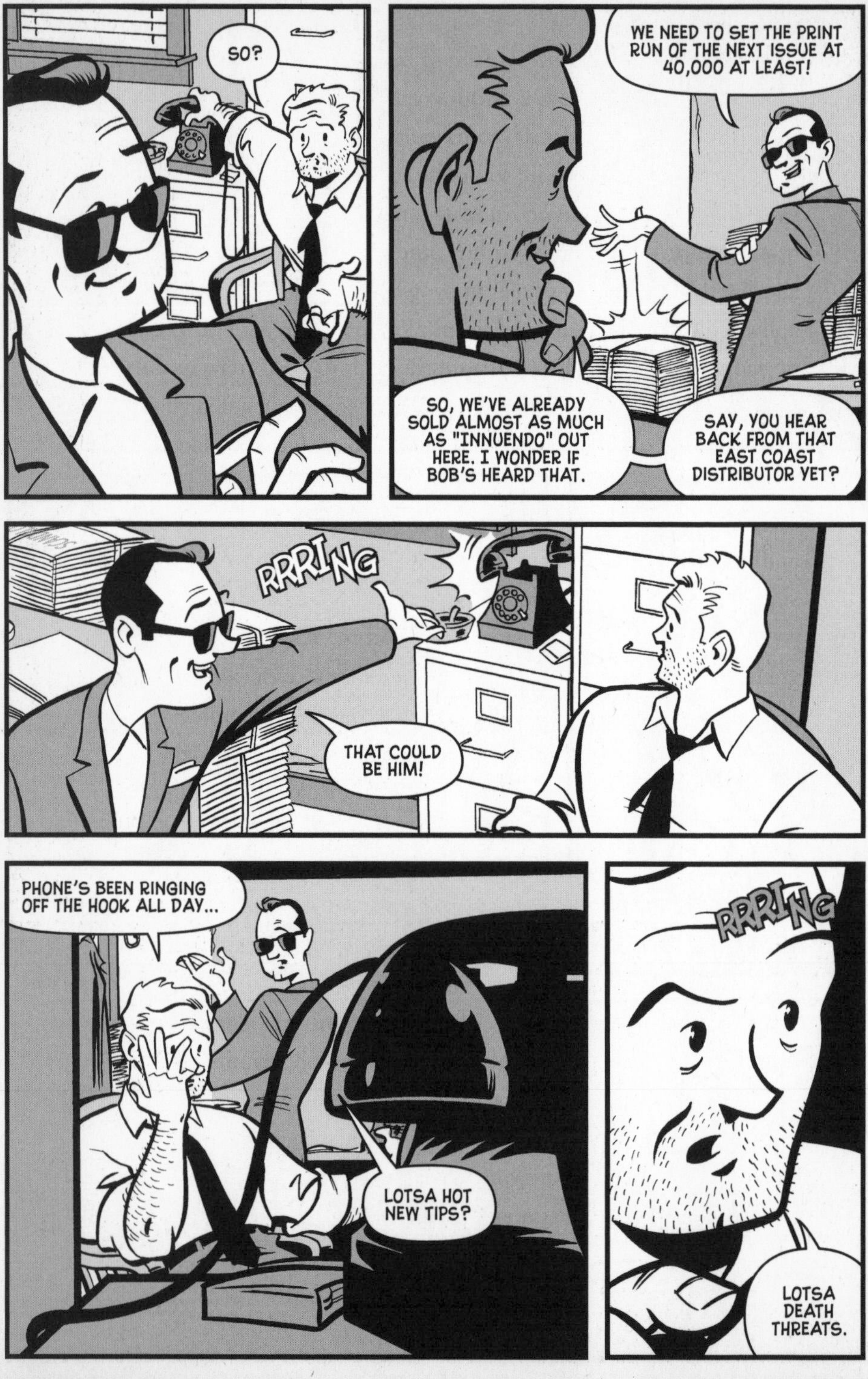
SO?
WE NEED TO SET THE PRINT RUN OF THE NEXT ISSUE AT 40,000 AT LEAST!
SO, WE'VE ALREADY SOLD ALMOST AS MUCH AS "INNUENDO" OUT HERE. I WONDER IF BOB'S HEARD THAT.
SAY, YOU HEAR BACK FROM THAT EAST COAST DISTRIBUTOR YET?
RRRING
THAT COULD BE HIM!
PHONE'S BEEN RINGING OFF THE HOOK ALL DAY...
LOTSA HOT NEW TIPS?
RRRING
LOTSA DEATH THREATS.

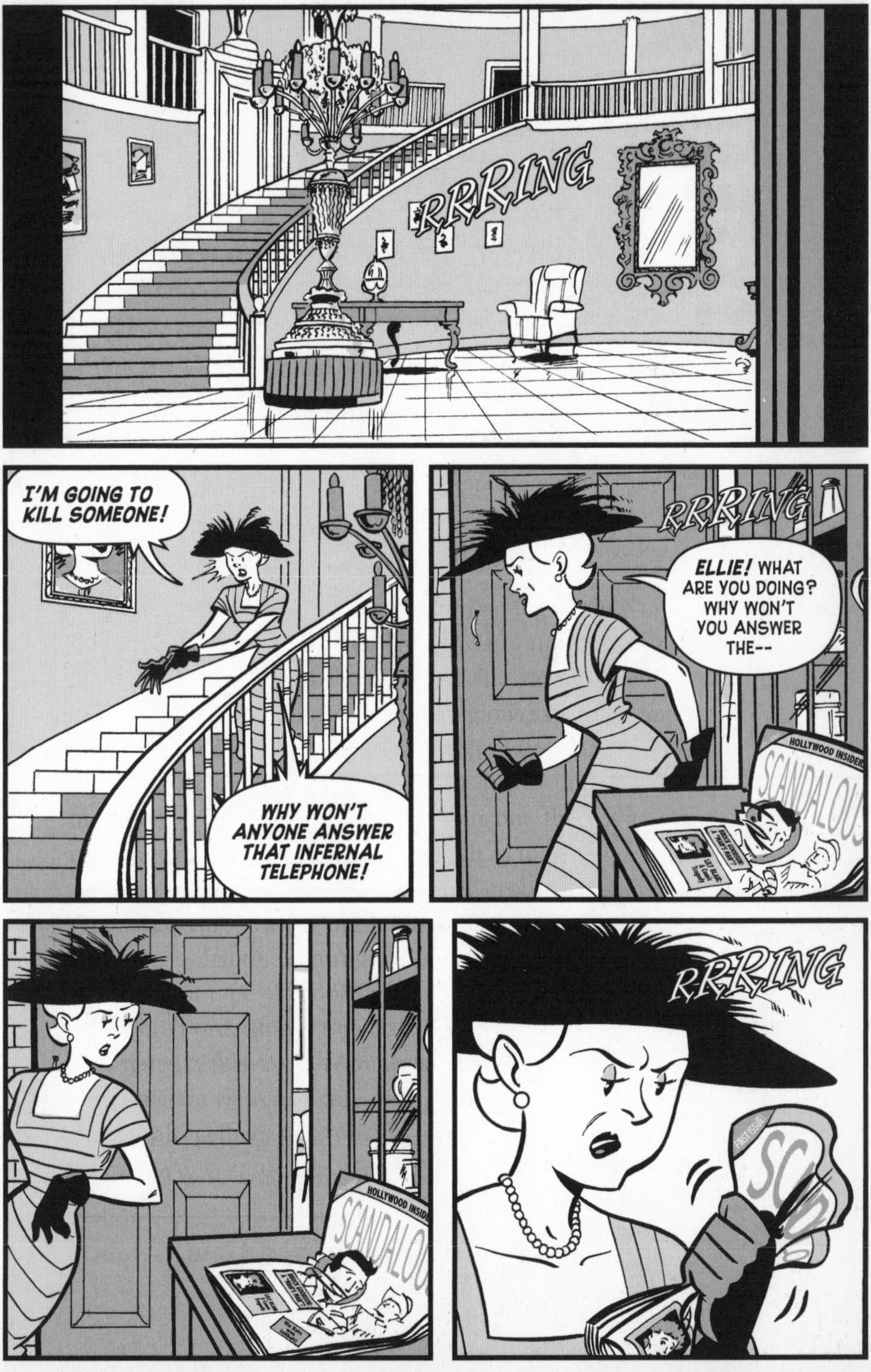
RRRING
I'M GOING TO KILL SOMEONE!
WHY WON'T ANYONE ANSWER THAT INFERNAL TELEPHONE!
RRRING
ELLIE! WHAT ARE YOU DOING? WHY WON'T YOU ANSWER THE--
HOLLYWOOD INSIDER
RRRING
FIRST ISSUE!

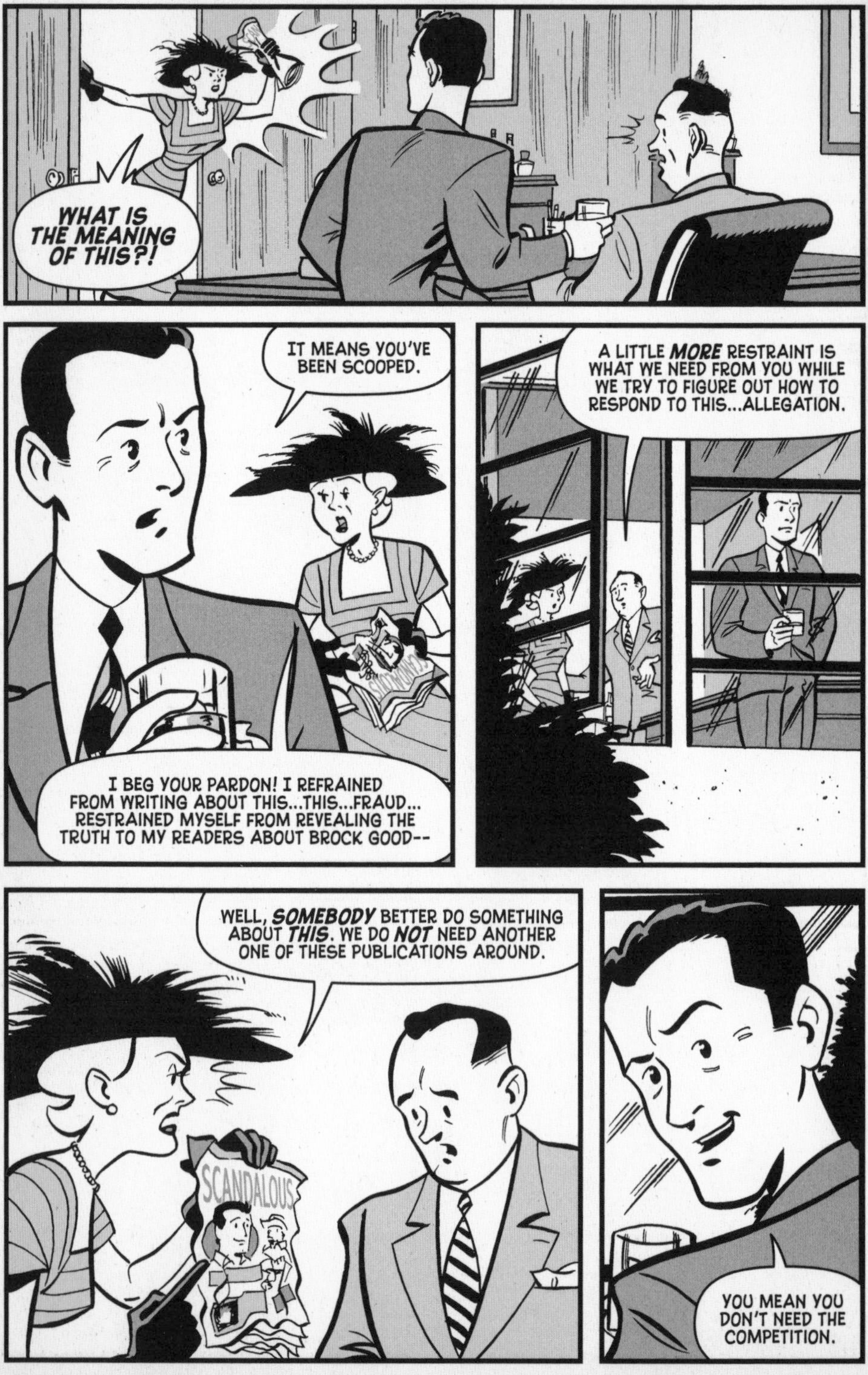
WHAT IS THE MEANING OF THIS?!
IT MEANS YOU'VE BEEN SCOOPED.
I BEG YOUR PARDON! I REFRAINED FROM WRITING ABOUT THIS...THIS...FRAUD... RESTRAINED MYSELF FROM REVEALING THE TRUTH TO MY READERS ABOUT BROCK GOOD--
A LITTLE MORE RESTRAINT IS WHAT WE NEED FROM YOU WHILE WE TRY TO FIGURE OUT HOW TO RESPOND TO THIS...ALLEGATION.
WELL, SOMEBODY BETTER DO SOMETHING ABOUT THIS. WE DO NOT NEED ANOTHER ONE OF THESE PUBLICATIONS AROUND.
SCANDALOUS
YOU MEAN YOU DON'T NEED THE COMPETITION.

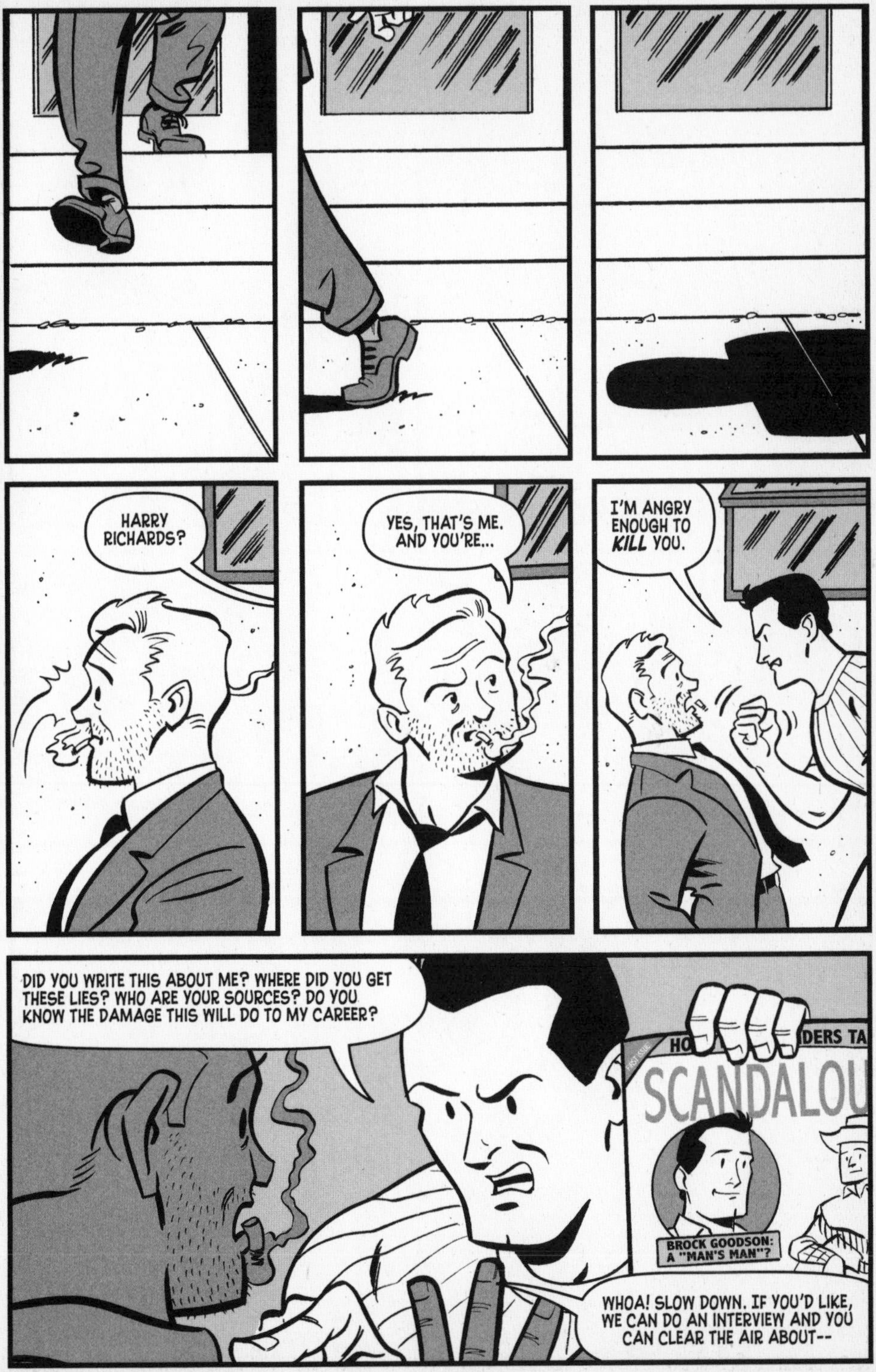

HARRY RICHARDS?
YES, THAT'S ME. AND YOU'RE...
I'M ANGRY ENOUGH TO KILL YOU.
DID YOU WRITE THIS ABOUT ME? WHERE DID YOU GET THESE LIES? WHO ARE YOUR SOURCES? DO YOU KNOW THE DAMAGE THIS WILL DO TO MY CAREER?
SCANDALOU
BROCK GOODSON: A "MAN'S MAN"?
WHOA! SLOW DOWN. IF YOU'D LIKE, WE CAN DO AN INTERVIEW AND YOU CAN CLEAR THE AIR ABOUT--

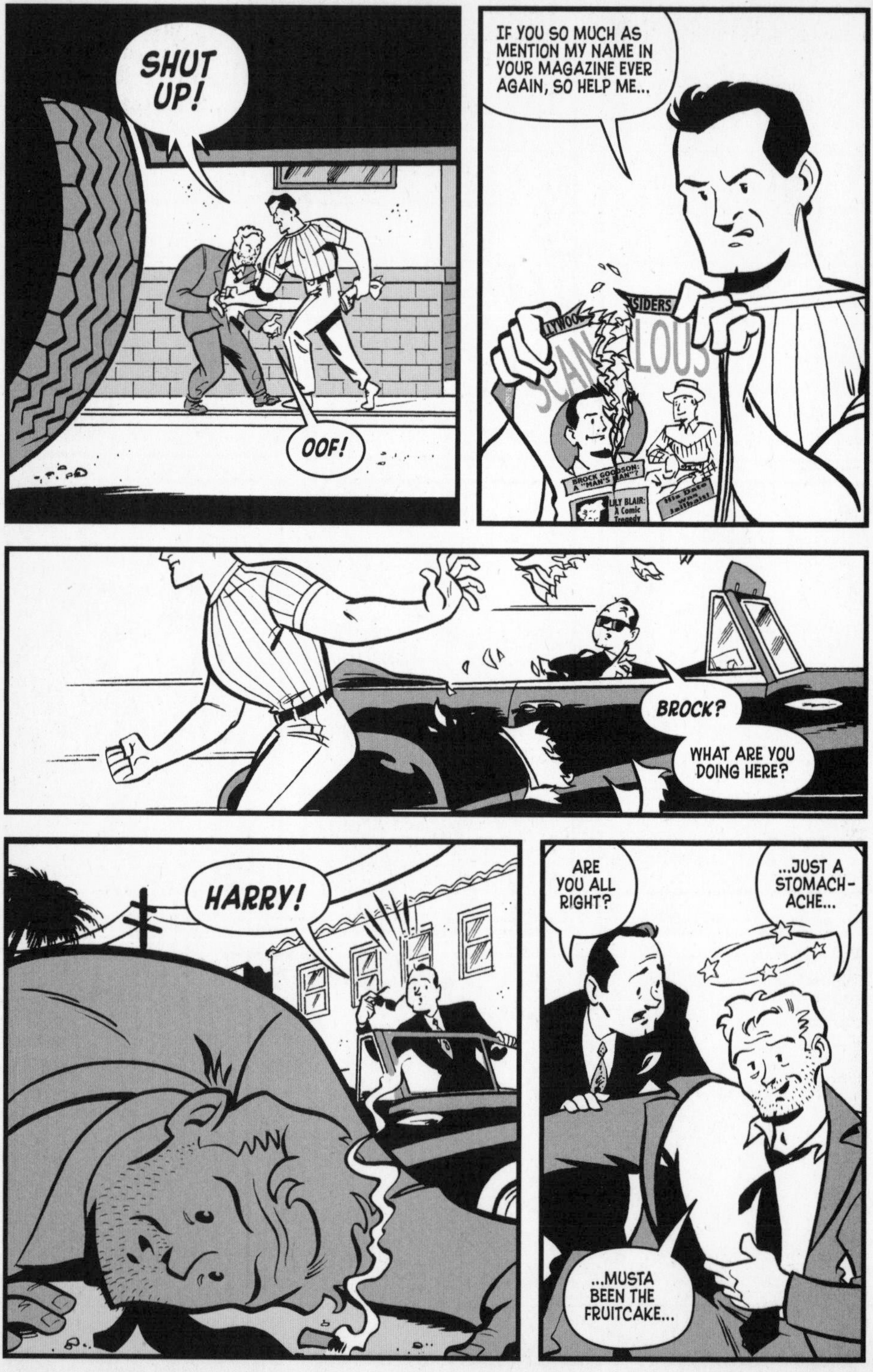
SHUT UP!
OOF!
IF YOU SO MUCH AS MENTION MY NAME IN YOUR MAGAZINE EVER AGAIN, SO HELP ME...
SIDERS
LOUS
BROCK GOODSON: A "MAN'S MAN"?
LILY BLAIR: A Comic Tragedy
BROCK?
WHAT ARE YOU DOING HERE?
HARRY!
ARE YOU ALL RIGHT?
...JUST A STOMACH-ACHE...
...MUSTA BEEN THE FRUITCAKE...

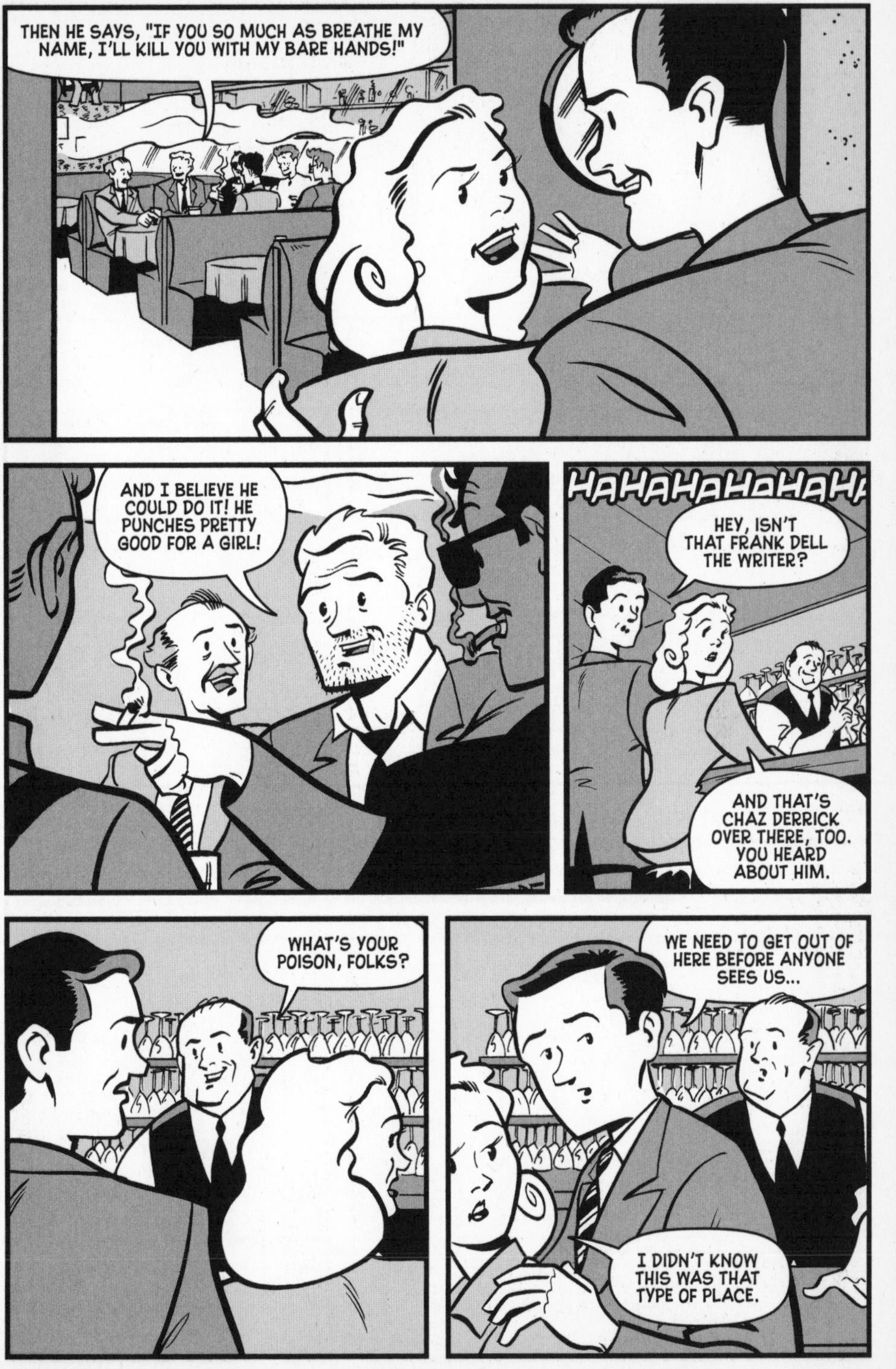
THEN HE SAYS, "IF YOU SO MUCH AS BREATHE MY NAME, I'LL KILL YOU WITH MY BARE HANDS!"
AND I BELIEVE HE COULD DO IT! HE PUNCHES PRETTY GOOD FOR A GIRL!
HAHAHAHAHAHAH
HEY, ISN'T THAT FRANK DELL THE WRITER?
AND THAT'S CHAZ DERRICK OVER THERE, TOO. YOU HEARD ABOUT HIM.
WHAT'S YOUR POISON, FOLKS?
WE NEED TO GET OUT OF HERE BEFORE ANYONE SEES US...
I DIDN'T KNOW THIS WAS THAT TYPE OF PLACE.

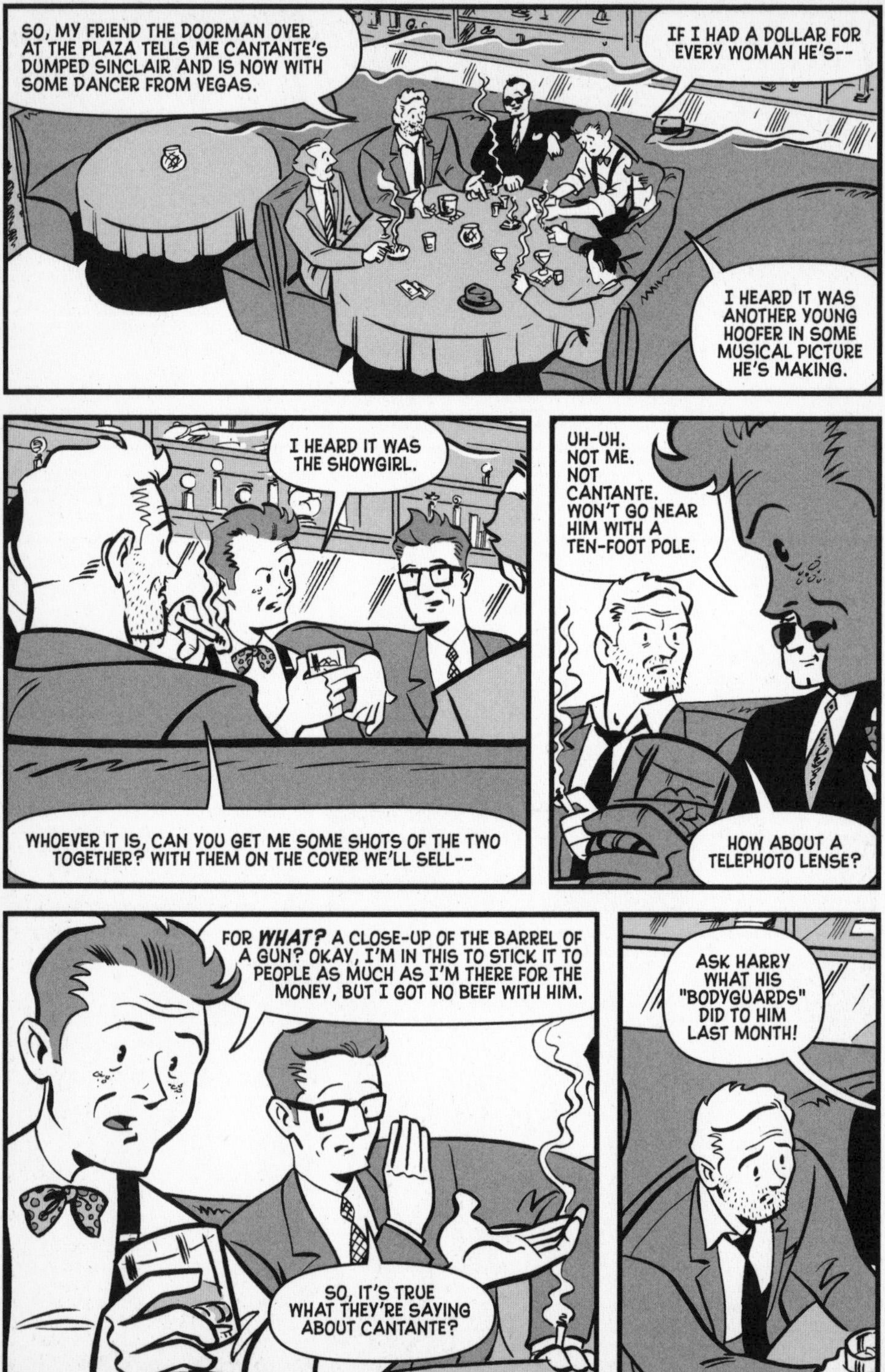

SO, MY FRIEND THE DOORMAN OVER AT THE PLAZA TELLS ME CANTANTE'S DUMPED SINCLAIR AND IS NOW WITH SOME DANCER FROM VEGAS.
IF I HAD A DOLLAR FOR EVERY WOMAN HE'S--
I HEARD IT WAS ANOTHER YOUNG HOOFER IN SOME MUSICAL PICTURE HE'S MAKING.
I HEARD IT WAS THE SHOWGIRL.
WHOEVER IT IS, CAN YOU GET ME SOME SHOTS OF THE TWO TOGETHER? WITH THEM ON THE COVER WE'LL SELL--
UH-UH. NOT ME. NOT CANTANTE. WON'T GO NEAR HIM WITH A TEN-FOOT POLE.
HOW ABOUT A TELEPHOTO LENSE?
FOR ***WHAT?*** A CLOSE-UP OF THE BARREL OF A GUN? OKAY, I'M IN THIS TO STICK IT TO PEOPLE AS MUCH AS I'M THERE FOR THE MONEY, BUT I GOT NO BEEF WITH HIM.
SO, IT'S TRUE WHAT THEY'RE SAYING ABOUT CANTANTE?
ASK HARRY WHAT HIS "BODYGUARDS" DID TO HIM LAST MONTH!

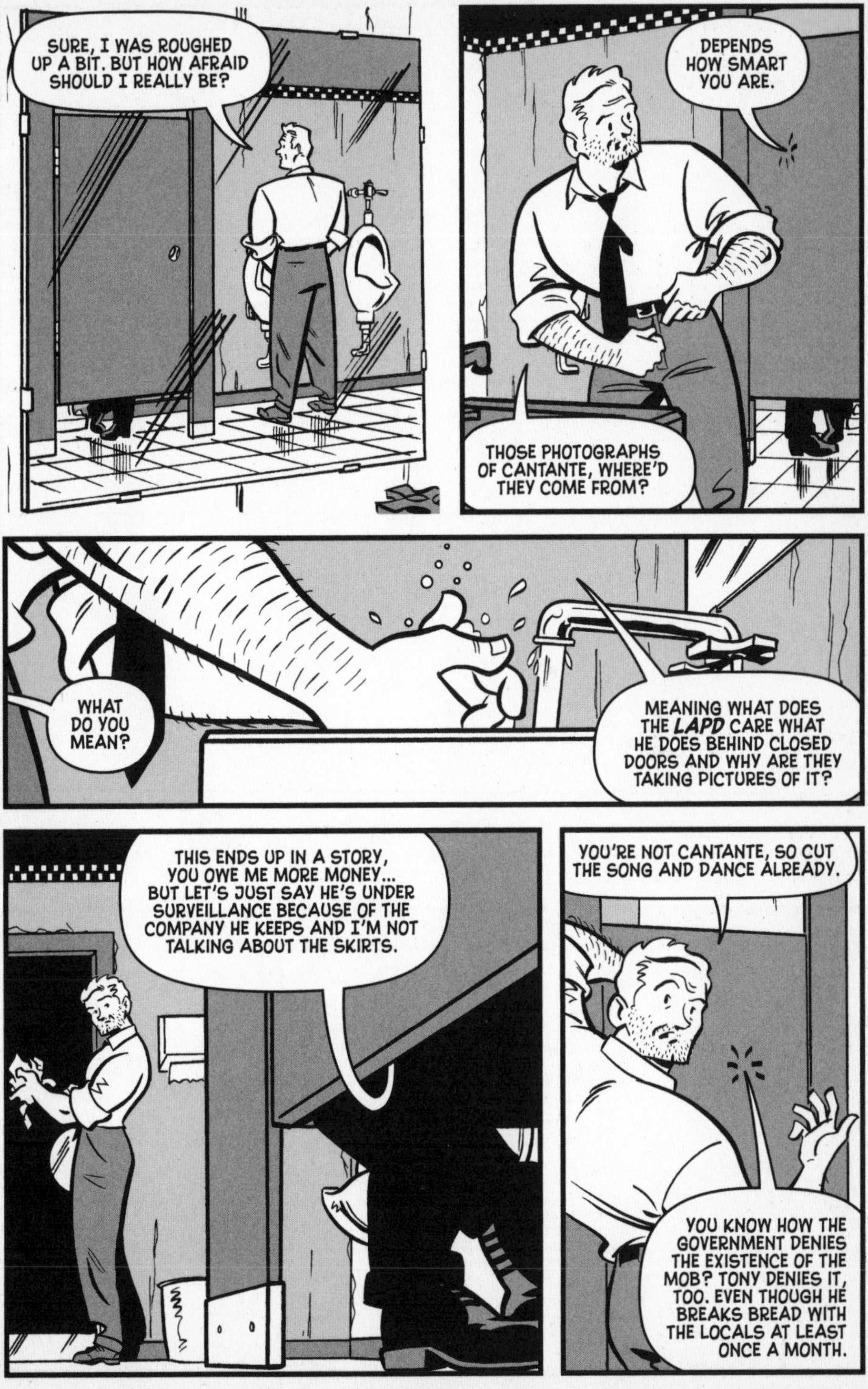

SURE, I WAS ROUGHED UP A BIT. BUT HOW AFRAID SHOULD I REALLY BE?
DEPENDS HOW SMART YOU ARE.
THOSE PHOTOGRAPHS OF CANTANTE, WHERE'D THEY COME FROM?
WHAT DO YOU MEAN?
MEANING WHAT DOES THE LAPD CARE WHAT HE DOES BEHIND CLOSED DOORS AND WHY ARE THEY TAKING PICTURES OF IT?
THIS ENDS UP IN A STORY, YOU OWE ME MORE MONEY... BUT LET'S JUST SAY HE'S UNDER SURVEILLANCE BECAUSE OF THE COMPANY HE KEEPS AND I'M NOT TALKING ABOUT THE SKIRTS.
YOU'RE NOT CANTANTE, SO CUT THE SONG AND DANCE ALREADY.
YOU KNOW HOW THE GOVERNMENT DENIES THE EXISTENCE OF THE MOB? TONY DENIES IT, TOO. EVEN THOUGH HE BREAKS BREAD WITH THE LOCALS AT LEAST ONCE A MONTH.

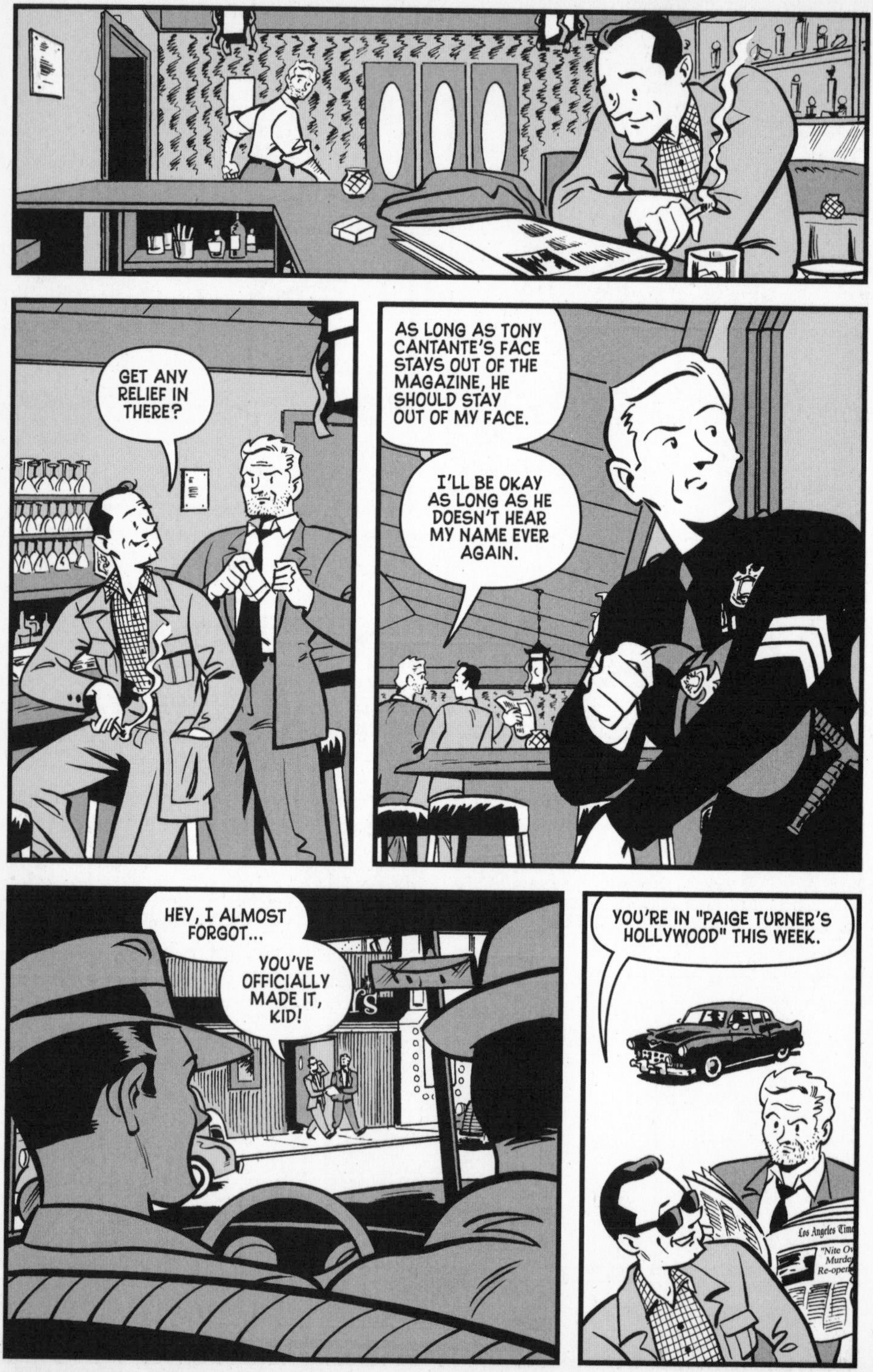
GET ANY RELIEF IN THERE?
AS LONG AS TONY CANTANTE'S FACE STAYS OUT OF THE MAGAZINE, HE SHOULD STAY OUT OF MY FACE.
I'LL BE OKAY AS LONG AS HE DOESN'T HEAR MY NAME EVER AGAIN.
HEY, I ALMOST FORGOT...
YOU'VE OFFICIALLY MADE IT, KID!
YOU'RE IN "PAIGE TURNER'S HOLLYWOOD" THIS WEEK.

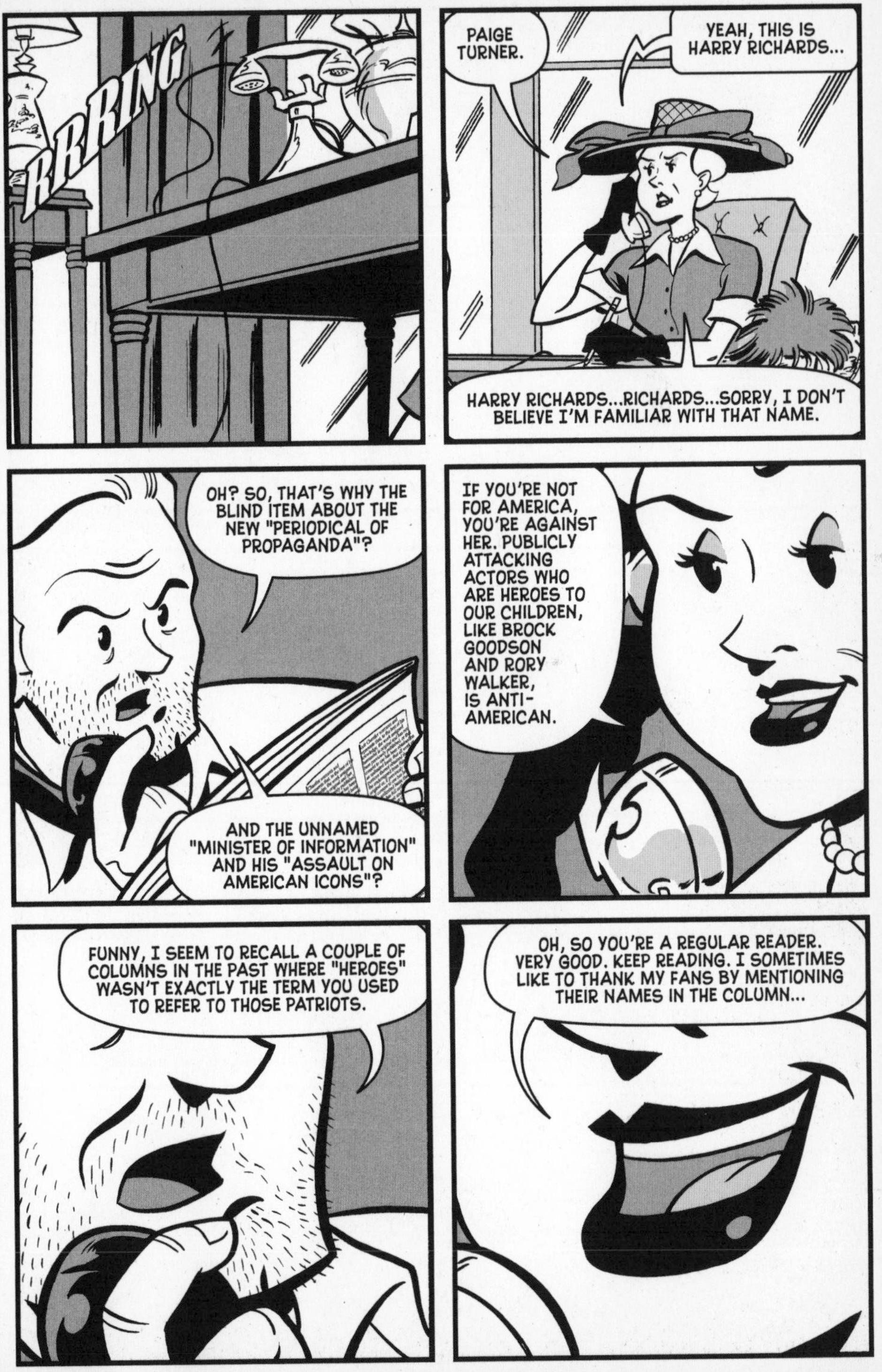
RRRING
PAIGE TURNER.
YEAH, THIS IS HARRY RICHARDS...
HARRY RICHARDS...RICHARDS...SORRY, I DON'T BELIEVE I'M FAMILIAR WITH THAT NAME.
OH? SO, THAT'S WHY THE BLIND ITEM ABOUT THE NEW "PERIODICAL OF PROPAGANDA"?
AND THE UNNAMED "MINISTER OF INFORMATION" AND HIS "ASSAULT ON AMERICAN ICONS"?
IF YOU'RE NOT FOR AMERICA, YOU'RE AGAINST HER. PUBLICLY ATTACKING ACTORS WHO ARE HEROES TO OUR CHILDREN, LIKE BROCK GOODSON AND RORY WALKER, IS ANTI-AMERICAN.
FUNNY, I SEEM TO RECALL A COUPLE OF COLUMNS IN THE PAST WHERE "HEROES" WASN'T EXACTLY THE TERM YOU USED TO REFER TO THOSE PATRIOTS.
OH, SO YOU'RE A REGULAR READER. VERY GOOD. KEEP READING. I SOMETIMES LIKE TO THANK MY FANS BY MENTIONING THEIR NAMES IN THE COLUMN...

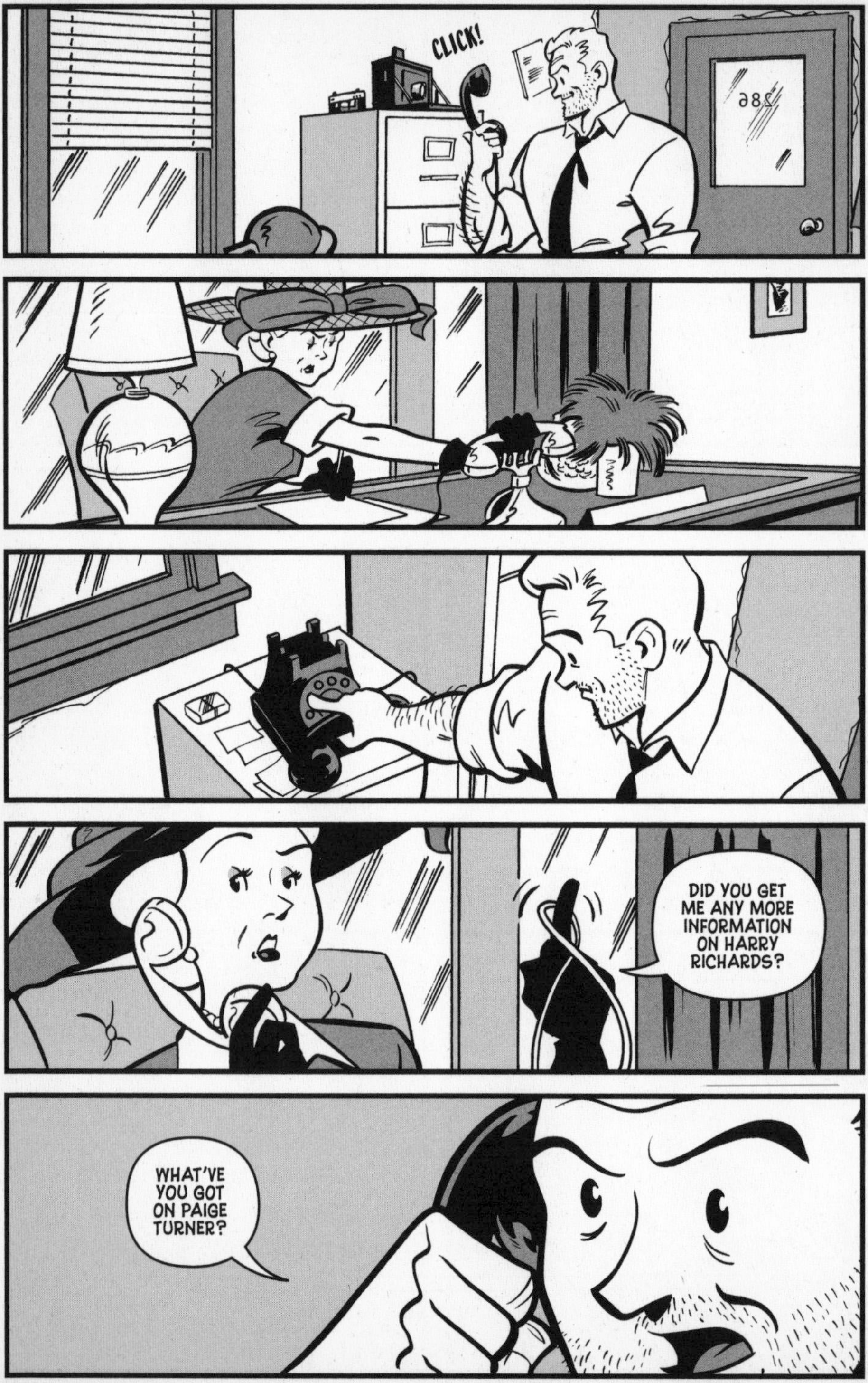
CLICK!
286
DID YOU GET ME ANY MORE INFORMATION ON HARRY RICHARDS?
WHAT'VE YOU GOT ON PAIGE TURNER?

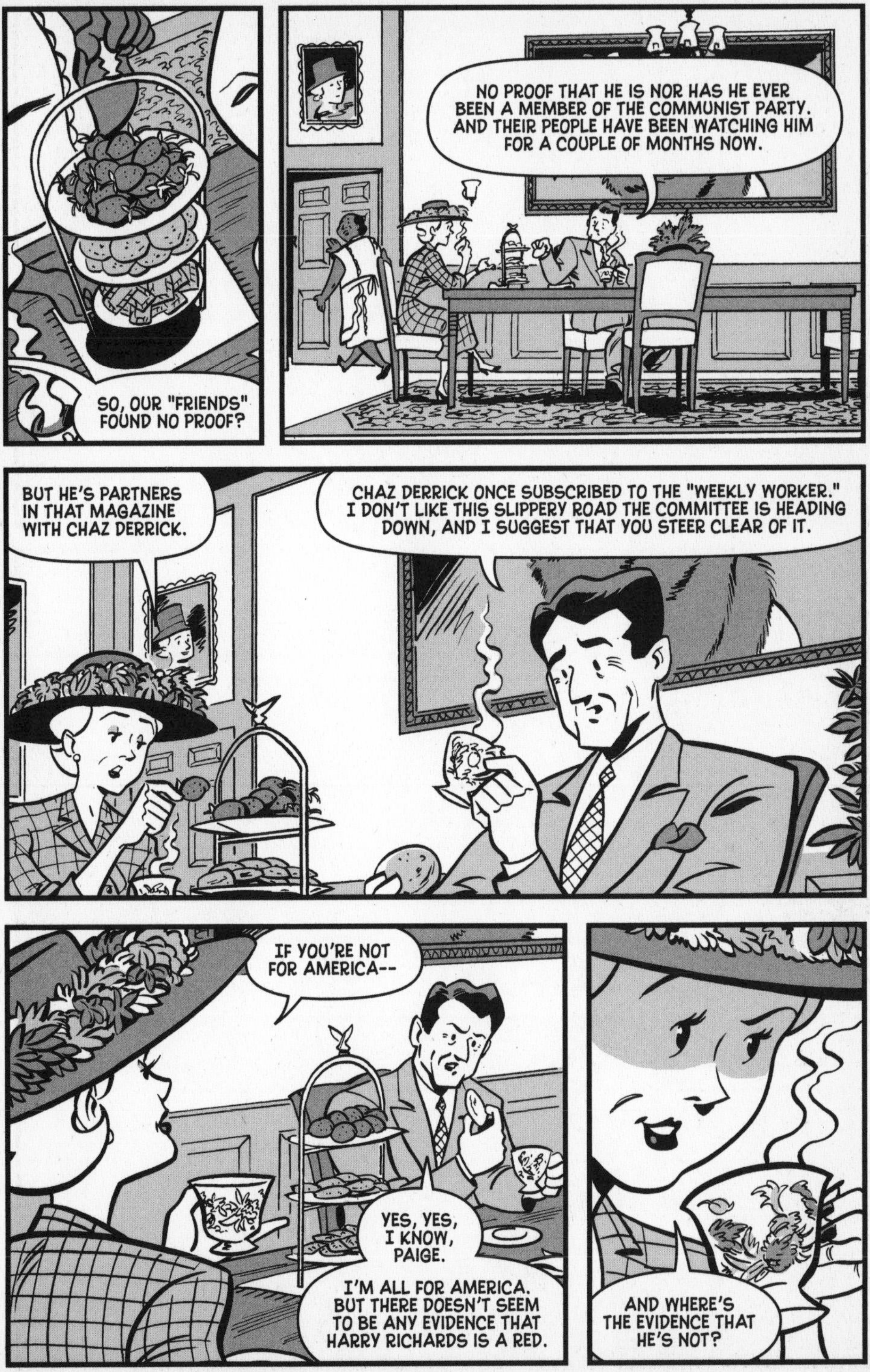
SO, OUR "FRIENDS" FOUND NO PROOF?
NO PROOF THAT HE IS NOR HAS HE EVER BEEN A MEMBER OF THE COMMUNIST PARTY. AND THEIR PEOPLE HAVE BEEN WATCHING HIM FOR A COUPLE OF MONTHS NOW.
BUT HE'S PARTNERS IN THAT MAGAZINE WITH CHAZ DERRICK.
CHAZ DERRICK ONCE SUBSCRIBED TO THE "WEEKLY WORKER." I DON'T LIKE THIS SLIPPERY ROAD THE COMMITTEE IS HEADING DOWN, AND I SUGGEST THAT YOU STEER CLEAR OF IT.
IF YOU'RE NOT FOR AMERICA--
YES, YES, I KNOW, PAIGE.
I'M ALL FOR AMERICA. BUT THERE DOESN'T SEEM TO BE ANY EVIDENCE THAT HARRY RICHARDS IS A RED.
AND WHERE'S THE EVIDENCE THAT HE'S NOT?

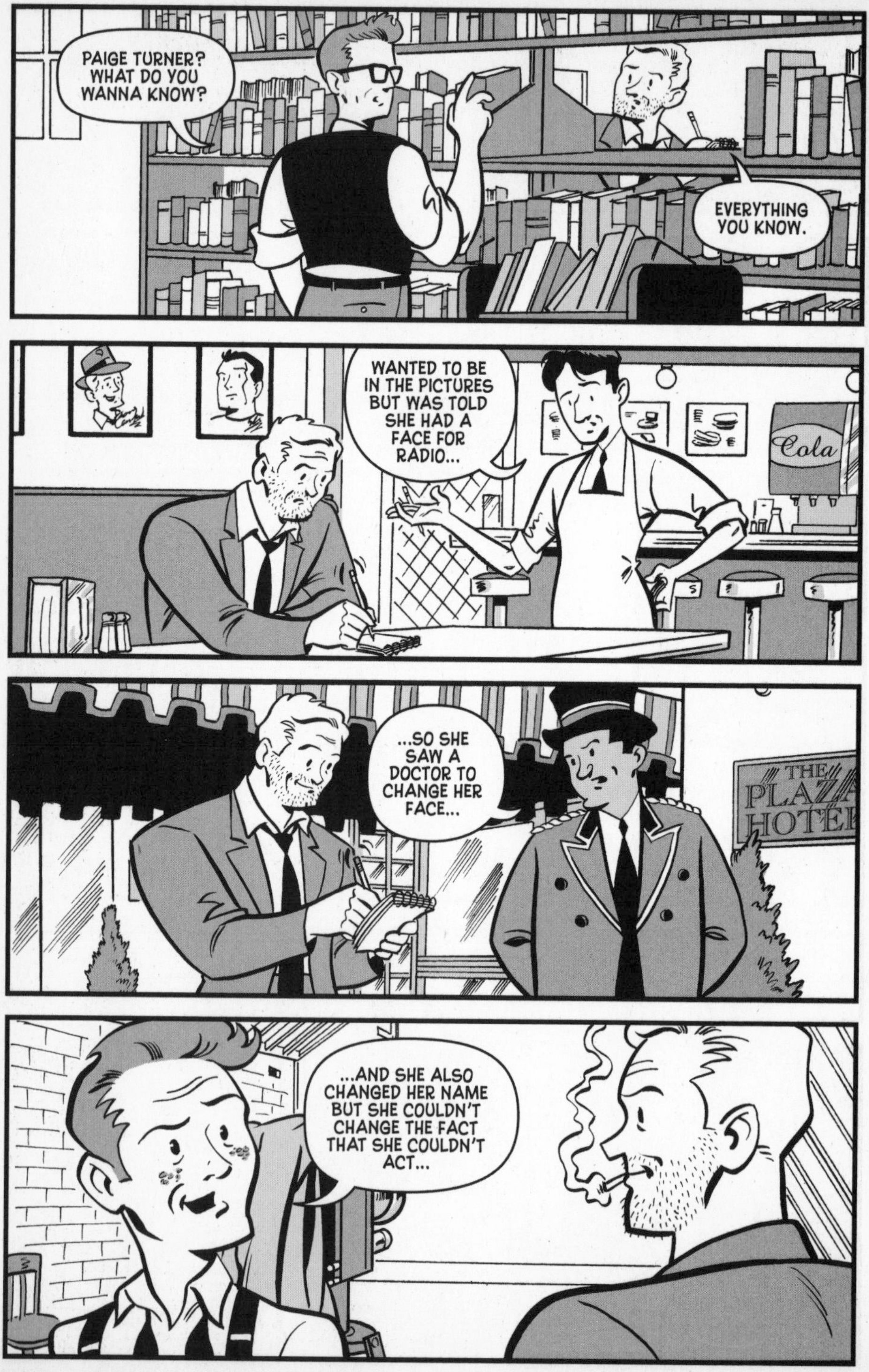
PAIGE TURNER? WHAT DO YOU WANNA KNOW?
EVERYTHING YOU KNOW.
WANTED TO BE IN THE PICTURES BUT WAS TOLD SHE HAD A FACE FOR RADIO...
Cola
...SO SHE SAW A DOCTOR TO CHANGE HER FACE...
...AND SHE ALSO CHANGED HER NAME BUT SHE COULDN'T CHANGE THE FACT THAT SHE COULDN'T ACT...

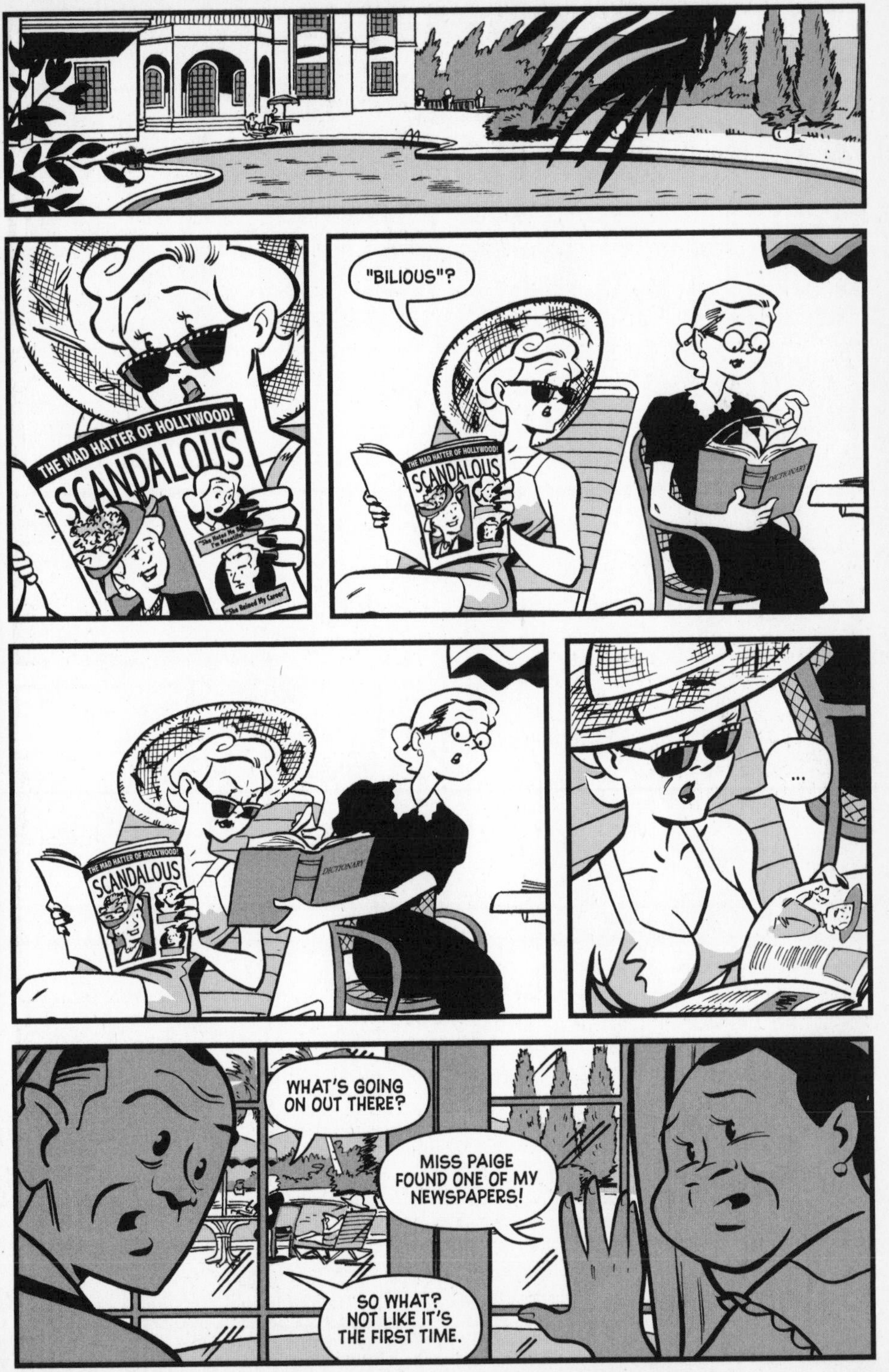
THE MAD HATTER OF HOLLYWOOD!
SCANDALOUS
"She Ruined My Career"
"BILIOUS"?
DICTIONARY
...
WHAT'S GOING ON OUT THERE?
MISS PAIGE FOUND ONE OF MY NEWSPAPERS!
SO WHAT? NOT LIKE IT'S THE FIRST TIME.

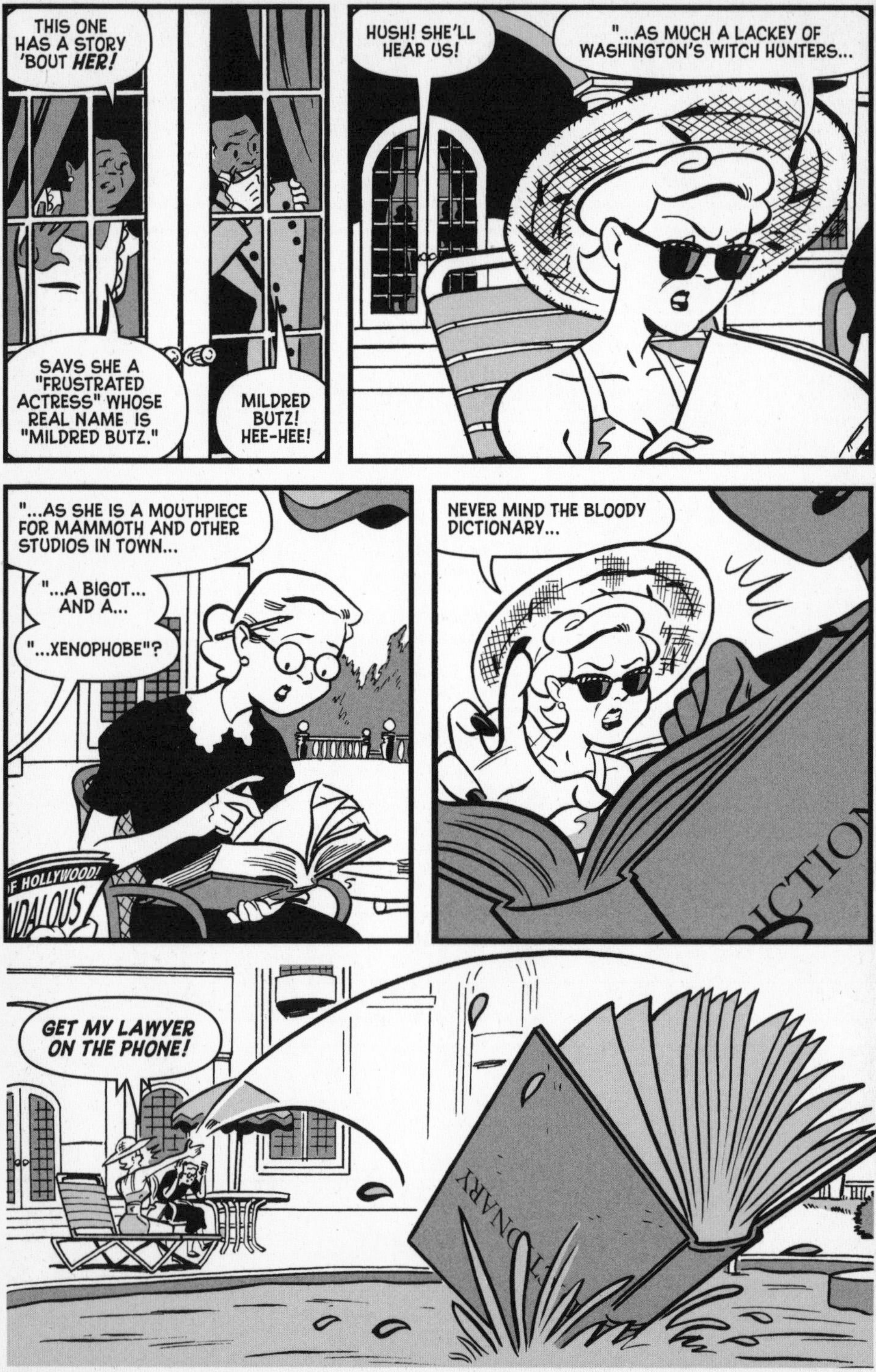
THIS ONE HAS A STORY 'BOUT ***HER!***
SAYS SHE A "FRUSTRATED ACTRESS" WHOSE REAL NAME IS "MILDRED BUTZ."
MILDRED BUTZ! HEE-HEE!
HUSH! SHE'LL HEAR US!
"...AS MUCH A LACKEY OF WASHINGTON'S WITCH HUNTERS...
"...AS SHE IS A MOUTHPIECE FOR MAMMOTH AND OTHER STUDIOS IN TOWN...
"...A BIGOT... AND A...
"...XENOPHOBE"?
OF HOLLYWOOD!
NDALOUS
NEVER MIND THE BLOODY DICTIONARY...
DICTION
GET MY LAWYER ON THE PHONE!

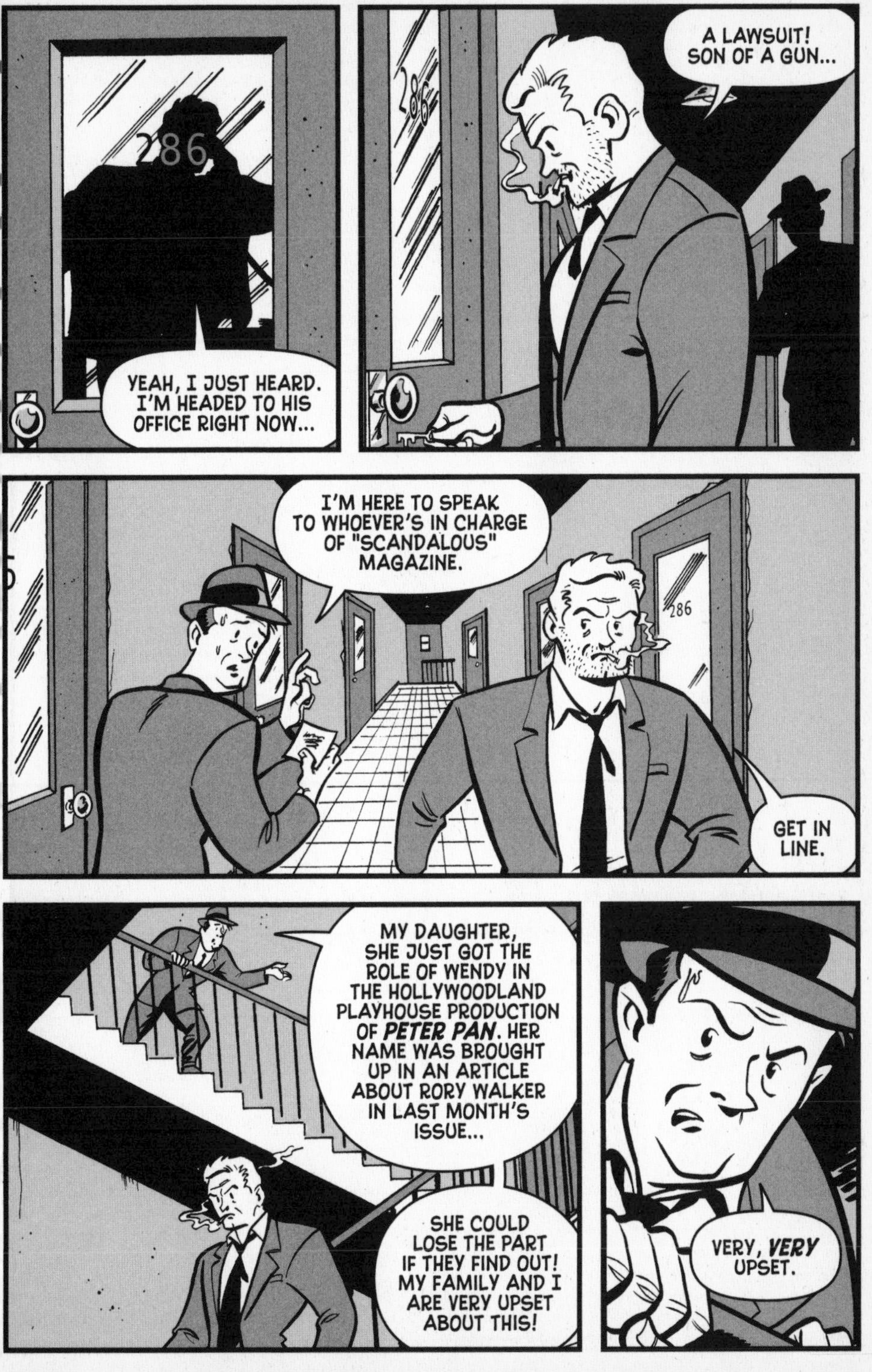
286
YEAH, I JUST HEARD. I'M HEADED TO HIS OFFICE RIGHT NOW...
A LAWSUIT! SON OF A GUN...
I'M HERE TO SPEAK TO WHOEVER'S IN CHARGE OF "SCANDALOUS" MAGAZINE.
GET IN LINE.
MY DAUGHTER, SHE JUST GOT THE ROLE OF WENDY IN THE HOLLYWOODLAND PLAYHOUSE PRODUCTION OF PETER PAN. HER NAME WAS BROUGHT UP IN AN ARTICLE ABOUT RORY WALKER IN LAST MONTH'S ISSUE...
SHE COULD LOSE THE PART IF THEY FIND OUT! MY FAMILY AND I ARE VERY UPSET ABOUT THIS!
VERY, VERY UPSET.

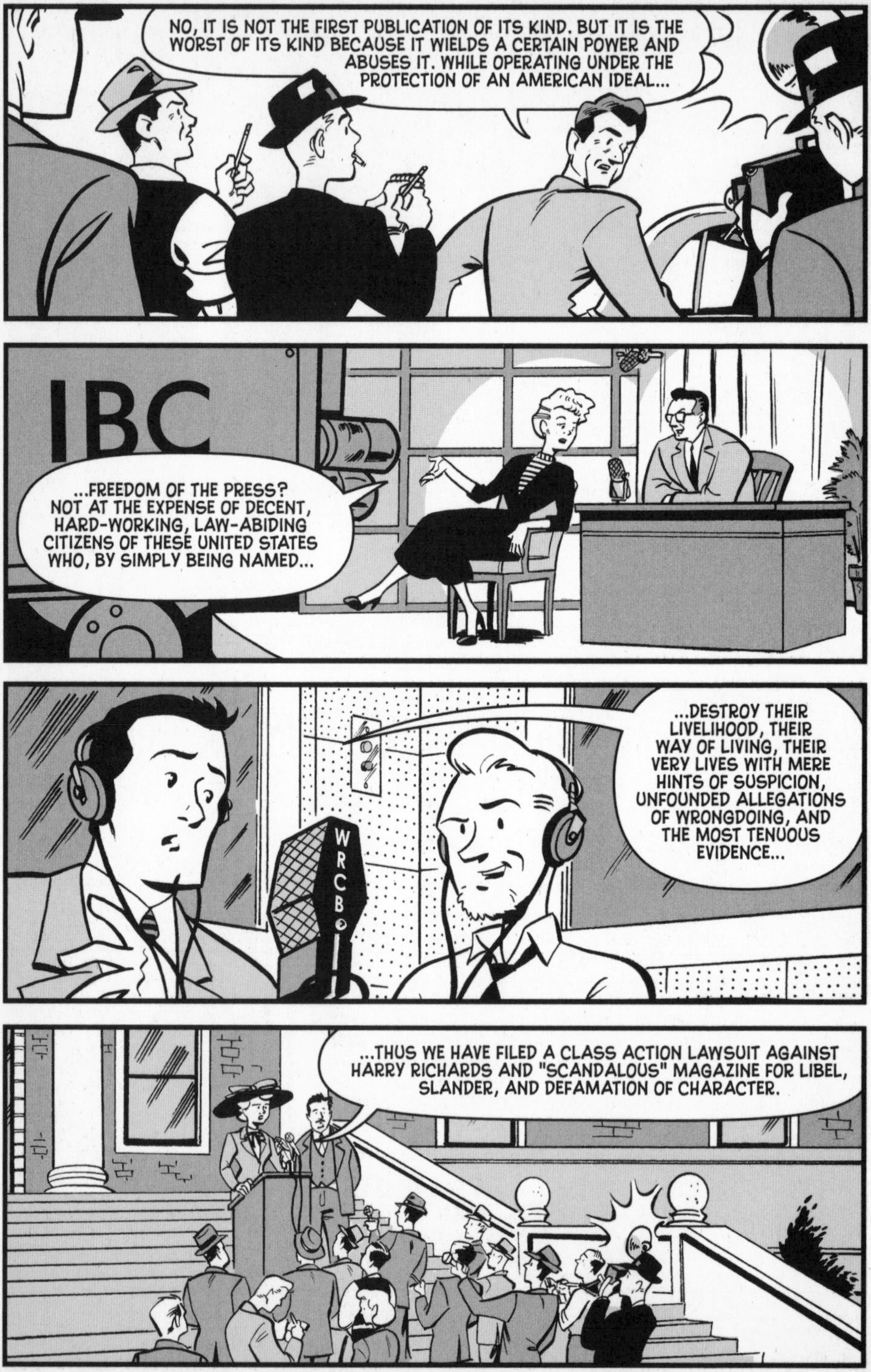
NO, IT IS NOT THE FIRST PUBLICATION OF ITS KIND. BUT IT IS THE WORST OF ITS KIND BECAUSE IT WIELDS A CERTAIN POWER AND ABUSES IT. WHILE OPERATING UNDER THE PROTECTION OF AN AMERICAN IDEAL...
IBC
...FREEDOM OF THE PRESS? NOT AT THE EXPENSE OF DECENT, HARD-WORKING, LAW-ABIDING CITIZENS OF THESE UNITED STATES WHO, BY SIMPLY BEING NAMED...
WRCB
...DESTROY THEIR LIVELIHOOD, THEIR WAY OF LIVING, THEIR VERY LIVES WITH MERE HINTS OF SUSPICION, UNFOUNDED ALLEGATIONS OF WRONGDOING, AND THE MOST TENUOUS EVIDENCE...
...THUS WE HAVE FILED A CLASS ACTION LAWSUIT AGAINST HARRY RICHARDS AND "SCANDALOUS" MAGAZINE FOR LIBEL, SLANDER, AND DEFAMATION OF CHARACTER.

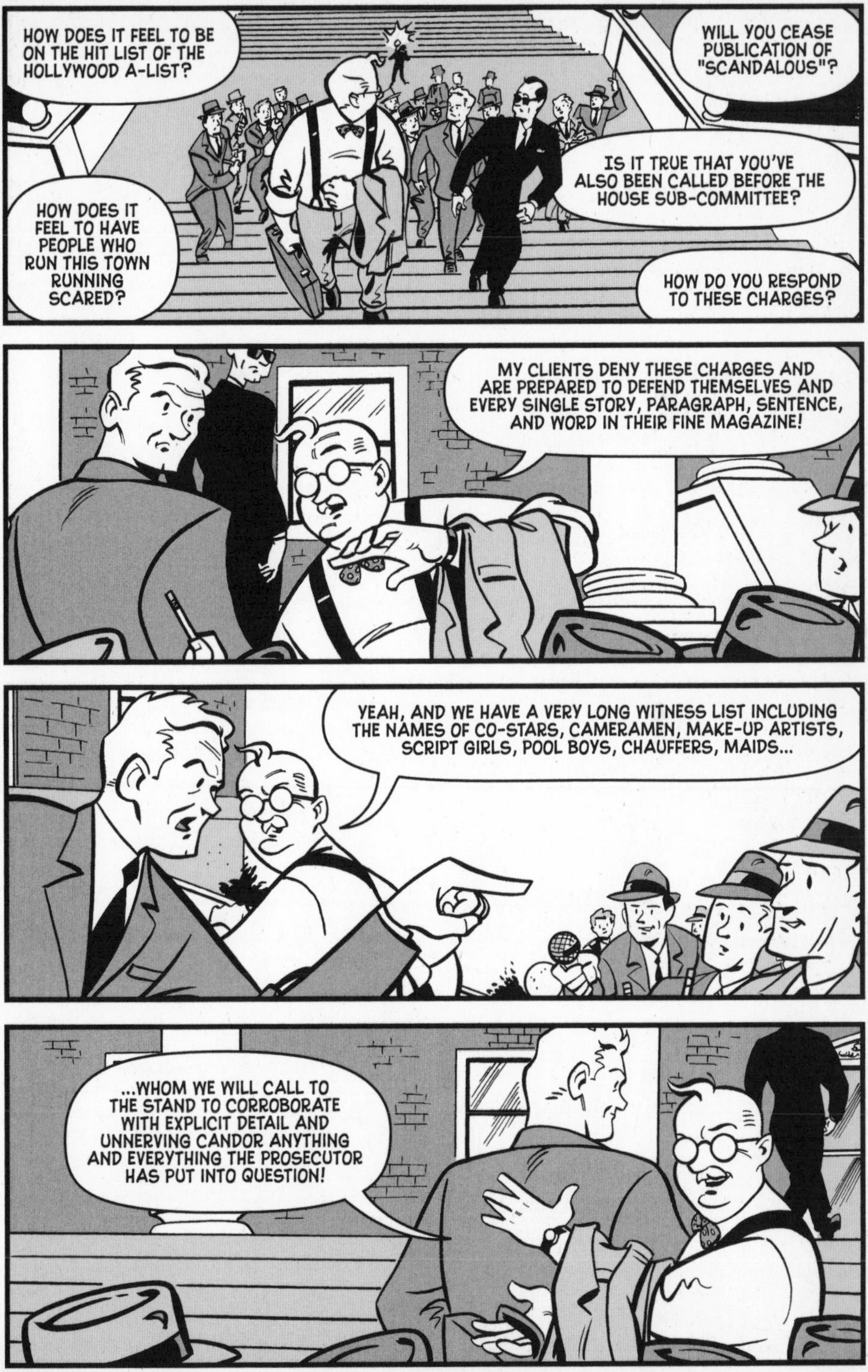

HOW DOES IT FEEL TO BE ON THE HIT LIST OF THE HOLLYWOOD A-LIST?
WILL YOU CEASE PUBLICATION OF "SCANDALOUS"?
IS IT TRUE THAT YOU'VE ALSO BEEN CALLED BEFORE THE HOUSE SUB-COMMITTEE?
HOW DOES IT FEEL TO HAVE PEOPLE WHO RUN THIS TOWN RUNNING SCARED?
HOW DO YOU RESPOND TO THESE CHARGES?
MY CLIENTS DENY THESE CHARGES AND ARE PREPARED TO DEFEND THEMSELVES AND EVERY SINGLE STORY, PARAGRAPH, SENTENCE, AND WORD IN THEIR FINE MAGAZINE!
YEAH, AND WE HAVE A VERY LONG WITNESS LIST INCLUDING THE NAMES OF CO-STARS, CAMERAMEN, MAKE-UP ARTISTS, SCRIPT GIRLS, POOL BOYS, CHAUFFERS, MAIDS...
...WHOM WE WILL CALL TO THE STAND TO CORROBORATE WITH EXPLICIT DETAIL AND UNNERVING CANDOR ANYTHING AND EVERYTHING THE PROSECUTOR HAS PUT INTO QUESTION!

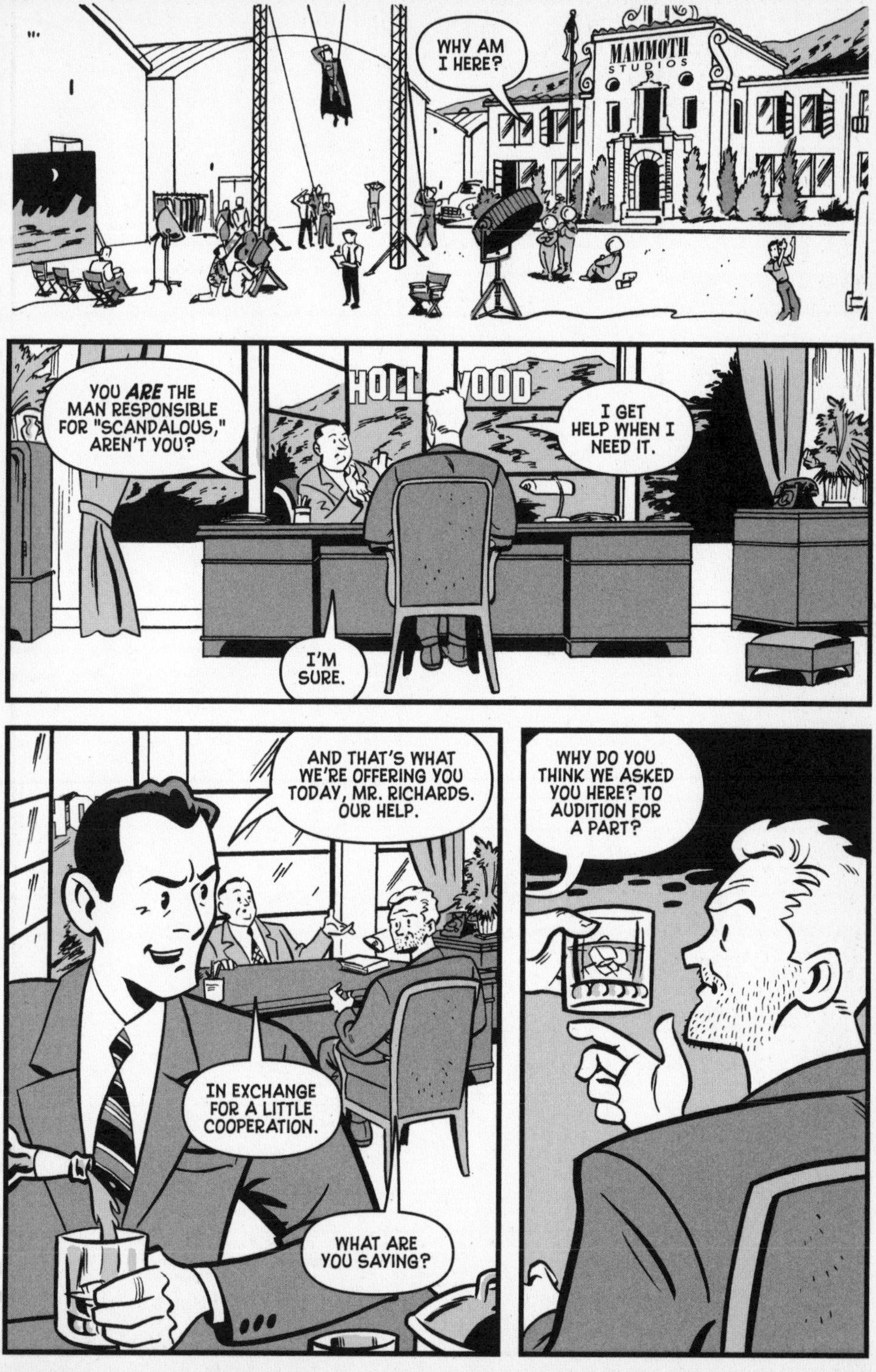

MAMMOTH STUDIOS
WHY AM I HERE?
HOLL VOOD
YOU ARE THE MAN RESPONSIBLE FOR "SCANDALOUS," AREN'T YOU?
I GET HELP WHEN I NEED IT.
I'M SURE.
AND THAT'S WHAT WE'RE OFFERING YOU TODAY, MR. RICHARDS. OUR HELP.
IN EXCHANGE FOR A LITTLE COOPERATION.
WHAT ARE YOU SAYING?
WHY DO YOU THINK WE ASKED YOU HERE? TO AUDITION FOR A PART?

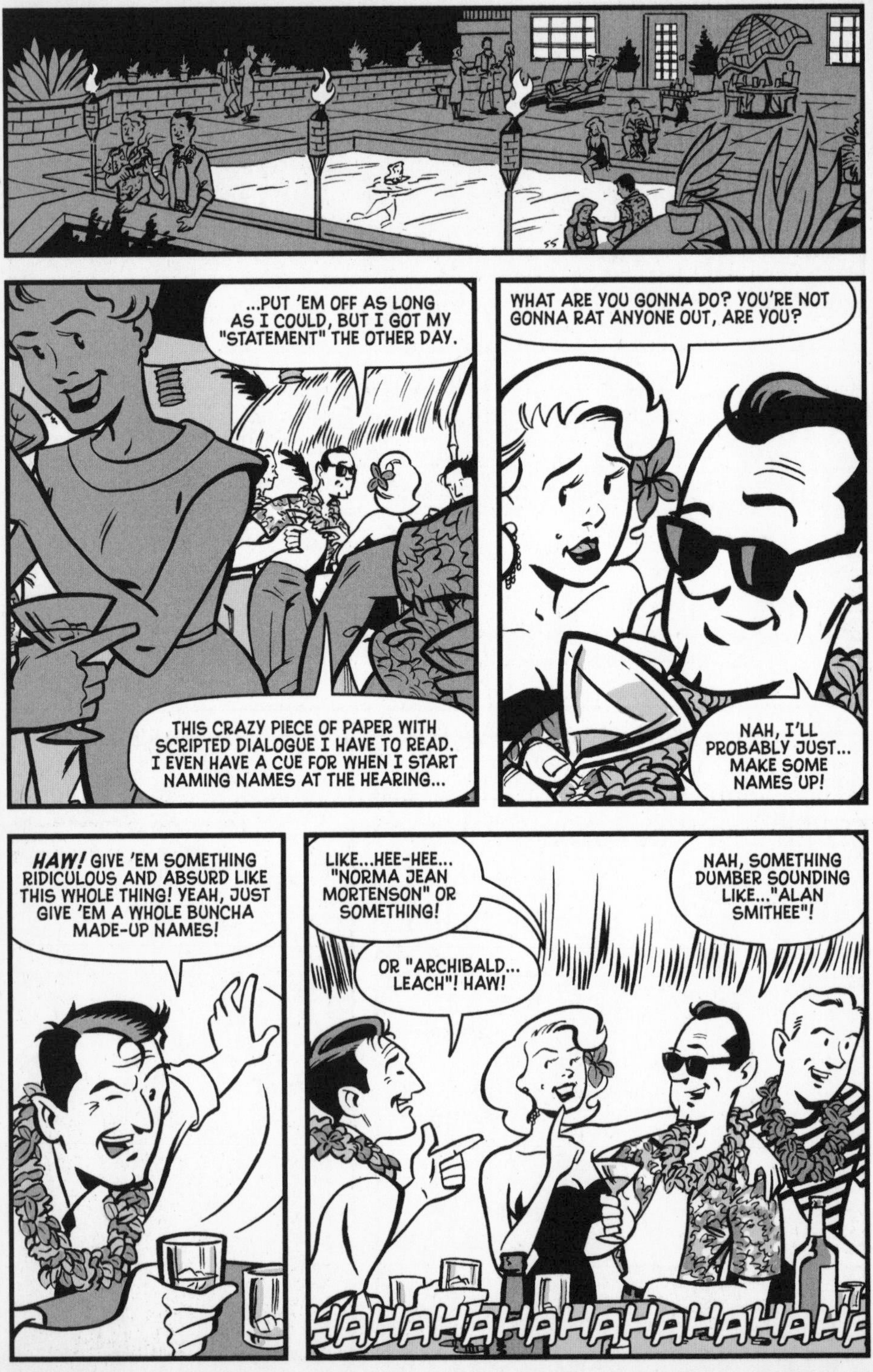
...PUT 'EM OFF AS LONG AS I COULD, BUT I GOT MY "STATEMENT" THE OTHER DAY.
THIS CRAZY PIECE OF PAPER WITH SCRIPTED DIALOGUE I HAVE TO READ. I EVEN HAVE A CUE FOR WHEN I START NAMING NAMES AT THE HEARING...
WHAT ARE YOU GONNA DO? YOU'RE NOT GONNA RAT ANYONE OUT, ARE YOU?
NAH, I'LL PROBABLY JUST... MAKE SOME NAMES UP!
HAW! GIVE 'EM SOMETHING RIDICULOUS AND ABSURD LIKE THIS WHOLE THING! YEAH, JUST GIVE 'EM A WHOLE BUNCHA MADE-UP NAMES!
LIKE...HEE-HEE... "NORMA JEAN MORTENSON" OR SOMETHING!
OR "ARCHIBALD... LEACH"! HAW!
NAH, SOMETHING DUMBER SOUNDING LIKE..."ALAN SMITHEE"!
HAHAHAHAHAHAHAHAHAHAHAHAHA

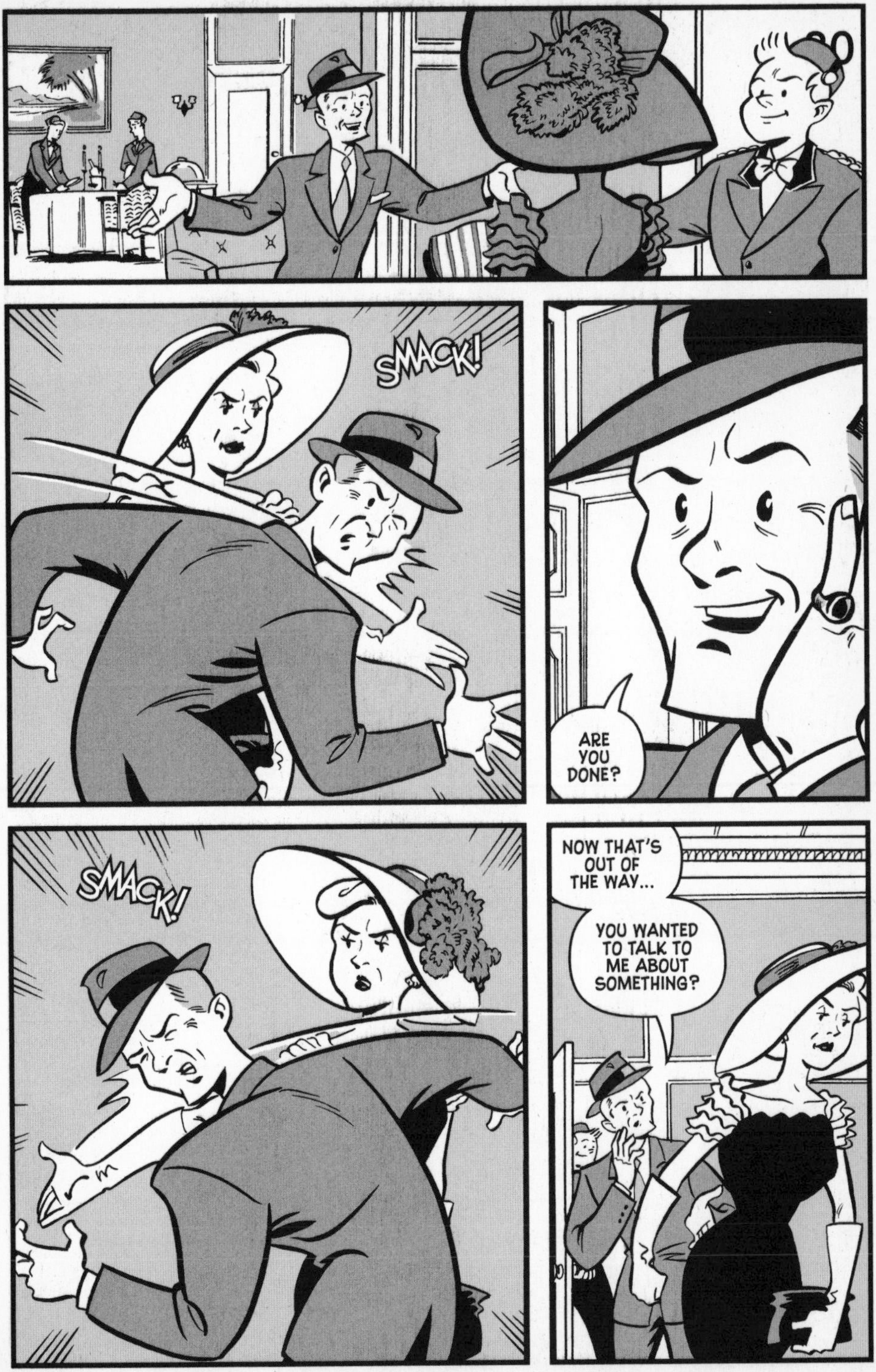
SMACK!
ARE YOU DONE?
SMACK!
NOW THAT'S OUT OF THE WAY...
YOU WANTED TO TALK TO ME ABOUT SOMETHING?

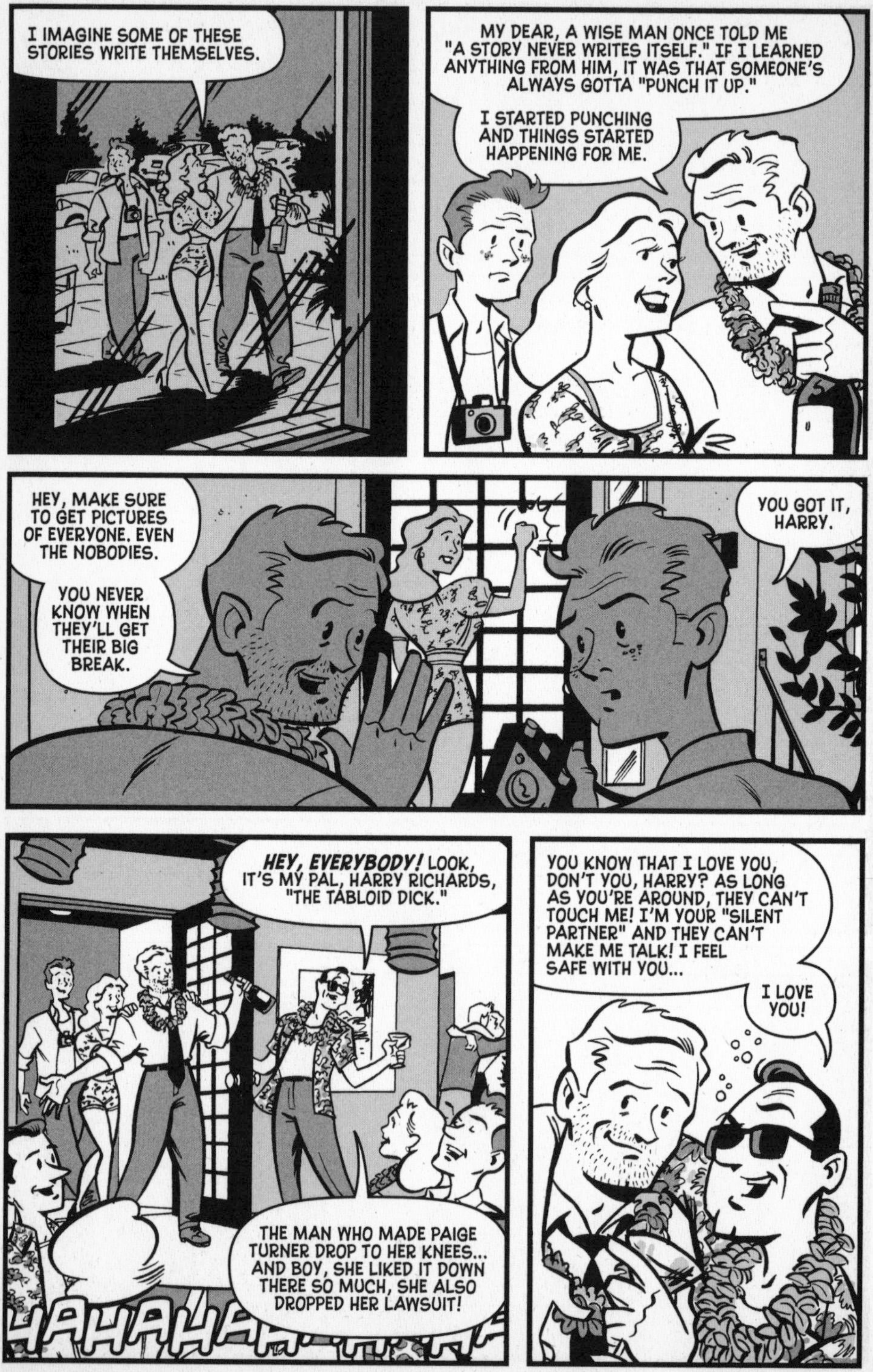
I IMAGINE SOME OF THESE STORIES WRITE THEMSELVES.
MY DEAR, A WISE MAN ONCE TOLD ME "A STORY NEVER WRITES ITSELF." IF I LEARNED ANYTHING FROM HIM, IT WAS THAT SOMEONE'S ALWAYS GOTTA "PUNCH IT UP."
I STARTED PUNCHING AND THINGS STARTED HAPPENING FOR ME.
HEY, MAKE SURE TO GET PICTURES OF EVERYONE. EVEN THE NOBODIES.
YOU NEVER KNOW WHEN THEY'LL GET THEIR BIG BREAK.
YOU GOT IT, HARRY.
HEY, EVERYBODY! LOOK, IT'S MY PAL, HARRY RICHARDS, "THE TABLOID DICK."
THE MAN WHO MADE PAIGE TURNER DROP TO HER KNEES... AND BOY, SHE LIKED IT DOWN THERE SO MUCH, SHE ALSO DROPPED HER LAWSUIT!
HAHAHAHA
YOU KNOW THAT I LOVE YOU, DON'T YOU, HARRY? AS LONG AS YOU'RE AROUND, THEY CAN'T TOUCH ME! I'M YOUR "SILENT PARTNER" AND THEY CAN'T MAKE ME TALK! I FEEL SAFE WITH YOU...
I LOVE YOU!

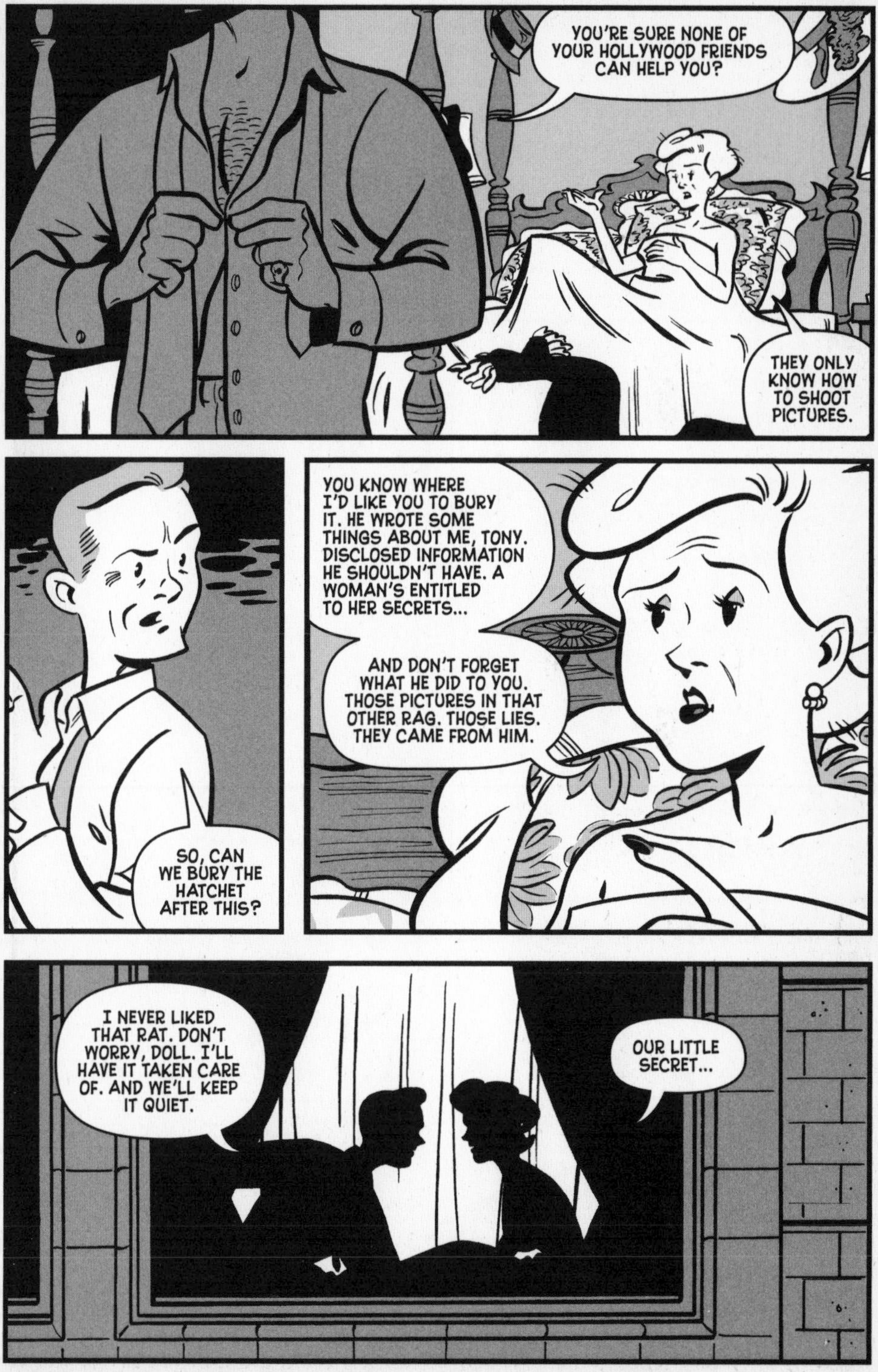
YOU'RE SURE NONE OF YOUR HOLLYWOOD FRIENDS CAN HELP YOU?
THEY ONLY KNOW HOW TO SHOOT PICTURES.
SO, CAN WE BURY THE HATCHET AFTER THIS?
YOU KNOW WHERE I'D LIKE YOU TO BURY IT. HE WROTE SOME THINGS ABOUT ME, TONY. DISCLOSED INFORMATION HE SHOULDN'T HAVE. A WOMAN'S ENTITLED TO HER SECRETS...
AND DON'T FORGET WHAT HE DID TO YOU. THOSE PICTURES IN THAT OTHER RAG. THOSE LIES. THEY CAME FROM HIM.
I NEVER LIKED THAT RAT. DON'T WORRY, DOLL. I'LL HAVE IT TAKEN CARE OF. AND WE'LL KEEP IT QUIET.
OUR LITTLE SECRET...

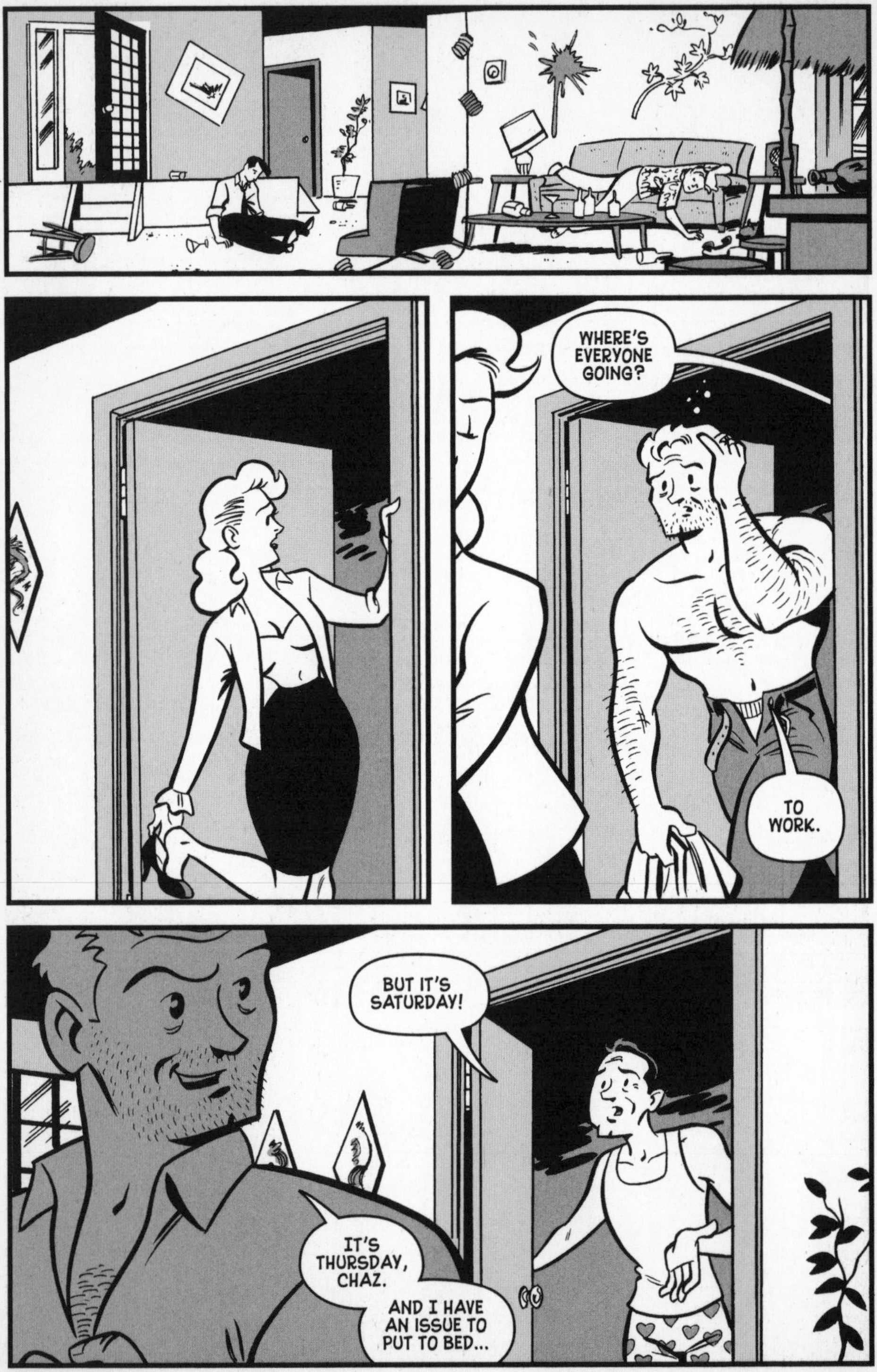
WHERE'S EVERYONE GOING?
TO WORK.
BUT IT'S SATURDAY!
IT'S THURSDAY, CHAZ.
AND I HAVE AN ISSUE TO PUT TO BED...

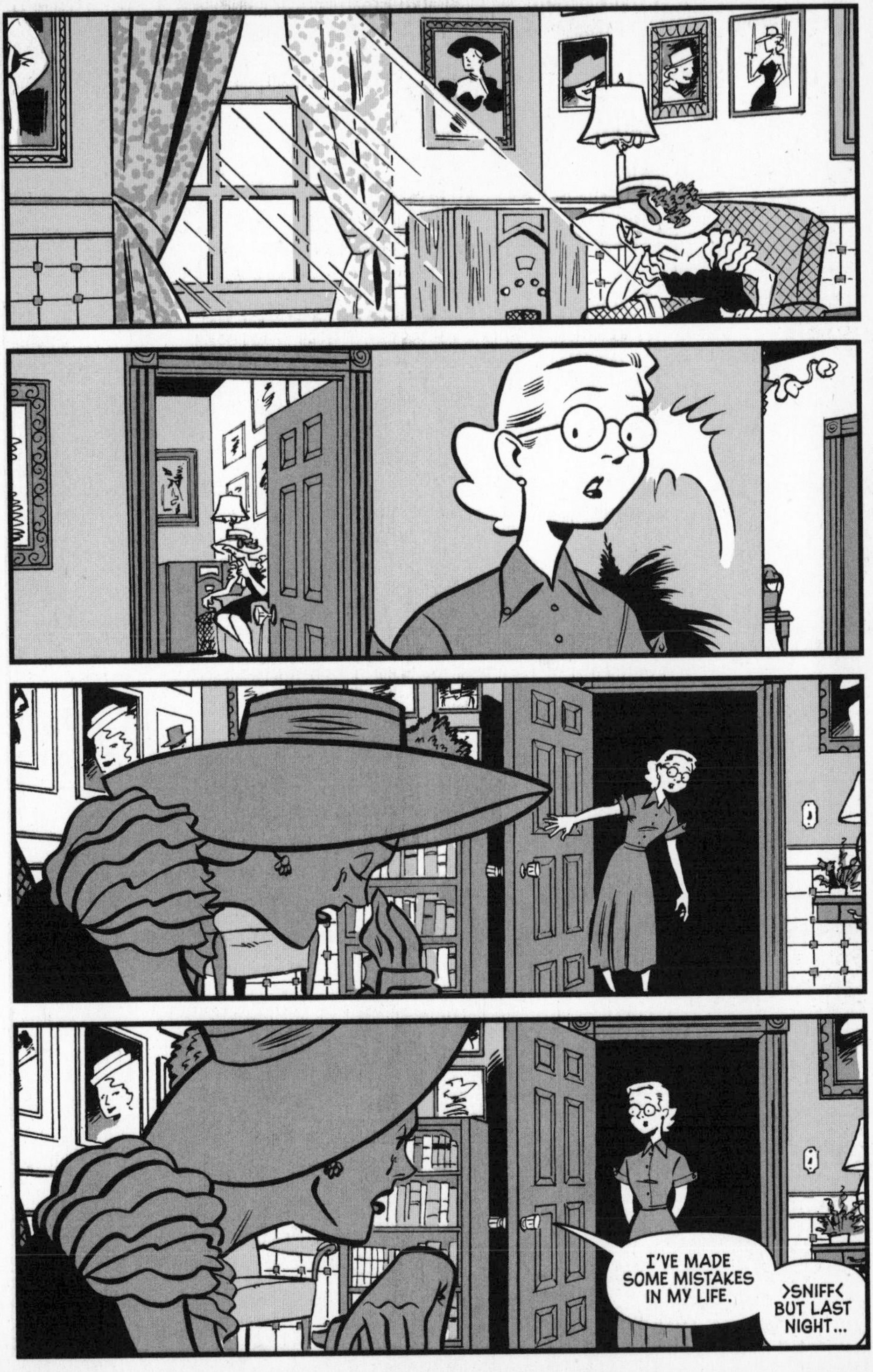
I'VE MADE SOME MISTAKES IN MY LIFE.
>SNIFF< BUT LAST NIGHT...

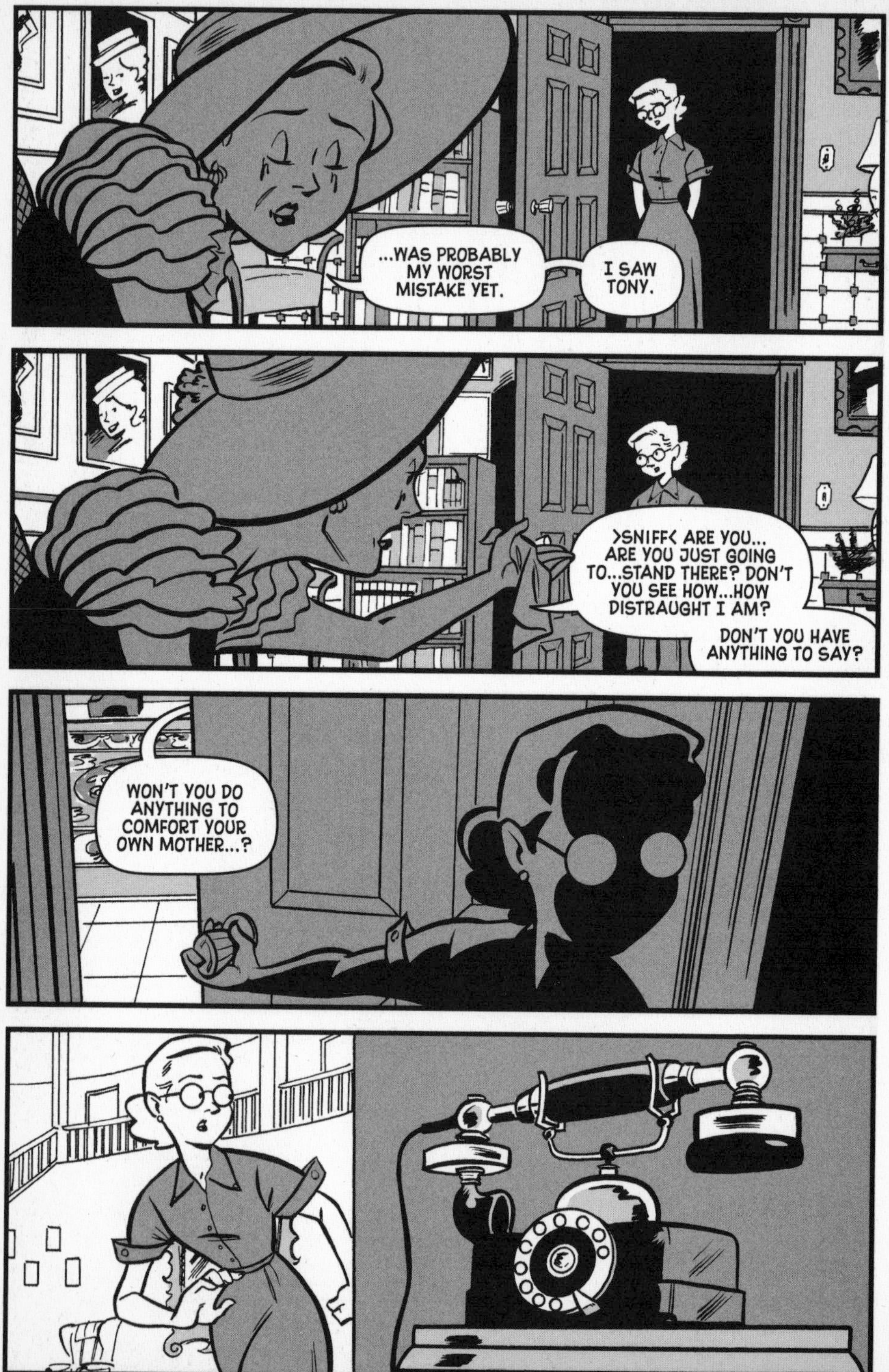
...WAS PROBABLY MY WORST MISTAKE YET.
I SAW TONY.
>SNIFF< ARE YOU... ARE YOU JUST GOING TO...STAND THERE? DON'T YOU SEE HOW...HOW DISTRAUGHT I AM?
DON'T YOU HAVE ANYTHING TO SAY?
WON'T YOU DO ANYTHING TO COMFORT YOUR OWN MOTHER...?

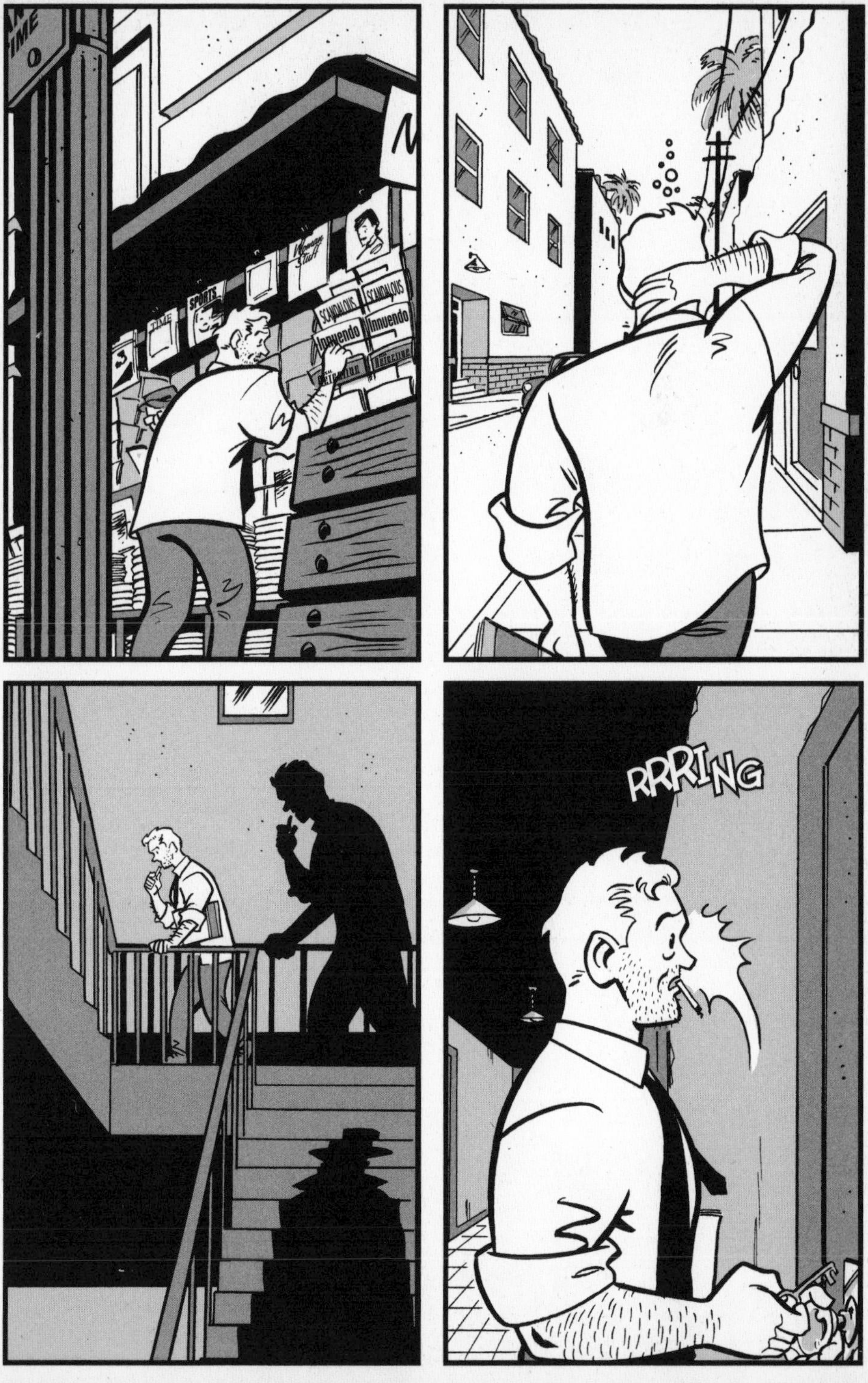
TIME
Woman Stuff
SPORTS
SCANDALOUS
SCANDALOUS
Innuendo
Innuendo
RRRING

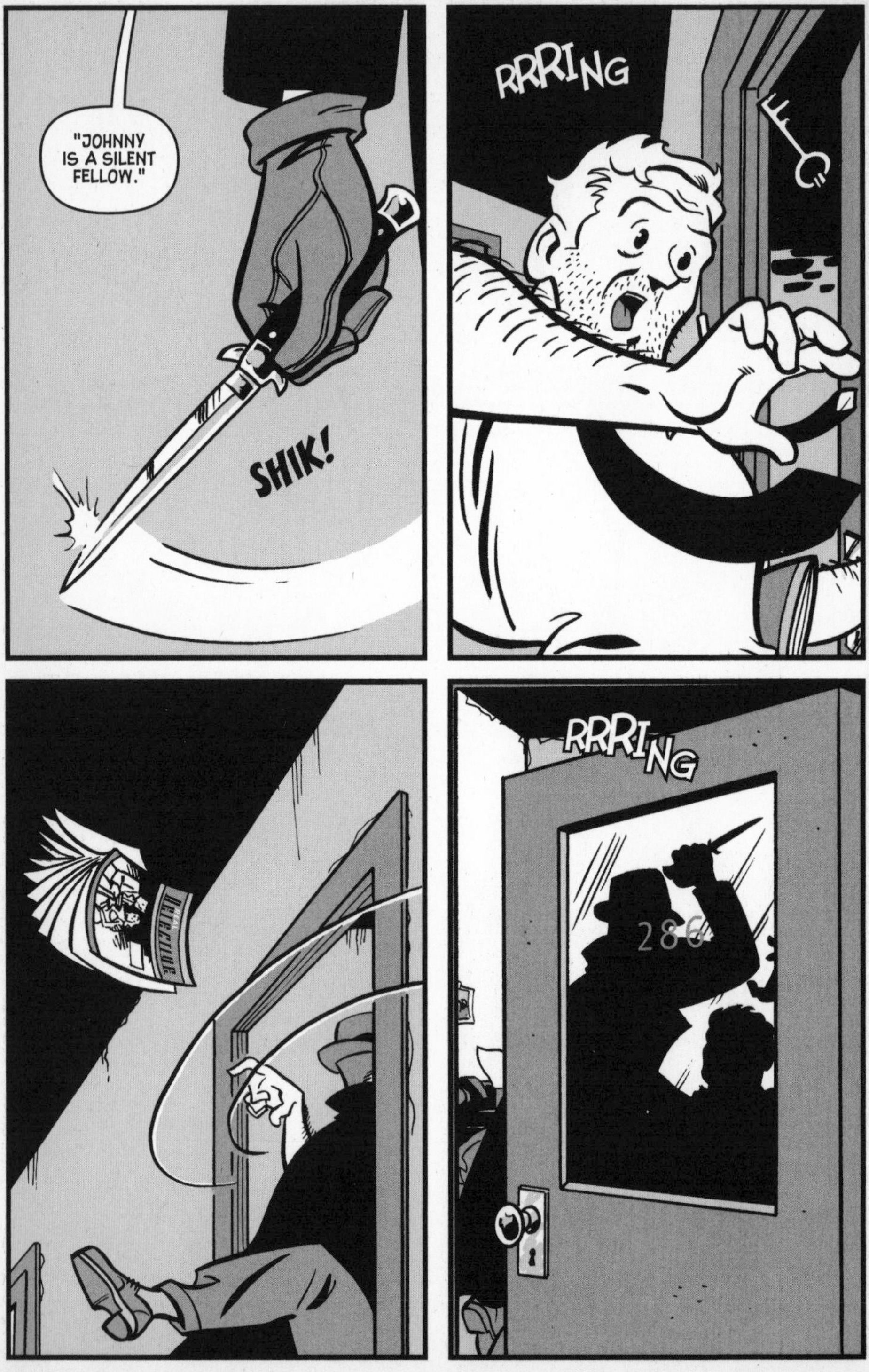
"JOHNNY IS A SILENT FELLOW."
SHIK!
RRRING
RRRING

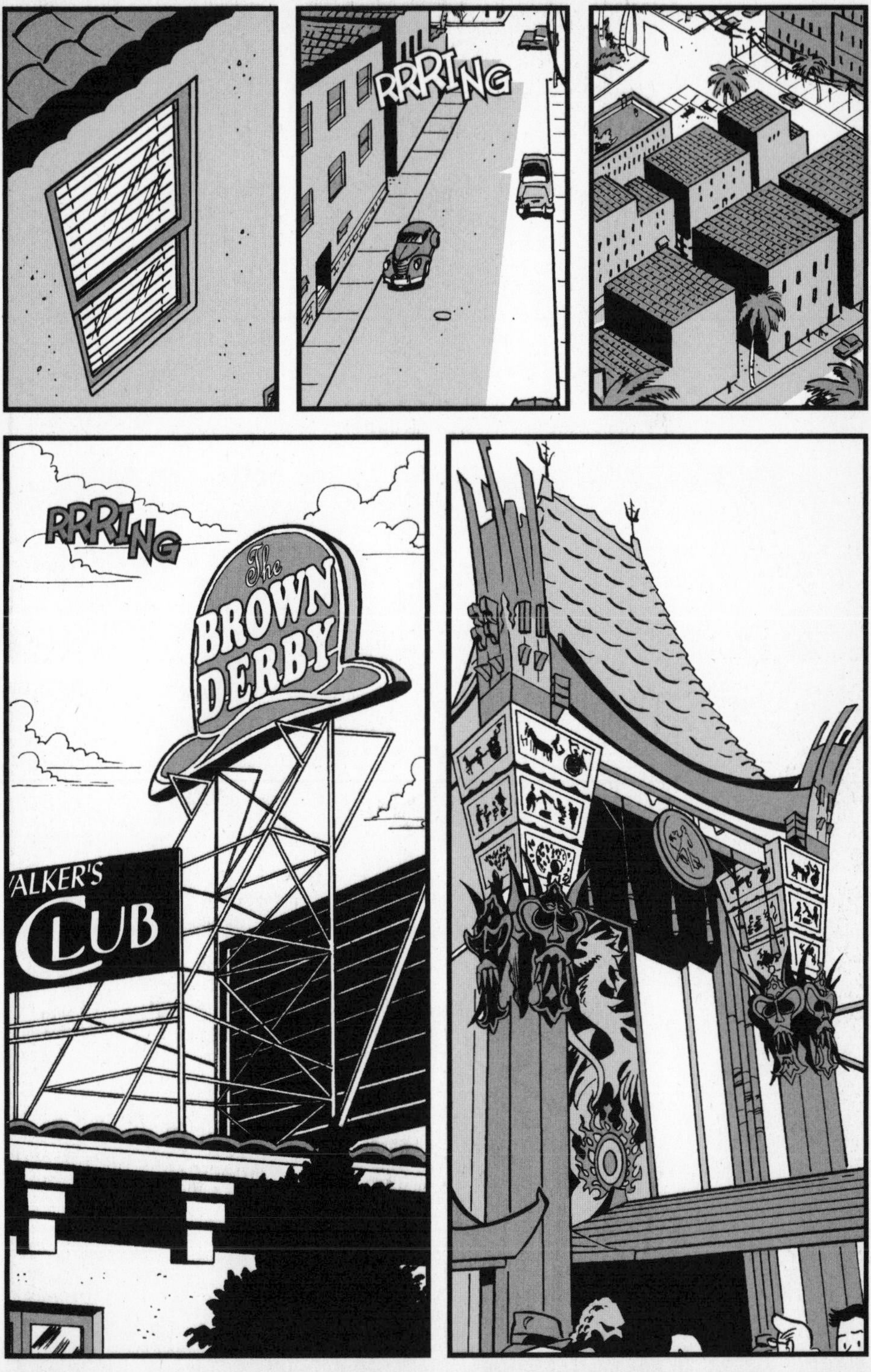

RRRING
RRRING
The BROWN DERBY
ALKER'S
CLUB

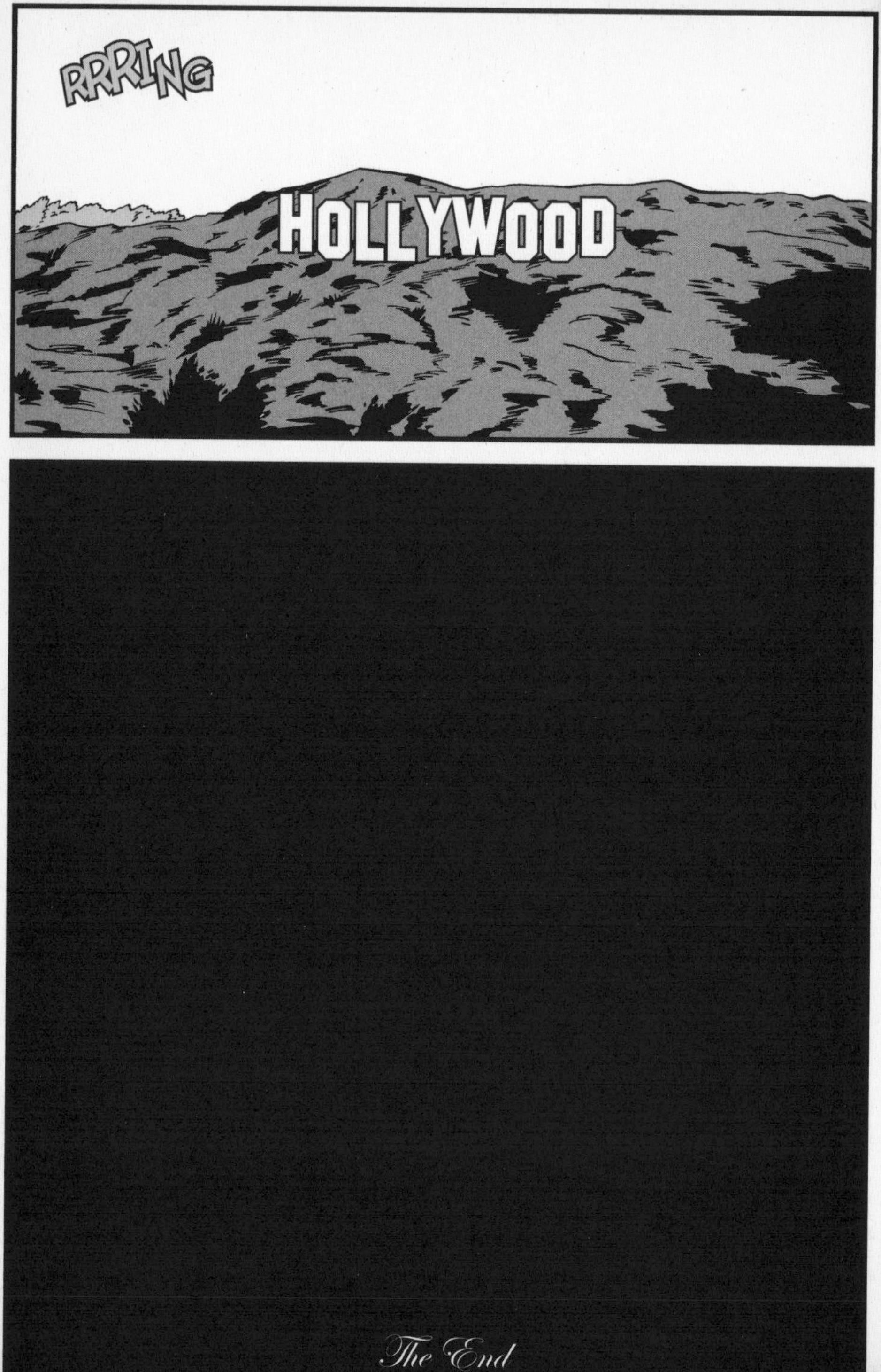
RRRING
HOLLYWOOD
The End

Afterword

by Ande Parks

In 1946, Orson Welles was asked to consider running for a senate seat in his home state of Wisconsin. Although interested in politics, he declined the opportunity. As a man who had been both divorced and known as a provocative entertainer, Welles reasoned that he had no future as a national statesman. Had Welles decided to pursue his political interests on a more full-time basis, we might have been robbed of some brilliant art. Even with the "greatest film ever made" five years behind him, Welles still had much to offer. On the other hand, Welles the politician might have saved the nation a great deal of suffering. The man who won the seat that would have been contested by Welles was Joseph McCarthy.

With few exceptions, every generation tends to look back with some degree of envy upon the world in which their parents grew up. In my case, when attempting to figure out insurance deductibles with an orange alert hanging over my family, a shaky retirement plan in place and the social security system nearing collapse, it is the relatively simple post-war years that beckon. It doesn't help that the cigars sitting on my bookshelf are known to cause eleven types of cancer, and getting drunk just isn't as glamorous as it used to be. Dear God, give me the days of a secure, lifelong job with its generous pension plan and all-inclusive health coverage. A cigar was… well, maybe not harmless, but it's only one or two a day, fer chrissakes. As for liquor, how could a man of means be expected to enjoy his quiet evening at home without a shaker of martinis at his side?

Of course, pinning down that golden era can be a might tricky. Too many veterans returning to an uncertain future... depressing. Just after the war is no good. Jump too far ahead, though, and you run smack into that pesky battle for equal rights. Somewhere in between lies the golden age of post-war prosperity and domestic innocence. America ruled the world, and we had a general in the White House to prove it. Our productivity, spurned to new heights by the war effort, now turned its focus to flooding the free world with consumer goods. Rosie the Riveter could trade in her tool belt for a stroller. Dad had seen the horrors of war, but he assured little Johnny, as he tucked him in at night, that the world was now a different place… safer and better. There was something troubling going on in Korea, but it wasn't really a war. Our boys were still getting drafted, but they'd be home safe after a little "policing."

Cue that McCarthy fellow I mentioned earlier. Four years into his first term, the junior senator began accusing the state department of harboring communists. Upon winning a second term, McCarthy assumed the chairmanship of the Senate's Government Operations Committee and took the national stage. Waving alleged lists of names, McCarthy convinced Middle America that their country was under assault from within. He didn't do it alone, though. Among his most vocal and noticeable allies was the immensely influential voice of Walter Winchell.

The power of Winchell is almost impossible to overstate. People of my generation may remember him as the fast-talking guy who narrated *The Untouchables* on TV, but we are likely to know little of the impact he had as a national columnist, both in newspapers and on radio. Winchell has been credited with the creation of the gossip column, and he did it nearly twenty years before McCarthy started his public witch hunt. By 1950, Winchell could make or break showbiz careers with a few words.

As McCarthy trained his sights on the alleged reds that lurked within the Washington power structure, Winchell took up the cause on another front… Hollywood. By the fifties, Winchell, still an undeniable national force, no longer dominated the gossip scene as he once had. Hedda Hopper and Louella Parsons wielded power nearly equaling the once-unrivaled master of the form. Scandal sheets such as *Hush-Hush* and *Hollywood Confidential* also began to flourish. Perhaps it was desperation that drove Winchell to so wildly and carelessly attack Hollywood players he deemed un-American. His over-reaching support for McCarthy's cause would result in several libel suits.

For McCarthy and Winchell, it was all over by 1954. McCarthy had been humiliated on national TV and censured by the Senate. Three years later, he would be dead of acute hepatitis at the age of 48. Winchell had gone too far, become too malicious for his audience. His media outlets dwindled, and his once awesome power vanished. Winchell would live until 1972, but he was forgotten by the end of the fifties.

Forgotten.

That is a problem. There is boundless wisdom in the cliché that history repeats itself. If we don't remember the likes of McCarthy and Winchell, we will have no chance to recognize them the next time they roll around. To that end, we should thank J. Torres and Scott Chantler. Books like *Scandalous* are not only a delight, they are vitally important. By doing his research, by knowing the world in which he set his compelling story, Torres allows us to lose ourselves in the tale without necessarily noticing that we've either learned about or been reminded of an important era in our not-so-distant past. Chantler's work is so charming that one cannot help feel for the book's characters. The bold, graphic nature of the art, in fact, pulls you into their world, drawing you into the story's shorthand so efficiently that you may not realize you're there until the tale has been told. This is the type of comic book (call it a graphic novel if you like, but it is still a big, fat, glorious comic book) we don't have enough of… the type that needs to be encouraged. Wonderful entertainment, characters you can't help but relate with, and a dose of history that tastes like pure cane sugar.

Scandalous presents us with both sides of the early fifties… the glorious optimism and the insidious fear. A grand age of opportunity, bookended by the horror of the world's worst war and the onset of the greatest civil unrest America had seen since its civil war. Torres uses Paige Turner and Harry Richards to expertly express these themes. Their ambitions, and their fates, mirror the time in which their story is set.

As effective as they are, words and pictures on a page may not be able to pay adequate tribute to those who suffered at the hands of McCarthy and his ilk. Works like *Scandalous*, however, can do the next best thing by keeping their story alive. As I did research for this piece, I came across a web site that gave me the names of The Hollywood Ten, a group of artists found in contempt for refusing to name names in front of the House Un-American Activities Committee (HUAC), along with a list of their credits. I'm going to pour myself a drink, light up a hand-rolled Dunhill cigar, and enjoy the work of these artists… names such as Edward Dmytryk, who directed *The Caine Mutiny*; Ring Lardner, Jr., who wrote *M*A*S*H*; and Dalton Trumbo, who wrote and directed *Johnny Got His Gun*. I may even watch my favorite Orson Welles film, *Touch of Evil*. Welles made the movie in 1958. It was the first film he was allowed to make in Hollywood in ten years. He had been blacklisted in 1950.

Ande Parks
July, 2004

Known primarily as an inker, Ande Parks wowed the comic book world with Union Station, his first graphic novel as a writer. Union Station is also a period piece, examining the evidence of a violent shootout in Kansas City, 1933. His next work as a writer is a project about Truman Capote's time in Kansas researching *In Cold Blood*. He also continues to ink the monthly Green Arrow series for DC Comics.

Biography

J. Torres was born in Manila, raised in Montreal, and currently lives in Toronto where his life continues to inch westward towards Hollywood. A long-time comic book fan when he and artist Tim Levins debuted *Copybook Tales* in 1996, Torres quickly went on to become too indie for mainstream comics and not cool enough for the alternative scene of the time. However, despite much more downbeat slice-of-life comics being much more popular back then, the much more nostalgic and optimistic *Copybook Tales* struck a chord with readers who would one day become editors willing to hire Torres. An eclectic list of creator-owned projects followed, including the Eisner-nominated *Alison Dare*, the ALA-listed *Days Like This* (with Scott Chantler), the recently optioned for television *Jason & the Argobots*, and the Harvey-nominated *Sidekicks*.  Other writing credits include Marvel's *Black Panther*, *X-Men: Ronin*, and *X-Men Unlimited*; Tokyopop's *Dragon Hunter*; and *Teen Titans Go!*, his current ongoing assignment for DC Comics.

Upcoming projects include *Love as a Foreign Language* with Eric Kim for Oni Press, *Horus* with Rjohn Bernales for NBM, and a wedding with Young for...late 2005? Now, do yourselves a favor and rent *The Sweet Smell of Success* and *Sunset Boulevard*.

Scott Chantler was born on a frozen February morning in Deep River, Ontario, in 1972 and still hates the cold. After spending most of his childhood in St. Thomas, Ontario--a city best known for having run down Jumbo the elephant with a train--he moved to Waterloo, Ontario, where he studied Fine Arts and Film at the University of Waterloo. By the time of his graduation in 1995, he had already embarked on a successful career as an illustrator and animator. His work has appeared in such publications as *The New York Daily News*, *Atlanta Magazine*, and *Maclean's*, TV shows such as *Shoebox Zoo* (premiering fall 2004), as well as in books, comics, and advertising for some of North America's largest corporations. His first animated short film, *Gone With the Wind in Sixty Seconds*, was an audience favourite at Siggraph 2003. He is currently tackling his first professional writing gig, a historical adventure graphic novel for Oni Press due next summer.

Scott still lives in Waterloo, with his wife Shari, son Miles, and an excitable mutt named Cubby. When he isn't drawing, he enjoys movies, reading, history, canoe trips, poker games, jazz, and the occasional expensive cigar.

J. and Scott previously collaborated on the original graphic novel *Days Like This*, an uplifting tale based on stories about '60s girl groups.

OTHER BOOKS FROM J. TORRES AND ONI PRESS...

DAYS LIKE THIS™
by J. Torres & Scott Chantler
96 pages, black-and-white interiors
$8.95 US
ISBN: 1-929998-48-1

THE COMPLETE COPYBOOK TALES™
by J. Torres & Tim Levins
240 pages black-and-white interiors
$19.95 US
ISBN: 1-929998-39-2

SIDEKICKS: THE TRANSFER STUDENT™
by J. Torres & Takeshi Miyazawa
144 pages, black-and-white interiors
$11.95 US
ISBN 1-929998-76-7

THE COLLECTED ALISON DARE™
by J. Torres & J. Bone
96 pages, black-and-white interiors
$8.95 US
ISBN 1-929998-20-1

**JASON & THE ARGOBOTS
VOL. I: BIRTHQUAKE™**
by J. Torres & Mike Norton
112 pages, black-and-white interiors
$11.95 US
ISBN: 1-929998-55-4

**JASON & THE ARGOBOTS
VOL. 2: MACHINA EX DEUS™**
by J. Torres & Mike Norton
104 pages, black-and-white interiors
$11.95 US
ISBN: 1-929998-56-2

**LOVE AS A FOREIGN LANGUAGE™
Vol. 1**
by J. Torres & Eric Kim
72 pages, black-and-white interiors
$7.95 US
ISBN: 1-932664-06-8
Available November 2004!

**LOVE FIGHTS™
vol. 1**
by Andi Watson
168 pages, black-and-white interiors
$14.95 US
ISBN: 1-9299998-86-4
Afterword by J. Torres & B. Clay Moore!

FORTUNE & GLORY™
A True Hollywood Comic Book Story
by Brian Michael Bendis
136 pages, black-and-white interiors
$14.95 US
ISBN: 1-0200008-06-6

UNION STATION™
by Ande Parks & Eduardo Barreto
120 pages, black-and-white interiors
$11.95 US
ISBN: 1-929998-69-4

Oni Press graphic novels are available at finer comics shops everywhere. For a comics store near you, call 1-888-COMIC-BOOK, or visit www.the-master-list.com.